Digital Fabrication and the Design Build Studio

This book explores the connection between digital fabrication and the design build studio in both academic and professional studios.

The book presents 17 essays and cases studies from well-known scholars and practitioners, including Kengo Kuma, Joseph Choma, Dan Rockhill, Keith Zawistowski, and Marie Zawistowski, whose theoretical and practical work addresses design build at various levels. Four introductory essays trace the history of the design build movement, exploring the emergence of design build in the pedagogy of the Bauhaus, the integration of technology into architectural design, and the influence of the act of making on the design build studio. The rest of the book is divided into two parts; the first part looks at traditional pedagogical models for the design build studio, and the second part focuses on experimental methods used in design build programs. Together, these works discuss human behavior, social-cultural trends, and motivations in socially minded studios which are based on a service-learning model. They look at component-based studios where innovation allows for an increased level of research and testing of new materials and assemblies, sustainable principles, and zero-energy prototypes.

Illustrated with over 200 color images, this book will be valuable resource for architecture students, educators, and practitioners seeking to explore the impact of digital fabrication on the global design build movement.

William Carpenter, FAIA, PhD, DPACSA, is the founder and president of the internationally recognized Lightroom Studio in Atlanta. William is also a Professor of Architecture and Urbanism at Kennesaw State University. He has made a lasting, indelible, and meaningful impact and contribution to international architectural pedagogies in education and practice through his influential writings, lectures, teaching, leadership, and research on design build education and multidisciplinary practices. His internationally award-winning firm, Lightroom, has designed many projects in Atlanta and works in several disciplines, including film production, graphic design, branding and websites, and modern architecture. He is past president of AIA Atlanta and AIA Georgia and received its highest honor, the Rothschild Medal. He was awarded the National Distinguished Professor Medal, one of the highest honors an educator can receive, from the Association of Collegiate Schools of Architecture, and served as the chancellor of the College of Distinguished Professors with this organization. He is currently serving as part of the editorial and curatorial team for the Biennale di Venezia Italian Pavilion in Venice, Italy. He recently delivered a keynote address at Ars Electronica in Linz, Austria, one of the most respected design conferences in Europe. He currently serves on the AIA Gold Medal and Firm Award nominations council.

Arief Setiawan is an educator, researcher, and designer based in Atlanta, Georgia. He teaches design studios and history and theory of architecture in Kennesaw State University, USA. His research interests include design thinking and methodology, design pedagogy, hybrid and alternative modernity in architecture and urbanism, and in the congruence of social, cultural, political, and technological factors in informing designs of contemporary built environments. He also works on design projects that problematized the relationship to a place, including a hospital for the underprivileged, educational facilities, and places of worship.

Chris Welty, AIA, is a professor in the College of Architecture and Construction Management at Kennesaw State University, for the 2022–23 academic year he served as the Interim Chair for the Architecture Department. Over his academic career, he has coordinated the professional program sequence, the thesis sequence, second-year design studios, and the design communication sequence. He has served as the KSU Architect Licensing Advisor for the National Council of Architectural Registration Board. His research centers on learning by making, integrating digital technologies within the design process while embracing the craft of making. His design studio projects have covered a wide range of topics from light and materiality to virtual computer environments and design-build. His professional practice class provides graduates with a road map for setting up and managing a design firm. In 2014, Chris was awarded an outstanding faculty award for his teaching excellence and was honored as the SPSU Teacher of the Year for the 2014–15 academic year.

Chris is a registered architect in Georgia and an active member of the American Institute of Architects (AIA). In 2015, he was awarded the AIA Georgia Bronze Medal for his service as State Treasurer for developing the strategic investment policy and the long-term strategic investment plan for reserve revenue, leading to the current Innovation Grant Award Program. Chris served as the 2019 President of AIA Atlanta and is an active member of the Architecture Foundation of Georgia Board. He is a graduate scholar of the Christopher Kelly Leadership Development Program.

When not teaching, Chris heads his small multimedia design firm, weltyWORLD, which consults in the architecture and construction field. Their work specializes in creating and analyzing spatial experiences linking virtual computer environments and physical installations.

Digital Fabrication and the Design Build Studio

**Edited by
William Carpenter,
Arief Setiawan and
Christopher Welty**

NEW YORK AND LONDON

Designed cover image: Photo by Bobby Vance.
Cover design: Catherine Burton and William Carpenter.

First published 2024
by Routledge
605 Third Avenue, New York, NY 10158

and by Routledge
4 Park Square, Milton Park, Abingdon, Oxon, OX14 4RN

Routledge is an imprint of the Taylor & Francis Group, an informa business

© 2024 selection and editorial matter, William Carpenter, Arief Setiawan and Christopher Welty; individual chapters, the contributors

The right of William Carpenter, Arief Setiawan and Christopher Welty to be identified as the authors of the editorial material, and of the authors for their individual chapters, has been asserted in accordance with sections 77 and 78 of the Copyright, Designs and Patents Act 1988.

All rights reserved. No part of this book may be reprinted or reproduced or utilised in any form or by any electronic, mechanical, or other means, now known or hereafter invented, including photocopying and recording, or in any information storage or retrieval system, without permission in writing from the publishers.

Trademark notice: Product or corporate names may be trademarks or registered trademarks, and are used only for identification and explanation without intent to infringe.

Library of Congress Cataloging-in-Publication Data
Names: Carpenter, William J., 1962– editor.
Title: Digital fabrication and the design build studio / edited by William Carpenter, Arief Setiawan and Christopher Welty.
Description: New York, NY : Routledge, 2024. | Includes bibliographical references and index.
Identifiers: LCCN 2023018672 | ISBN 9780367766696 (hardback) | ISBN 9780367766702 (paperback) | ISBN 9781003168003 (ebook)
Subjects: LCSH: Architectural practice—Case studies. | Design-build process (Construction industry)—Case studies. | Architecture—Technological innovations—Case studies. | Computer integrated manufacturing systems—Case studies.
Classification: LCC NA1995 .D63 2023 | DDC 724/.7—dc23/eng/20230727
LC record available at https://lccn.loc.gov/2023018672

ISBN: 978-0-367-76669-6 (hbk)
ISBN: 978-0-367-76670-2 (pbk)
ISBN: 978-1-003-16800-3 (ebk)

DOI: 10.4324/9781003168003

Typeset in Adobe Garamond
by Apex CoVantage, LLC

Printed in the UK by Severn, Gloucester on responsibly sourced paper

Contents

Acknowledgments — vii
List of Contributors — viii
Foreword: Learning by Doing at the Bauhaus by William Carpenter — xii
Preface: Informality and Temporality by William Carpenter — xxi
Introduction by William Carpenter — xxxiii
Art of Making by Jim Burton and William Carpenter — xl

1 Pedagogical Models — 1

Design-build Program at KSU — 3
William Carpenter, Arief Setiawan, and Christopher Welty

Making to Construct Design Thinking — 26
Arief Setiawan and Christopher Welty

Folding Research Into Teaching — 40
Joseph Choma

Beyond (the) Building: Fabricating a Design Build Program on the Arabian Peninsula — 52
Michael Hughes

2 Experimental Methods — 63

Studio 804, Inc. — 65
Dan Rockhill

Virginia Tech — 79
Jim Burton and William Carpenter

La Riviera Bistro — 106
Gabriel Esquivel

Practicing for Practice — 114
Keith Zawistowski and Marie Zawistowski

Two Scales of Approach, Tulane's Design Build Programs — 128
Byron J. Mouton and Emilie Taylor Welty

	Borboletta	**139**
	Eric Goldemberg	
	Poetic Systems—the Art of Transformation	**148**
	Stefan Mittlböck-Jungwirth-Fohringer	
	Energy Flow Across Enclosures	**153**
	Joseph Lstiburek	
3	**Conclusion**	**163**
	Digital Fabrication by Kengo Kuma	**165**
	Professor Kengo Kuma	
	Conclusions: The Significance of Design Build Studios	**178**
	William Carpenter	

Index　　　　*186*

Acknowledgments

The author would like to thank his book team: Chris Welty AIA and Dr. Arief Setiawan and James Burton AIA. Thank you to Jake Millicheap, our supportive and fearless editor, and the entire Routledge team. Thanks to Gregory Luhan, FAIA and Edwin Akins for supporting during my time in residency as visiting scholar and professor.

Thank you to my Topaz Medallion Nominator James Fausett for your enduring encouragement and belief in my research, teaching, and legacy.

Thank you to Celma for believing in me and encouraging me through this entire process. I could not do this without you.

Thanks to the Lightroom Atlanta, Lightroom 30a, and Lightroom Brasil teams, especially Chad and Julie Reineke and Samuel Rosa and the entire Rosa family.

This formative study was made possible due to the encouragement and endless support of numerous individuals and institutions during the course of the research. Special thanks go to my parents, Cathy and Billy Joe Carpenter, Esme and Mirette Carpenter, Norman Jaffe FAIA, Lance Brown FAIA, Samuel Mockbee FAIA, Christopher Risher, Gregory Hunt FAIA, Robert Ford FAIA, Dr. Wilson Barnes AIA, Alessandro Melis, the enigmatic Michael and Donna Waterhouse, Dr. Noha Nasser. and the luminaries Alan Green and Anne Brown, who helped me in the United Kingdom.

Heartfelt thanks go to Ginger Massey who seemed to read my mind and give me valuable and insightful critiques. My thesis advisor Professor Thomas Muir, who worked closely with me through the entire process to bring rigor and depth to the study. He encouraged me to look more critically and for more global implications in academia.

This study is dedicated to my teacher, Robert Fisher of Deerfoot Path, Cutchogue, New York. He guided a misfit seventh-grade student onto an alluring path of architecture and education.

Contributors

Jim Burton is the managing principal of Carter + Burton Architecture PLC. As an AIA design award winning designer, his unique experience has included experimentation with design build projects such as Studio Loggerheads and Boxhead. He has been a contributing writer in critical theory books *Learning by Building* and *Sustainable Modern House* authored by Dr. William Carpenter. His designs testing sustainability and critical regionalism is being celebrated at the 2023 Architecture Biennale in Venice, Italy.

Joseph Choma serves as the director of the Florida Atlantic University School of Architecture. Joseph Choma is the founder and director of the Design Topology Lab, an interdisciplinary practice which conducts design research and provides consultation relating to material innovation, unconventional means and methods of construction, and the role of geometry in the built environment. Current topics of exploration include foldable structures and materials, lightweight deployable shelters, ultra-thin formwork for concrete casting, stay-in-place formwork for shell structures and concrete slabs, and advancements in natural fiber textiles. As a researcher, he uses mathematics, folding, structure, and materials as generative design devices to imagine new ways to design and build more sustainably.

Gabriel Esquivel was born and educated as an architect in Mexico City with a degree from the National University (UNAM) and received his master's degree in architecture from The Ohio State University. He previously taught architecture and design at the Knowlton School of Architecture and the Design Department Ohio State University. After joining the architecture faculty at Texas A&M University, he has investigated the benefits and vehicles of a heterogeneous model that integrates both technology and architecture's proprietary devices. Gabriel began to explore different possibilities of research through fabrication in partnership with the Department of Aerospace Engineering. He has created a new advanced research fabrication lab that deals with the concept of robotic-assisted fabrication. Gabriel is the director of the T4T Lab at Texas A&M University since 2010 where he examines the integration of digital technology to exchange architectural information and its connection to contemporary theory. He was the moderator of Interface 2017, the discussion between Patrik Schumacher and Mark Gage, as well as the curator of the Deep Vista Conference in 2018, and most recently in DigitalFutures.world, he moderated the talk about agency, borders, and immigration.

Eric Goldemberg is an artist and architect, with a professional degree from the University of Buenos Aires and a master of science in advanced architectural design from Columbia University, New York. He worked for Peter Eisenman as Senior Designer for the City of Culture of Galicia, Spain, as well as heading design teams in several competitions. He was also project architect for Asymptote Architecture (Hani Rashid and Lise Anne Couture) on projects in Malaysia, The Netherlands, and the Guggenheim Museum in Guadalajara, Mexico. In Buenos Aires he collaborated with Clorindo Testa and Estudio STAFF—the latter founded by his parents Jorge Jose Goldemberg and Teresa BIelus, with over 2,000,000 m2 of social housing projects built in South America. In 2004, he co-founded MONAD Studio with his wife, Veronica Zalcberg. The principals of MONAD Studio have lectured about their projects at very prestigious institutions worldwide. They are the authors of the book *Pulsation in Architecture*, which highlights the range and complexity of sensations involved in constructing rhythmic ensembles. Goldemberg is an associate professor and digital design coordinator at Florida International University in Miami, where he teaches graduate studios and advanced digital design and fabrication courses. Previously he taught at Pratt Institute, Columbia University, New York Institute of Technology, New Jersey Institute of Technology, and University of Buenos Aires.

Michael Hughes began his teaching at Cornell University after working professionally in the Los Angeles offices of Richard Meier and Frank Gehry. He is also co-principal of Catovic Hughes Design. Hughes' research, teaching, and creative activities involve a combination of design, community outreach, tectonics, and material exploration. These interests inform a pedagogical agenda focused on an integrated approach to architectural education that emphasizes hands-on learning, sustainable practices, and civic responsibility.

Kengo Kuma (隈 研吾, *Kuma Kengo*, born 1954) is a Japanese architect and professor in the Department of Architecture (Graduate School of Engineering) at the University of Tokyo. Frequently compared to contemporaries Shigeru Ban and Kazuyo Sejima, Kuma is also noted for his prolific writings. He is the designer of the Japan National Stadium in Tokyo, which was built for the 2020 Summer Olympics. He is a prolific writer and scholar and is one of the most respected architects in the world.

Joseph Lstiburek is a forensic engineer, building investigator, building science consultant, author, speaker, and widely known expert on building moisture control, indoor air quality, and retrofit of existing and historic buildings. Lstiburek is an adjunct professor of civil engineering at the University of Toronto, an industry consultant specializing in rain penetration, air and vapor barriers, building durability, construction technology, and microbial contamination—and an advisor on numerous prominent building envelope failures. He consults regularly on building code and industry standards. Widely known for his "Perfect Wall" concept, Lstiburek identified four key control layers within the building envelope (rain, air, vapor, and thermal) critical to a building's behavior, long-term performance, and viability. He is a proponent of understanding the concepts that allow older buildings to survive over time in harsh climates—and mimicking those concepts with contemporary construction.

Stefan Mittlböck-Jungwirth-Fohringer has been a member of the Ars Electronica Futurelab since 2001. He studied painting and graphics at the Art University of Linz and, as a trained electrician, brings with him technical and manual skills. His diploma thesis dealt with the question of the absence of time in moving pictures. He is an artist, producer, and key researcher. He is working on the topic of poetic systems, which is the field of his artistic research in the context of art and architecture within the Ars Electronica Futurelab.

■ Contributors

Byron J. Mouton is an established architect, educator, New Orleans native, and alumnus of Tulane University. He has traveled a path from New Orleans through Harvard's Graduate School of Design to professional practice in Central Europe, and eventually back at home. He now finds himself committed to building his locally based practice BILD Design, in conjunction with his academic role as professor of practice at Tulane's School of Architecture, director of the school's design/build program URBANbuild. From 2011 to 2014, he served as one of the founding endowed social entrepreneurship professors in the university-wide program in Social Innovation and Social Entrepreneurship (SISE). With more than 20 years of experience in the fields of architecture and construction, several award-winning projects, and exposure in national and international publications, Byron is committed to critical assignments that exemplify a collaborative planning approach and a dedication to the regional remediation of New Orleans. As a local, Byron understands the impact of pre-Katrina problems on a post-Katrina world and the challenges set forth. The comprehensive nature of such tasks fuels his investigations in pursuit of progressive contextual infill possibilities that encourage and advance the revitalization of New Orleans' urban fabric. Over the past 14 years, as Principal of BILD, Byron has explored alternative models for affordable housing within the context of the city's sometimes peculiar setting, and he continues to offer the city progressive options for domestic growth in the face of ongoing challenges.

Dan Rockhill is an ACSA distinguished professor of architecture and the JL Constant distinguished professor of architecture at the University of Kansas and executive director of Studio 804. He and his students have designed and built 15 LEED (Leadership in Energy and Environmental Design) Platinum buildings in Kansas and have also completed three passive institute certifications. They have won numerous international design awards, including three American Institute of Architect's Honor Awards, two Wood Design Awards, two-time winner of the NCARB Prize, two-time winner of *Architecture Magazine*'s "Home of the Year," and multiple leadership awards from the USGBC (United States Green Building Council). In addition, the work of his firm, Rockhill and Associates, is tightly bound to the natural milieu and culture of the Kansas region. In the spirit of regionalism, the areas archetypal forms, Spartan aesthetics, frugal methods, and relationship to nature permeate the results. They are the recipients of numerous awards, most recently; *Residential Architect* magazine's Firm of the Year.

Emilie Taylor Welty brings experience and praxis in the making and teaching of design. She is a leader in the design/build field, and at Small Center, she focuses on teaching students how to be better designers, makers, and citizens. When she's not wrangling Small Center's Design/Build studios, Emilie helps provide structure, schedule, and nifty graphics for projects we're working on. Emilie's wordy titles include professor of practice at Tulane School of Architecture and Design/Build Manager at Small Center, but she prefers to think of herself as a doer of things. One of those current things is a book project in the works titled *Fieldwork; Designbuild Education's Past, Present, and Potentials*. A native of southern Louisiana, Emilie knows the difference between Cajun and Creole and is adapted to our humid swampland. Emilie's side hustles include principal at Colectivo, and she is currently working on a book about design build education.

Keith Zawistowski was born in New Jersey, USA, and studied architecture at Virginia Tech. Marie Zawistowski was born in Paris, France, and studied architecture at the Ecole d'Architecture Paris Malaquais. They met at Auburn University's Rural Studio while working as students with architect Sambo Mockbee to design and build a charity house for Lucy Harris and her family. In 2005, they received a Graham Foundation Grant for "Traditions of Today and Tomorrow," their study of traditional building practices in Ghana, West Africa. They have since married and established on-site to continue their collaboration, making buildings, which are deeply rooted in the unique identity of people and place. Their work has received significant recognition, including the prestigious "Prix Françoise Abella" from the French Beaux Arts Academy and the "AJAP" young architects award from the French Minister of Culture. The Virginia Society of the American Institute of Architects recently recognized Keith with the Award for Distinguished Achievement and Marie with Society Honors "for their extraordinary joint efforts to advance the art and science of architecture," and Public Interest Design listed them among "the top 100 individuals and teams working at the intersection of design and service." Marie and Keith also share a passion for teaching. They are currently tenured faculty at the national architecture school in Grenoble, France. Their professional practice course "Designing Practice" has received the National Council of Architectural Registration Boards' Grand Prize for the Creative Integration of Practice and Education in the Academy, and the design/buildLAB, which they co-founded was recognized by the Association of Collegiate Schools of Architecture with their inaugural Design/Build Education Award for "best practices in design/build education."

Foreword: Learning by Doing at the Bauhaus

William Carpenter

Throughout the history of architecture, architects have transformed abstract ideas into tangible, built, and meaningful reality. In these buildings of the past, an inseparable unity of design and construction processes existed. Today, however, a complex and segmented process nearly separates the architect from the builder. In recent years, design build has swept through the building industry as a delivery method offering faster and more cost-effective buildings. These buildings, for the most part, have lost the connection to design that once existed in buildings of the past. These buildings tend to emphasize cost savings and efficiency over design process and rigor. This study is a wake-up call to academia and industry to again see the connection between design and workmanship in architectural education.

Architectural education, especially in North America, has mirrored this segmented process existing in architectural practice. It is very rare for architecture students to actually build something they design. In some cases, such as at the Dessau Bauhaus, students were encouraged to build in order to learn and pursue design intentions. This was Walter Gropius' intention as he set up the school as an antithesis to the Ecole des Beaux Arts educational system.

Only an Idea has the power to spread so far.
—Ludwig Mies van der Rohe (Naylor, 1968)

INTRODUCTION

The work of the Bauhaus has offered influential design and pedagogical influences to architects and to architectural education. This chapter discusses the "learning by doing" workshops at the Bauhaus taught by Johannes Itten and Josef Albers. These workshops offered students the chance to experiment with materials in an open-ended format, which emphasized rigorous process and intuitive design methods. Students were challenged to work directly with materials in the design process. Itten and Albers differed slightly in their approaches as they developed their own ideas about architectural education. Political forces at the time of the Bauhaus make it a unique educational model for study. Because the school was reacting to political and social forces in Nazi Germany, learning objectives and student output were affected. More specifically, an emphasis on the economy of materials is evident.

THE BAUHAUS

In considering architectural education and construction, it is helpful to discuss the inherent theoretical differences between schools of thought. At the Parisian Ecole Polytechnique, C. N. Durand, the first tutor in architecture, sought to establish a universal building methodology.

This was an architectural counterpoint to the Napoleonic code by which economic and appropriate structures could be created through the modular permutation of fixed plan types and alternate elevations (a sort of stock plan theory). After winning the Prix de Rome, Henri Labrouste spent five years at the French Academy devoting much time in Italy and studying temples at Paestum. The education of the Beaux Arts architect put an emphasis on the picturesque, an attitude toward the monumental and archival use of history for emotional affect, and a sort of "hands off" approach. This approach appeared to lead to an elitist attitude, as architects were concerned with drawing elaborate elevations of unbuilt palaces for the wealthy and opulent. In the Deutsche Werkbund movement, which lasted from 1898 to 1927, Gottfried Semper stated that the depreciation of materials results from its treatment by machine lead. Frampton and Semper, at the same time, were asking how industrialization might affect the quality of architecture. Semper wondered if the handcraft would be lost.

> Let us create a new guild of craftsmen, without the class distinctions, which raise an arrogant barrier between craftsman and artist. Together, let us conceive and create the new building of the future, which will embrace architecture, sculpture and painting in one unity and which will rise one day toward heaven from the hands of a million workers like the crystal symbol of a new faith.
>
> (Gropius—Proclamation Weimar Bauhaus, 1919)

Bauhaus educator Bruno Taut stated that within a new art of building, each separate discipline would contribute to the final form, and there would be no boundaries between the crafts, sculpture and painting. This revolution of Gesamtkunstwerk was amplified even in the word Bauhaus. Walter Gropius was intentionally recalling the medieval Bauhatte, or masons lodge. He was realigning the architect with the craftsman. In a 1922 letter to his colleague Oskar Schlemmer, he wrote about his vision of a workshop system inspired by the cathedral building lodges. Swiss painter Johannes Itten was influenced by a system of learning design that is based on sparking individual creativity by constructing collages of varying materials, textures, and assemblies. Influenced by Froebel and Maria Montessori, he believed in "learning by doing"—a phrase first coined by American John Dewey—in the Voukurs, or preliminary class. In 1922, Gropius modified the craft orientation of Bauhaus by integrating the notion of mass production. He argued that its education was a means to prepare students for a world of mass production. Thus, students would learn skills to work with machinery, to grow to be a master, and to address problems in a rounded manner (Wick, 2000). This caused the immediate resignation of Johannes Itten and ushered in the new Bauhaus. Moholy Nagy replaced Itten, which put him in charge of both the preliminary course and the metal workshop. He introduced students to "constructivist elementarism," a concept that describes the economy of the designed object. He introduced students to wood, metal, wire, and glass. He was not interested in collages and contrast of materials. Rather, he was interested in light and space.

The first design build projects were two houses built on the campuses and furnished by the students. The Sommerfeld House, designed by Gropius and Adolf Meyer, and the "Veruchshaus," or experimental house, were designed as traditional "Heimatstil," or log houses, with interiors of carved wood and intricate stained glass. The second house was a production object or living machine. The house was organized around an atrium space. All of the fittings, windows, doorframes, furniture, and light fixtures were built by the students in the workshops of new materials. Josef Albers designed the stained glass and built the installation with student help in 1922. Further, the design utilized salvaged teak as its primary

■ Foreword: Learning by Doing at the Bauhaus

material (Droste, 1990). The design was not generated and supplied by students but by their professors, Walter Gropius and Adolf Meyer. The foreman on the project, Fred Forbat, was a recent graduate. The interiors were completed in collaboration with the mural-painting, textile, and woodworking workshops. The ceremonies for laying the foundation and topping out the villa celebrated the collaboration (Droste, 1990).

The Breuer foyer table deserves examination. The table sits here as an element for the photograph only. Breuer moved the chair, which he designed, out of the way and placed the table here. It normally sat across from this space near the entry doors. It appears that this was done in order to reflect the explosive Tautian geometries into the polished stone top. The diagonal corner posts are pulled out away from the top and appear to be in dialogue with each other. Overall, the table has an unfinished quality. In the upper-right corner of the image, one can see intricate carved patterns evocative of Wright's Barnsdall House in Los Angeles, which are repeated as a pattern up the rail and newel post of the staircase. However, the project also posed a problem with its continuously rising budget. Other projects done this manner also went over budget (Whitford, 1984).

Marcel Breuer designed some of the furnishings for the house as part of his journeyman's examination. He designed chairs and an entrance table in the foyer of the house. The design itself owes much to the work of Frank Lloyd Wright, De Stijl, and the Crafts Movement, particularly the work of William Morris. The curious blending of the explosive geometries, expressionist paintings, and architecture of Bruno Taut can be seen in the diagonal geometries of apparently knot-free, clear wood. The wood was recycled, and this may have led to the use of short pieces. There is also an apparent conflict between the diagonal geometries of the walls, stairs, and the floor pattern, which does not harmonize with the explosive geometries.

The furniture also appears to be at odds with the space. In the work of Frank Lloyd Wright, the furniture grows out of the wall or is made of materials and geometric patterns similar to the design of the building. Here, the furniture appears to stand out from the walls and even block, or partially block, passage to the staircase flow.

The colored glass mural in the stair hall at the Sommerfeld House is one of the most exciting pieces created at the Bauhaus. This early work of Joseph Albers exhibits derived influences from Paul Klee and his grid paintings and landscape-inspired collages. The overall composition of the piece is designed to be in harmony with the diagonals of the walls and exterior of the building. The angled and inflected geometry of the glass is expressed both in the stair hall and the exterior of the building. Abstractions, of what appear to be open books, are interspersed through the piece, which make the statement about historical precedent and the importance of past knowledge. This also goes against Walter Gropius' proclamation that history was not relevant to the Bauhaus. It also related to an inherent conflict between the professors and students and the office of Walter Gropius. This conflict caused, during the construction of the house, the resignation of Johannes Itten. The root of this was the different views between Gropius and Itten about industrialization and mass production. Itten cherished individual crafts, while Gropius embraced the necessities of the industrialized production (Droste, 1990). The Sommerfeld House can be viewed as a prototype that Walter Gropius created to express his vision of the school. This was the school working in partnership with Gropius' own firm, and he wanted it to express ideas of school-based practice. The choice of client, however, was unfortunate. The client was a wealthy businessman, which created the image that the school was catering to elitist patrons. The idea of the Live Project, or school-based commissions, was pivotal to the Bauhaus. Gropius constantly sought contact with outside industry and potential clients.

The educational situation that forged the Bauhaus in Germany after WWI showed the chaos of postwar society compounded by the vestiges of a traditional, rigid division between the (academic) arts and (practical) crafts. Walter Gropius created the first Bauhaus in Weimar. In his Bauhaus Manifesto, Gropius declared that "the ultimate aim of all creative activity is the building." The building was jointly erected and embodied both the arts and the crafts, which were taught side by side at the Bauhaus. Students started as apprentices, progressed to journeymen, then completed their studies as young masters. Students had two master mentors: one for form (art) and the other for craft. In contrast with both history and other cultures, the Bauhaus embraced design for an industrial society, as opposed to a craft society. Its pedagogy was a leap forward that fused the best from the predecessor approaches and bridged gaps, art versus craft, for example, and academics versus practitioners.

In 1922, Gropius documented this pedagogy as a group of concentric circles depicting workshops of increasing skill and art as the student moved inward and deeper into mastery. Bauhaus students spent their first six months in the basic workshop studying fundamentals of form and materials by making arts and crafts. Those selected to continue spent three years studying "components" of design and building. In all stages of learning, students actually built what they designed. Speaking to American educators later in his career, Gropius discussed the DBS as an educational model. He stated that a designer should be a visionary equipped with professional skills because they had to integrate various social, technical, economic, and formal problems related to the design and construction of a building. Crucially, industrializations, along with social and scientific progress, were inevitable. This mode of production implied specialization and method. Hence, he underlined his concentric pedagogical model that emphasized relationship. This model started from the simultaneous introduction to design element and basics of constructions. It would be followed by a design and construction studio that simulated field experiences. This approached aimed at integrating design and constructions, as well as collaborative work. He also pointed to the importance of developing skills through individual experiences and feedback. This educational approach would prepare students to work with constraints. Further, he sought a balance between developing technical skills and enjoyment. This emphasis on learning design from constructing a structure necessitate suspending learning from historical cases. He argued that the latter would lead to simply imitating historical precedents. However, The Bauhaus was closed by the Nazis in 1933, only 14 years after being founded, and having produced less than 500 graduates. These students had very progressive attitudes toward architecture and collaborative design. These attitudes reflected Gropius' vision of an education that embodied the advance of time, including in technical, scientific, intellectual, and aesthetic terms, in order to meet both spiritual and material conditions of human beings (Naylor, 1968).

> Let us create a new guild of craftsmen, without the barrier between craftsman and artist. Together let us conceive and create a new building of the future, which will embrace architecture and sculpture and painting in one unity which will one day rise toward heaven from the hands of a million workers, like the crystal symbol of a new faith.
>
> (Gropius, 1919)

■ Foreword: Learning by Doing at the Bauhaus

These words could have been written by William Morris 50 years earlier. In England, the first country to feel the effects of the Industrial Revolution, Joseph Paxton was creating a new aesthetic vocabulary in iron and glass. The influential view in architecture of Paxton's time was that of Ruskin, who rejected demands for new styles. Along this line, William Morris, in "The Seven Lamps of Architecture," expressed his dislike of the Machine Age. He believed in the artist's responsibility to society and in the possibility of improving man by improving his environment. Morris rejected the machine on aesthetic and social grounds. He believed in the necessity of the improvements of social life through the collaboration of art, industry, and the crafts, which united artists, craftsmen, experts, and patrons (Naylor, 1968).

When Walter Gropius took over the Bauhaus, he was 31. Even having grown up without the benefits of the Machine Age, he embraced technology. He studied architecture in Berlin and Munich. He trained with Peter Behrens beginning in 1907. Behrens' office was a training ground for other architects, including Mies van der Rohe and Le Corbusier, who

FIGURE 0.0.1
Bauhaus curriculum diagram.

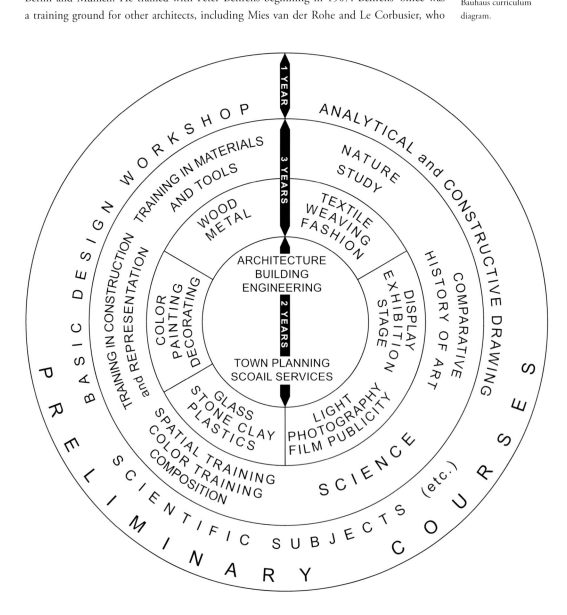

greatly influenced Gropius. In Behren's office, they learned about logical and systematical design process that reflected modern time. It was a contrast to academic design based on classical styles and order that were a common practice at that time. Gropius had demonstrated his ability to grasp the potentials of the new materials and techniques that were becoming available to architects and to suggest entirely new ways of using them. He also demonstrated foresight in the recognition of outstanding talent and the potential for talent. One of the most distinguishable aspects of the Bauhaus is the exceptional talent that he was able to assemble in such a short period of time. This talent, in architecture, industrial design, graphics and art, would later change the future of architecture profoundly.

JOHANNES ITTEN

> The ability to invent through construction and to discover through observation is developed, at least at first, by undisturbed, uninfluenced and unprejudiced experiment that is a playful tinkering with concrete goals and experimental work.
>
> (Itten, 1932)

Johannes Itten was one of the most influential Bauhaus professors. His inventive ideas involved integrating materials to enhance the design process. The institution of the preliminary course, as a step in artists' training, was not an invention of the Bauhaus or of Johannes Itten. Rather, it goes back, as we have seen, to the nineteenth century, and it was expressly encouraged in the early twentieth century by numerous art school reformers. The objectives of his courses started from developing creativity from experiences, rather than from historical conventions. It related to the second objective that focused on experiences from engaging with materials. This point encouraged students to discover their materials of choice. Further, it would equip students with principles of composition based on the laws of form and color. These principles would provide a means of objectivity (Wick, 2000). According to Itten, everything perceptible is perceived through difference, and so a general theory of contrast formed the basis of the entire course. Contrast could appear through chiaroscuro, different materials, colors, shapes, and dimensions. Itten uses materials to teach design. It is through the process of montage that he lets these materials be understood as a learning tool. In a sense, each material is seen as a different representation of building materials. In order to heighten the students' senses, both optically and haptically, Itten carried out studies with materials and textures in his course that were taken over, in modified form, by his successor Laslo Moholy-Nagy. Itten put attentions to tactile engagements with materials. The design process, according to Itten, sharpens the ability of the senses to recognize and to expand concrete thinking. He once expressed this connection in a concise formula but did not further explain: "sharp senses exact real thinking." Itten was not concerned with anatomically precise reproduction of an external reality but with finding the typical "expressive form" and "inner movement." Dimensions of the optic, as well as the haptic, were followed around 1922–23 by a series of glass windows that reveal a strictly geometric, formal construction as well as a return to a traditional technique of craftsmanship, namely, lead glazing. Examples include the glass windows in the Sommerfeld House in Berlin-Dahlem that was furnished by the Bauhaus workshops, which was one of their first design build studios. The process of making objects, including cutting and sandblasting, informed the designs.

Even at Weimar, the glass workshop, which was initially under the direction of Johannes Itten and then under Paul Klee in 1922–23, had difficulty asserting itself. After the Bauhaus moved from Weimar, it was not thought necessary to continue the glass workshop at the Dessau Bauhaus. Albers actually created his single-disk glass pictures, with their technical and formal innovations, without any institutional support, somewhat against the official trend, and without any connection to architectural tasks. However, Itten's Vorkurs also drew criticism, calling it a brainwashing, where students were to forget everything they had learned before the course (Whitford, 1984). Josef Albers had enrolled in Itten's preliminary course and was the same age as his teacher. Walter Gropius asked Albers to remain at the Bauhaus because Itten had praised Albers' work as a student.

JOSEF ALBERS

Josef Albers' view of the Bauhaus was unique. He saw education in the beginning of the twentieth century as attempts to incorporate scientific progress. Thus, they added science course into the previous models that offered basic knowledge in arithmetic, language, and writing. However, this contemporary educational models relied on routines and rote memorization. He found it detrimental in design, in which students imitating historical examples instead of designing. He called for a shift design education to privilege exercises in making things (Wick, 2000). In this line of thought, Albers was fascinated by the properties of materials and their potential when shaped. A piece of paper when cut and folded is remarkably strong and rigid. Insights gained from experimentation with sheets of paper, metal, and fabric were used in his course. He stressed on developing creativity through continuous inventions that would be facilitated by the understanding of methods of working with a substance. In other words, it was process of experimentations accompanied by observations. It would take longer to educate designers (Wick, 2000). The pedagogical ideas of John Dewey (1859–1952) had a profound influence on Albers, as evidenced by his belief in the process of learning based on trial and error as well as on discoveries. With these two points, Albers demonstrated that he was an educator who took the progressive educational ideals of the pedagogical reform movement of the period around and after 1900 and productively applied them to the field of artists' training. Dewey's writings on pedagogy, including *The School and Society* and *Democracy and Education*, were published during the first two decades of the twentieth century in German translation and were helpful for the reform pedagogy movement, especially for Kerschensteiner. Dewey's pedagogical pragmatism, which he himself characterized as "instrumentalism," can be summarized briefly as follows: the school should prepare students for practical life; consequently, dead book knowledge (ancient languages, to some extent mathematics as well) should be abandoned. Thus, "learning by doing" is the fundamental pedagogical principle.

Albers saw his own view of practical instruction in deliberate contrast to the practical instruction of the work school, which was focused only on craft skills. These skills in crafts encompassed many aspects, including woodworking, tailoring, and bookbinding. Although Albers was drawn to the handicrafts, he tried to expand the dimension of the creative, which he considered essential. In his "Werklicher Formunterricht" (instruction in form through work), Albers rigorously limited the use of tools at first in order to order to activate the students' creative energies and to counteract a tendency to fall into actions guided by tradition. He used a sheet of paper to explain this point. We tended to treat paper simply a flat sheet.

However, he showed that we could transform into new expressions, including standing up and become sculptural (Wick, 2000).

In contrast to the official opinion at the Bauhaus (as stated in the founding manifesto) that art cannot be taught, Albers took a somewhat modified standpoint on the issue. He believed that art could not be taught directly, but that it could be "learned." This linguistic nuance contains that which distinguishes the principles of Albers' concept of education from the practical training of the old school, as manifested in the activities of the art academies. The teaching of design by Josef Albers and his intention to abolish hierarchy and integrate the arts remains the core belief at the Bauhaus. Albers' teaching methods were very different than those of his colleagues. Albers was more concerned with exposing his students to making and later inferring theoretical principles. Albers promoted the notion of flexible teaching, by which experimentation is encouraged and failure acceptable.

Hired in 1923 by Walter Gropius to teach one section of the preliminary course, Albers was asked to expose his students to materials and methods of craft. Where Itten encouraged students to make collages using different materials, Albers limited the students to a single material. This reductive process allowed for the students to learn about basic design elements such as texture, surface, structure, space, and form. Many of these exercises were done in paper or cardboard and offered an open-ended approach. In 1929, Albers wrote a description for the course that included the phrase "inductive learning experiences" without instructed leadership, to achieve one's own experiences through self-selected and directed assignments. Albers was not interested in all the students following the same method; instead he allowed each student to find his own way of solving a problem. Understanding the difference between "material studies" (Materialstudie) and "matter studies" (Materiestudie) is helpful for grasping Albers' method. In the material studies, the students made projects that emphasized the materials' inner energies or capacity. In the matter studies, students studied the materials' external image and concentrated on texture, form, and contrast. These materials included a range of industrial materials, such as metal, wood, and glass. He was not interested in the students' prior knowledge. He wanted them to be inventive and work without preconception through direct experience. Albers' studio visited the workshops of box-, chair-, and basket-makers, of carpenters and cabinet-makers, of coopers and cart wrights, in order to learn the different uses of wood; the different characteristics of flat grain and quarter-sawing, split, bent, and laminated wood; and to learn the various methods of joining: gluing, nailing, pegging, and screwing. The exercises with matiere show that Albers was building on the work of Itten and Moholy-Nagy. Later in Moholy-Nagy's course, the equilibrium studies were given more time than the exercises with tactile and surface aspects; in Albers's course, by contrast, the real emphasis was placed on the material exercises. This practice was Albers' most original and unmistakable contribution to the pedagogy of the Bauhaus. Albers saw the inevitability of the industrial world in the considerations of functions and materials, in which materials informed functions.

This decision to abandon a basic instruction, in which students merely paint and draw, in favor of a systematic study of materials, of their constructional, functional, and economic requirements and possibilities, was didactically significant in that it related to the Bauhaus founding manifesto of 1919, which emphasized applied arts. The basic purpose of these material exercises was to develop the general ability of "constructional thinking," as construction does not relate exclusively to architecture. Hannes Beckmann, a student at the Bauhaus from 1928 to 1931, illustrated his impression of Albers' preliminary course, as told in Wick, 2000.

At the beginning of the course, Albers asked students to make anything out of a stack of newspaper. In response to varieties of child toys that students made from newspaper, Albers simply folded a piece of a newspaper to make it stood up. In a way, he showed students to work with properties of a material. Albers stressed optimal use, or doing as much as possible without loss or waste. Teaching economy of materials meant teaching rational, planned action. Economy of materials implies discipline, and cleanliness and exactness are the most important factors in discipline. Economy in the use of materials leads to an emphasis on lightness, which was a widely accepted goal at the Bauhaus (in Moholy-Nagy's course, for example). This was realized in the realm of product design by Marcel Breuer and his steel tube chair.

SUMMARY

The Bauhaus significantly influenced architectural education. Many of the professors migrated to the United States during World War II to teach and practice, profoundly affecting North American educational pedagogy. Both Johannes Itten and Joseph Albers taught in the United States and the concept of learning by doing was a central theme in their coursework. These professors revolutionized design education through the use of simple teaching methods, which did not emphasize preconceptions. Their interest in the nature of materials and the importance they placed on the basic understanding of these materials are paramount.

REFERENCES

Droste, M. (1990). *Bauhaus*. London: Taschen Press.
Itten, J. (1967). *Design and Form: The Basic Course at the Bauhaus*. London: Thames and Hudson.
Jencks, C. (1997). *Theories and Manifestoes of Contemporary Architecture*. Chichester: Wiley.
Naylor, G. (1968). *The Bauhaus*. New York: Studio Vista.
Whitford, F. (1984). *Bauhaus*. London: Thames and Hudson.
Wick, R. K. (2000). *Teaching at the Bauhaus*. Berlin: Hatze Cantz.

Preface: Informality and Temporality

Appropriation in Atlanta as a Prototype for Resilient Communities

William Carpenter

THE NATURE OF IDEAS

A strong and resonant concept in architecture and design inherently solves a problem or set of problems. As designers and artists, we all face the void of emptiness; of nothingness, the blank sheet of paper, a blank computer screen. So the first step is to clearly define the problem. The programmatic and site forces need to be defined during the research process and remember that the research process is a patient search, a creative search. There is a reciprocity between research and design.

So we have the following:

Site forces
Programmatic forces
Conceptual forces

As Steven Holl states, "A concept whether rationally explicit or subjective establishes an order, a field of inquiry and a limited principle."

The strength of a concept has to do with the clarity of its mandate to manage the scheme into a particular direction. How long the concept can continue to sustain potency through the design process. This reveals preconceptions quickly and allowed a concept to fatigue. A concept is a living thing, and the designer has to have the courage to let it fatigue and move through preconceptions. A natural order exists, and the concept has the strength to inform the overall mandate or premise and then move across scales to inform a system of assembly. Design is the confluence or assembly of programmatic, site, and conceptual forces. Therefore, this is an ordering system. A concept is an ordering system in spatial terms. When realized, a concept or network of concepts give direction and guidance to the designer at every scale. From the whole to the part or from the part to the whole. It provides us with a framework of position to experiment and innovate.

As Donald Judd tells us, "Order is reason made visible." In the same vain Giancarlo De Carlo states, "Architecture is the organization of from and physical space through (an framed) by the idea. This is the difference between building and architecture." As Samuel Mockbee states,

> The practice of architecture and urbanism not only required participation in the profession, but it also requires civic engagement. It has to address social values as well as aesthetic and technical values. the gift an architect has to address is his or her imagination, their intuition. we can therefore take something ordinary and elevate it into something extraordinary.

This is resilience.

> Architecture begins at the measurable, and the idea transcends it to the immeasurable.
>
> Louis I. Kahn (Tyng, 1984)

PROLOGUE

The design build studio (DBS) incorporating digital fabrication represents a watershed change in architectural education pedagogies, in academia, and in practical and practice-based applications as well. This has been my area of focus in research and scholarship for the past 37 years. My first book, *Learning by Building* (Routledge, 1997), was the first to describe the movement. This movement has now grown into an exciting and rigorous method of presenting tectonic experimentation and the foregrounded advancement of service-learning methods into design education. Some of the professors and students sat with me. Sitting in the front row presenting our ACSA papers on this subject in the early 1990s where a few attendees gathered in nearly empty rooms. Then, in 1992 with the advent of the Auburn University Rural studio founded by DK Ruth and Samuel Mockbee, you could feel an electricity in the air, a new pulse of architectural academia.

Now, you see the front row filled with deans and chairs of departments and colleges and interested students and faculty there; it was a charged atmosphere now with standing room only lecture halls. At that time, I worked closely with the AIAS and gave keynote speeches and seminars each year at the AIAS Forum and led a design build project for the flight 592 ValuJet memorial with John Cary and Elizabeth Pater Zyberk and the University of Miami students. The movement grew from 7 schools including Southern Poly to over 30 schools in just ten years. And now, globally we have over 90 schools with DBS programs.

The DBS allows for a multidisciplinary approach and for a haptic and cognitive process to occur within a team structure. This approach incorporates an integrated paradigm in simultaneity; where designing and building occur at the same time.

> The designer should become aware as a person of vision and of professional competency whose take it is to coordinate the many social, technical, economic and formal problems which arise in in the design of architecture. In this age of specialization; method is more important than information and students should work in collaborative e teams to build these skills.
>
> Walter Gropius FAIA, 1959 ACSA National Assembly Meeting Keynote Address, Director; Harvard Graduate School of Design

INFORMALITY AND TEMPORALITY

Working Definitions:

- **Informality**—Organic natural and manmade growth patterns in urban morphology which reconcile, or attempt to reconcile, the collision between certain natural systems such as topography, forests, rivers, infrastructure, and urban densities.
- **Temporary Appropriation**—The making of a thing (such as), urban spaces, building, shelter, public space into your own, which sometimes implies illegal or temporary use (Lara-Hernandez and Melis, 2018).

Framing—Our view of the world is defined by frames: doorframes, window frames, and surrounding paintings, screens, and cellular and television signals. Frames contain, order, and systematize their contexts (Porter, 2015).

Design Build—When designing and building occurs in relation to making. In architectural practice it usually relates to cost saving and speed of construction in building; in academia it normally relates to service-learning based projects or component-based material and systems-based artifact studies, which can be used in research or practice (Carpenter, 1997).

Simultaneity—When designing and building occurs at the same time or in overlapping sequences. Normally simultaneity is studied in relation to haptic cognition and materials-based learning and the neurosciences (Carpenter, 2003).

The Peccioli Charter proposes a bold global vision for the country of Italy as a "Nation of Resilient Communities," and it also creates a global network of practitioners and scholars of design centered in Peccioli on urban innovation. The new technical tools, such as digital fabrication and visualization, allows us to examine the environmental crisis in new ways. The charter for the new Italian Resilient Communities movement states as follows:

> We believe that sustainable development is not an obsolete option or concept, but a collective commitment that must be based on solid pillars of a new development paradigm that defines a new alliance between space and society, between individuals and community.

To highlight four of the main points of the Peccioli Charter, we can further understand how temporary appropriation and design build practices align and exponentially expand how to examine and implement these principles:

1. PROMOTE INNOVATION

"Innovation becomes an important catalyst in this thinking: Resilient Communities want to promote innovation, always and everywhere, sharing their experiences, their actions of resistance, their resilience practices, learning from each other and presenting themselves as new knowledge platforms."

2. REIMAGINE CITIES AND LIFE SPACES

"In the Resilient Communities each actor must promote a radical rethinking of the urban fabric, starting from the suburbs, and its environment to transform cities into virtuous non-erosive and dissipative systems that react actively to climate, economic, social and cultural changes, generating mitigations."

3. BE SENSITIVE AND EFFECTIVE

"The capacity for reaction and transformation of the urban fabric must characterize the Resilient Communities of the future, through timely actions that pass from the late reaction to effective prevention."

■ Preface: Informality and Temporality

4. BE POLYCENTRIC

"The Resilient Communities will facilitate relations between settlement systems based on territorial identity, specialization and the distribution of urban-rural functions in a polycentric and reticular perspective."

TEMPORARY APPROPRIATION AND INFORMALITY: A PROTOTYPE

With the organic growth of informal systems in cities creating a densification of interstitial suburban spaces occurs. This is an in-between condition of natural boundaries and urban density. It is this gray space between figure and ground, and this allows for areas of the city worthy of temporary appropriations. This gray zone is a healing condition of resiliency. For the Peccioli Charter, we emphasize innovation, sensitivity, and a polycentric approach. The following prototypes show partnerships the author has been involved in leading, which form a prototype that is transferable to other sites; each example helps to solve a specific urban issue or set of issues.

With the advent of Covid-19 and the worldwide protests regarding racism, we see a watershed change regarding temporary appropriation of urban space. For example, social distancing alone redefines and reframes our experience of each other and of the city.

SELECTED PROTOTYPES

As an architecture professor in Atlanta for the past 28 years, I have witnessed profound change in the city. After the 1996 Olympics, the city nearly doubled in size, to over 6 million people. The need for urban housing became foregrounded, and over 100,000 units have been built in the past 10 years. The following projects are a glimpse into some of the prototypes regarding temporary appropriation and design build approaches in the city. If we examine the urban plan of Atlanta, you will see three main grids which collide along a topographical ridge (Peachtree Street), which is a strong organizing device and a historical Indian trail.

Cutting through the historic urban grids is the interstate connector, which plows through the historic districts like a gouge and cuts off the Auburn Avenue district from the downtown, effectively damaging it for the past 50 years. The decision was intentional by the former state governor and certainly racially motivated.

Rem Koolhaas writes about Atlanta and informality:

> Less a city and more a landscape, Atlanta is a delicate and sparse carpeting of dwellings and supreme composition of small fields. In this photo essay, this non-city is examined through an incisive and questioning lens that focuses on the city's most important contextual references; vegetation and infrastructure. A new aesthetic operates in Atlanta: the random juxtaposition of entities that have nothing in common except their coexistence? **Atlanta** is a creative experiment, but it is not intellectual or critical: it has taken place without argument. It represents current conditions—without any imposition of program, manifesto, ideology.
>
> (Koolhaas and Mau)

Preface: Informality and Temporality

He goes on to describe Atlanta as a

> convulsive architecture that will eventually acquire beauty, instead of a navigable street grid, a sensible zoning code or a dominant housing type, it is green space, both public and private, that weave together our disparate neighborhoods and commercial monuments into something approaching a cohesive whole.

(Koolhaas and Prat)

The following projects are interventions into the urban context, which help reveal cultural and societal needs and allow for students and faculty to investigate learning objectives and outcomes which are complex, multilayered, and constantly evolving. The faculty member faced many obstacles in helping get these projects realized. The influence of several visits by Rem Koolhaas and Samuel Mockbee became formative in the direction and pedagogy for these projects.

MAD HOUSERS

The first example in Atlanta is a collaboration project between the homeless advocacy group "The Mad Housers" and my students at Kennesaw State University. This group is comprised of mainly military veterans who build their own shelters from recycled materials and create

FIGURE 0.1.1
Mad Housers Prototype: Temporary Appropriation of Urban Spaces. The prototype can be assembled in eight hours and includes a stove for heating, cooking, and rainwater collection. Southern Polytechnic State University, Mad Housers design build studio, size: 50 s.f., budget $348.00.
Photo credit: Author.

■ Preface: Informality and Temporality

encampments on illegally used land. Even though the land is considered, there are certain political structures that allow the city to "look the other way." For example, one resident has attached his dwelling to a railroad bridge, which is evocative of the Lebbeus Woods high houses in London. This leads to a stealth-like existence creating a guerilla camouflage that allows for a symbiotic relationship use of shelter and infrastructure. It is an understanding of sympathy and a verve for survival (Carpenter, 1997, 2009) (Madhousers.org).

Normally these units are four feet wide by eight feet deep and about ten feet high. The materials palette is usually recycled wood from demolished buildings or from donated sources. They are usually timber frame, and they contain a heat source woodstove which is also a cooking device devised by the group. This device has kept many of these homeless residents from freezing to death and has been emulated by many other homeless advocacy groups.

This project emphasizes the gray liminal spaces between urban infrastructure and the urban core. Many of these projects were prefabricated in the shop and then delivered to the sites at night.

MISS MATTIES GARDEN

The second example is that of a project in downtown Atlanta called "Miss Matties Garden." This project is a former garbage dump and drug sales house that was reappropriated into a community garden by my Design for Humanity studio. The project was temporarily occupied while construction took place without permits through a creative interpretation of the term "garden structure" in the building code. Because of this loophole, we were able to build the

FIGURE 0.1.2
Mad Housers Prototype; image with doors open.

Photo credit: Author.

xxvi

Preface: Informality and Temporality

FIGURE 0.1.3
Southern Polytechnic State University, Mad Housers design build hut, size: 50 s.f., budget $348.00.

project with a building permit. The project transformed this dump into a meaningful urban park that continues to patina and grow over time with meaning and sensitivity.

Juxtapositions of the temporal qualities of the site and materials of this project allow for a kind of freezing in time when one visits the site. The stone walls frame the site and topography, and the light wooden structures are organic and temporal. The project creates a meditative space through its winding paths and gathering spaces and allows for contemplative reflection of lost loved ones in this neighborhood.

This project still offers many transferable lessons. It has become an important gathering place for the community and has taken a dangerous site on this street and turned it into a desirable contemplative garden.

■ Preface: Informality and Temporality

FIGURE 0.1.4
Ms. Matties Garden, entry view from the street. Southern Polytechnic State University, Design Build Studio, size: .25 acres, budget: $6,000.00.
Photo credit: Author.

REYNOLDSTOWN GATEWAY PARK

This site turned one of the most dangerous areas of the city into a flourishing landmark and urban park as a design build studio involving simultaneity. The project uses the temporary appropriation of this area of the city and involves local graffiti artists in its creation. Local children created the detailed mosaics, and the steel was fabricated in a nearby steel plant where the students worked alongside local residents and steelworkers. The project now marks an important threshold of the city and announces this important neighborhood of former African-American slaves who moved to Atlanta after the United States Civil War. Many of these residents are well recognized and talented quilters, jazz musicians, hip hop artists, and visual artists known internationally.

Odd Lots (For Future Consideration)

The odd lots purchased by artist Gordon Matta Clark in New York, mainly at local tax auctions, reveal temporary appropriation in an interesting way. He was essentially buying small vestiges of land, some only centimeters wide, but they reveal temporary appropriation through the potential uses and reconciling of ownership of private and public entities. Matta Clark bought a total of 15 sites in the New York City area, and before his death he intended to use these for future use. The odd lots of Matta Clark are a form of informality and temporality appropriation; we can examine these examples in any city as they form a

Preface: Informality and Temporality

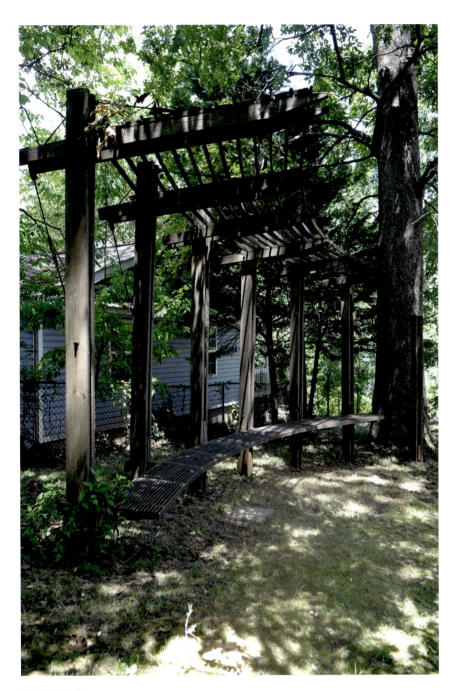

FIGURE 0.1.5
Ms. Matties Garden, reflection pavilion. Southern Polytechnic State University, Design Build Studio, size: .25 acres, budget: $6,000.00.

Photo credit: Author.

■ Preface: Informality and Temporality

FIGURE 0.1.6
Reynoldstown Gateway Park. Team leaders, students B. J. Goodman and Michael Rickman. Collaborators: James Fausett FAIA, Young Hughley Jr. (executive director of the Reynoldstown Revitalization Corporation), and Shannon Sanders Mcdonald AIA. Southern Polytechnic State University, Design Build Studio, size:.85 acres, budget $740,000.00.

Photo credit: Author.

FIGURE 0.1.7
Reynoldstown Gateway Park; steel entry pavilion.

Photo credit: Author.

Preface: Informality and Temporality

negotiation between urban overlays of public, private, and semi-private ownership. What are the leftover parcels/spaces, and how can they be energized and appropriated? This example offers us a transferable method to understand the dynamic morphology of the city and the notion of ownership.

FIGURE 0.1.8
Reynoldstown Gateway Park; steel pavilion with tile paving.

Photo credit: Author.

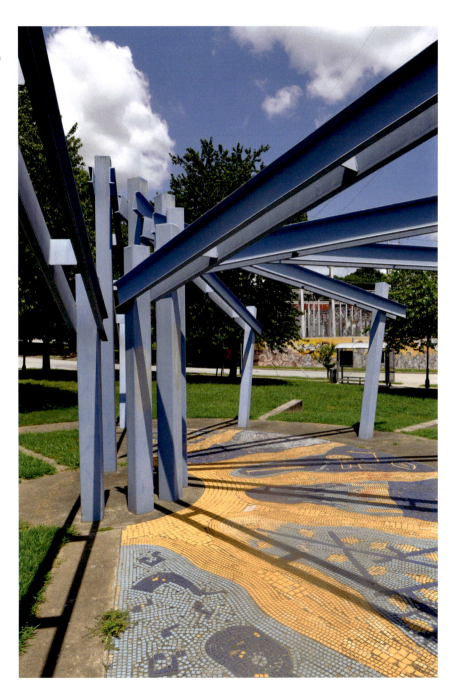

xxxi

CONCLUSIONS

These examples offer the Peccioli Charter as set of prototypes of how academic partnerships with local industries and practices can create projects that involve and expand the interstitial spaces of the cities and to solve complex urban problems in the design build studio.

Resilience and the self-healing city are compelling definitions of informality and its manifestation of temporary appropriation in urban morphologies and dynamic spatial systems. These Atlanta projects are examples of temporary appropriation and design build studios which allow for liminality and simultaneity to occur while also giving back to communities.

As we examine the ideas of informality and temporality appropriation, we should ask how the projects contribute to student learning, faculty exploration, and how the projects contribute to community. Each of these projects navigated or carefully avoided complex codes, and the teams worked closely with community members to achieve these goals.

REFERENCES

Carpenter, W. (1997). *Learning by Building*. New York: Van Nostrand Reinhold.
Carpenter, W. (2009). *Design Build Studio*. New York: Lightroom Press.
Di Raimo, A., Lehmann S. and Melis, A. (2021). *Informality Through Sustainability: Urban Informality Now*. London: Routledge.
Porter, J. (2005). *Archispeak An Illustrated Guide to Architectural Design Terms*. London: Spon Press.
Tyng, A. (1984). *Beginnings: Louis I. Kahn's Philosophy of Architecture*. New Jersey: Wiley.

Introduction

William Carpenter

The role of this essay is to describe some of the forefront process-based approaches in current engineering and architectural practice. Its purpose is to encourage and help reconcile DBS projects and faculty to consider syllabus design, which will incorporate some of these approaches. This will help push the educational learning objectives forward and allow the learning outcomes within the DBS to be focused and informed by some of these cutting-edge ideas in architectural practice.

The chapter allows us to forecast where architectural education might go in the future as DBS professors might include new materials such as carbon fibers, dichroic glass, sustainable methods, and CATIA design processes. These studios could also work with materials scientists and architectural practitioners to study new materials and test them before they come to market. Within the boundary of this study, this chapter is not a comprehensive look at these new ideas. Rather it is a survey of some of the ideas present which help act as vector forces for the DBS professors to analyze and consider.

Technology is reshaping the face of today's architectural practice. Email and videoconferencing is now routine, and geographic barriers that once prevented collaboration have now been removed. Design drawings can be priced more accurately because of the computer, and spaces can be visualized to a precise extent, including materials, lighting, and spatial perception. Technology has also changed architectural education. Students now use the computer to build study models and walk-throughs that simulate the experience of assembling and experiencing architecture. It appears, however, that architectural education is a step behind architectural practice. This chapter examines several cutting-edge methods being used in the field. Its purpose is to encourage DBS professors to align more closely with these trends so architectural students will be better prepared for practice.

TECHNOLOGY TRANSFER

Technology transfer has been one of the most exciting areas of research in the design build method. It is the practice of evaluating how technologies from one discipline can transfer to another, sometimes unrelated, discipline. Technology transfer is most typically used in the automotive, aerospace, and shipbuilding industries. Kieran Timberlake, a leader in this area of research, advocates an integration from four related disciplines involved in the construction process, which are architecture, construction, materials science, and product engineering (Kieran and Timberlake, 2003). Researchers believe this integration will transform the way architects practice. Further, transfer processes appear to reinvent the construction process. Timberlake contrasted automotive or aerospace with construction industries. The former integrated latest technological advancement, including integrated design and rapid prototyping, while the latter still relied on a linear process. For example, the design and construction industry still followed the line of the production of construction document that architects turned over to a contractor. In turn, the contractor passed that along to a fabricator then to a company (Kieran and Timberlake, 2003).

This circuitous task process is quickly being overtaken by computer modelling techniques, which are now combined with fabrication software that connect the architect directly to the fabricator. In the future, it is likely that the architect's precise computer model will become the shop drawing, and fabrication will be executed from this.

RAPID PROTOTYPING

Rapid prototyping refers to a wide range of state-of-the-art techniques in which a three-dimensional design specified by a computer file is fabricated in a machine that calculates the object's cross section, then sinters, laminates, or solidifies hundreds of very thin cross-sectional layers (Kieran and Timberlake, 2003). Rapid prototyping allows for the testing of materials and systems. These prototypes allow an architect to input size and shape data so that building details, such as a wall or roof connection, can be tested. The technique can also be used to test the overall performance of a building model, including its aerodynamics, solar patterns, and thermal efficiency. It allows for the quick testing of multiple conceptual frameworks early on in the design process, which appears encouraging. As an example, in automobile production, the assembly line has streamlined the way that cars are built. This streamline took advantages of integrations of computing technology as well as improvements in engineering precisions (Kieran and Timberlake, 2003).

PETER RICE AND FULL-SCALE MODELLING

The work of engineer Peter Rice offers an important process model. His intention is not to come up with surprises but to follow a process of discovery. A particularly helpful project to study is the Menil Collection in Houston, which was a collaboration between the architect Renzo Piano and the engineer Peter Rice of Ove Arup and Partners. The project involved housing an art collection for the DeMenil Family. The client's desire for natural light guided the project, in which natural light, such as the trajectory of the sun, would inform the lighting condition inside the museum (Rice, 1993).

During the time of Piano and Rice, we had experimented with various materials. Ferro-cement and ductile iron were two of these materials. In combining them we sought to weave together the porcelainlike fragility of the ductile iron with the soft, grainy like texture of the ferro-cement into a continuous melded whole. Renzo, with active support from me, decided that the Menil Gallery roof would be in ferro-cement. This is a highly reinforced thin sheet of concrete. Pier Luigi Nervi, the outstanding designer of the age in Italy in the 1950s, invented it. The ferro-cement, which is usually made by a plastering technique and its principal use is seen in boats, is a material dependent on very high-quality workmanship to make it sound and durable. In its normal condition, it is 1.5–4 centimeters in thickness with six to eight layers of wire mesh reinforcement. When it is used in boats, a steel cage is made to approximate the shape wanted. This cage, which has occasional longer rods to help keep its shape, becomes a rigid hull. Very dry mortar is then made, and the cage is plastered and then finished on the outside by wooden and steel towelling. It is very important for the quality of the final project that the plastering is done in a single continuous application and that no dry joints occur, that is, joints between the mortar which has already started to harden and wet mortar which is being applied (Rice, 1993).

The collaboration between Rice and Piano enhanced the design build process. The project is an amalgam of both of their ideas, and the ideas are totally and inextricably linked to the process of ferro-cement making. Its advantages are its strengths while requiring only a minimum amount of materials. Further, its thinness and fineness allow it to follow elegant shapes and surface quality. The construction process allows for inspection to maintain its qualities, including the density of mortar and the mesh. Rice stresses the importance of "material in an industrial environment" (Rice, 1993).

Rice and Piano's collaboration included input from lighting designers, the client, art consultants, and other related engineers. This amount of input at such an early stage of the projects could have confused other lead designers, but Piano and Rice incorporated this information into a clear and consistent whole. They also created a template, which included careful handcraft as well as the benefit of steel and ferro-cement prefabrication. Changes from Piano's sketch in which the ferro-cement louvers are a part of the structure into louvers as a separate element illustrate a dialogue between Piano and Rice (Rice, 1993).

Another Texas museum, designed about 20 years before by Louis I. Kahn, directly influenced this project. The lighting system implemented in the Kimbell Art Museum in Fort Worth, Texas, also used the notion of diffused light and naturally lit paintings. For this project, Kahn had full-scale mock-ups of the lighting diffusers made and ultimately chose the 50 percent perforations for the desired lighting effects. The illustrations at the end of this section include Kahn's sketch for these diffusers and the ultimate realization in the gallery space.

Rice points that the full-scale prototype model was a critical element in the design process. For example, they fabricated a fiberglass mold to test the density of mortar matrix. They also used similar approaches to experiment with the trussing structure. They tested the use of ductile iron (Rice, 1993).

ELECTRONIC MEDIA

In *Visions Unfolding: Architecture in the Age of Electronic Media* (1992), Peter Eisenman argues that architecture is out of pace with electronic age. He pointed to the shift from the mechanical to electronic modes of reproductions. It relates to the role of humans in the process, such as in photography and telefax. In photography, a person could control the image captured, while with fax, the reproductions came out without any human interference. In essence, the advance of media impacted our perceptions of reality. The description of reality, whether virtual or constructed, relates directly to the DBS, which is largely out of step with actual practice. Eisenman discusses the connection between vision and the designer, which is the primary reason that the DBS could be an important teaching tool. He pointed out to the long-standing notion that architecture represented the real thing. Further, metaphors such as "house and home" or "bricks and mortar" reinforce this stress on reality. Architecture also relates to efforts to overcome the force of gravity. However, the electronic age has presented us reality based on "media and simulation." It implied that appearance has taken over real things. He criticized the reluctance of architecture to acknowledge this shift in our perceptions of reality (Eisenman, 1992). In this line of thought, the DBS connects the abstract realm of envisioning with the haptic realm of hand-to-mind connection and material assembly. Envision is a way to relate seeing to thinking.

■ Introduction

Sight, which includes seeing the team on the project and seeing ideas turn to reality, is critical to the DBS. The electronic visualization methods allow these ideas to be seen more clearly. "Architecture, unlike any other discipline, concretised vision" (Eisenman, 1992).

FRANK O. GEHRY AND PARTNERS—CATIA PROCESSES

Computer-aided three-dimensional interactive application, or CATIA, was first used in the 1992 fish sculpture designed by Frank Gehry for the Vila Olimpica in Barcelona. This software was originally developed for the aerospace industry by Dessault Systemes of Paris, France, and has revolutionized the way that irregularly shaped buildings can be produced. According to a project architect in the Gehry office, Gerhard Mayer, "Gehry's designs are worked out at length in physical models, which are then laser scanned in three dimensions by a mechanical arm" (*Architecture Magazine*, 2002). Frank Gehry's experimentation involved using the computer as a design tool and working with cutting-edge engineering and fabrication contractors in order to reinvent the construction process. Gehry's design process incorporates a "skin-in" approach, meaning he works from the envelope of the building in, as opposed to the strict modernist doctrine of working from the structural grid out, such in Le Corbusier's architecture. This approach is linked to a paradigmatic approach to architecture as a whole. The modernist method was similar to an assembly line: pieces were developed that made up the machine/architecture, components were standardized, and the various systems (of architecture, plants, exterior panels) were made as autonomous and independent as possible. Gehry's method is relational: the secret is the relation between the parts instead of their independence. Underneath the curvature of his architecture lies an electronic system that Gehry developed.

In the early 1990s, the Gehry office had only three outdated computers, which were mainly used for accounting purposes. The office purchased discarded IBM computers at a garage sale and then began a computer revolution in architectural design. Frank Gehry was trained in an era when becoming an architect was an act of social responsibility. Gehry was 49 years old and had been practicing architecture for 16 years when he had designed his own house in Santa Monica, California, in 1978. When asked how he starts a project, he replies, "through drawing." When asked how he gets his ideas, he states, "We talk to the client, a lot." These self-effacing comments by Gehry himself and the tendency of others to dismiss his hard work to the exigency of genius hide the exceptionally efficient entity of his design process. Similarly, the designation of Gehry as an artist, and his work as sculptural, had unexplainably delayed the recognition that he and his office deserves in contributing to changes in architecture and architectural practice. His matter-of-fact manner also hides the obvious importance of the statements themselves—he does begin with a project through drawing, and he does talk "a lot" to his clients" (Lindsey, 2001).

Jim Glymph joined the firm in 1989 as an executive architect. He was hired because of the problems arising in the design of the Disney Concert Hall. The curvaceous form gives the design its prominent feature, such as doubly curving stone panel for its exterior walls. They were able to work out the complex geometry by working together with aerospace engineers who designed the Mirage fighter plane (Lindsey, 2001). The first digital project fully realized in the Gehry office was the Barcelona Fish. Glymph, with extensive experience as an executive architect, began to develop the in-house expertise to realize that increasingly exuberant formal developments of Gehry. A "technical genius," as described by Gehry, Glymph immediately saw the deeper potential for the computer to assist in the construction of more complex shapes. The first real test would come in a building for the 1992 Olympic Village in Barcelona—part of a residential and commercial master plan designed by Bruce Graham of Skidmore Owings and Merrill (SOM). The 54-meter-long and 35-meter-high fish-shaped canopy was part of a 14,000-square-meter commercial development designed by Gehry. The dynamic shape was to be realized in a steel frame clad in woven stainless steel. With an extremely tight construction schedule of ten months, Glymph faced a familiar architectural problem—how to build a complex object, in a short amount of time, within the budget allotted (Lindsey, 2001).

As Gehry's first fully digital project and a turning point in his design process, the Barcelona Fish project warrants elaboration. The design was initially developed from Gehry's sketches and translated into a wood and metal model. With the design work complete, the problem emerged: how to construct and support a fish. Glymph and the office worked with William Mitchell, professor of architecture and computer guru at Harvard, and student Evan Smythe to model the complex form with Alias software. They produced a digital model that was visually accurate but lacked the necessary information to construct the form. The surface of the Alias computer model, defined as a grid of polygons approximating the shape, did not allow for the precise spatial location of points on the surface. The majority of the software written for the architectural field at the time consisted of either two-dimensional drafting software or modelling software designed for visualization. This software could not support the connection of the digital model to computer-aided manufacturing that Glymph felt was an essential step in building the computer forms (Lindsey, 2001). Knowing that the software that could produce the required accuracy and depth existed in the automotive and aerospace industry, Glymph went searching for the right application. He found CATIA, a software company developed for the aerospace industry by Dessault, a French software company associated with IBM. With that, he became a pivotal figure in the development of the Gehry office. Not only did he have the foresight to adopt the CATIA program, he understood its value to Gehry in that irregular forms could be realized and linked to the construction process. Another of Glymph's contributions was recruiting Rick Smith, who previously worked in the aerospace industry (Lindsey, 2001).

Gehry's methods shifted radically at this time in his career. Using methods previously employed by his office to produce the tedious hand drawings—string, plumb bobs, and countless measurements—a digital model was produced. It was based on CATIA's complete numerical control, developing descriptions for the surface that were described by polynomial equations. The surface was literally "built" using the mathematical equations of descriptive geometry. This allowed the spatial location of any point on the surface to be determined precisely. Smith's digital model was used to generate a laser-cut paper stack model in order to verify the accuracy of the translation. It matched. Working from the surface of the digital model, Smith developed a series of connection points that located where the woven skin could be attached to the steel frame. These points were converted to AES format and used by the structural engineers of SOM to develop the structural skeleton. The skin was offset from the structure an average of ten inches and was supported from the frame with steel strakes of varying sizes. This system—a skin, a space for connection, and a space for the structure—was later used on the Guggenheim Museum in Bilbao (1991–97) and the Experience Music Project (EMP) in Seattle (1995–2000). The ability to work with the surface structures came out from figuring out the translation from complex three-dimensional form with two-dimensional drawings (Novitski, 1992). Smith flew to Italy and for 11 days worked with the construction team to "get it out." Working from the skin to the structure, they determined the exact dimensions of each strake and produced paper templates that were used. The next project developed in the CATIA design process model was the Hanover Bus Stop. This project, built for Expo 2000, allowed Gehry's team to further the design process begun with the Fish project and to completely build the project in CATIA without any other type of construction documents.

■ Introduction

TABLE 01 CATIA Process

Museo Bilbao Process Image	*CATIA Process in the Gehry Office*
	1 Step One Jim Glymph or CATIA engineer traces sketch model for digital input in the Gehry offices. 2 Step Two Surface model is created in CATIA from the digitized points. 3 Step Three Shaded surface model is created in CATIA from the surface model. 4 Step Four CNC-fabricated milled model is created to verify the accuracy of the computer model. 5 Step Five After verification and possible revisions, a model is created which designates the primary structural framing members in CATIA. 6 Step Six Immediately following the previous step, the secondary structure, such as purlins and skin attachment, is created. 7 Step Seven Frank Gehry and Jim Glymph and office staff examine the models again and check for aesthetic and functional soundness. Shop drawings of the frame are emailed to the office from the structural fabricator and carefully checked in the Gehry office. 8 Step Eight After about a five-month period of checking shop drawings and fabrication, the structural frame is assembled on-site and checked by the general contractor, project engineers, and architectural team. 9 Step Nine After about an eight-month period of construction, titanium cladding is applied to the secondary structure. 10 Step Ten The completed building is tested and occupied.

Digital information is malleable. Once the information of the final design model is in a digital form, it can play a number of other roles: simulation, direct detailing, and computer-aided manufacturing (CAM) being the most recent. While Smith recites an office rule, "model all and only necessary design information," the digital models have become increasingly more detailed. This occurs through the continued development of the model by the design team, as well as contributions by consultants and manufacturers who relay their work back.

Jim Glyph has stated, "The cost of producing and reviewing shop drawings in a large project far exceeds the architectural and engineering fees" (Cocke, 2000).

COMPUTER-AIDED MANUFACTURING

Perhaps the most innovative use of digital information in the Gehry office, and the most relevant to this study, is computer-aided manufacturing. It crosses the boundaries between design and construction, repositioning architects as the center of the process. Meanwhile, contractors assume the assembly and management roles. In this vein, manufacturers and the contractors turn into an important partner in the design team. This approach reconstitutes relationship between mass production, standardization, prefabrication and the industrial production of building component selection and arrangement in architecture. As a result, the field has shifted into "mass-customisation" (Lindsey, 2001). One of the other exciting new technologies that directly affects the future of the DBS is the three-dimensional printer. This technology has allowed for physical manifestations of the design, which could be enticing for clients.

TECHNOLOGY AND THE DBS

This chapter demonstrates that architecture is a rapidly changing practice. In just ten years, an entire design process and methodology within the Frank Gehry office changed. The production process of the architecture also changed. How does this type of inherent change affect architectural education? How does it inherently affect the concept of the DBS? It appears that if the DBS would more closely align with some of these practice-based changes, it might prepare the students in a more effective way for the rapidly changing practice. Most of the DBS programs that have been discussed use, for example, stick frame construction. This method is more than 100 years old and may need to be reevaluated in order to prepare students for new technologies.

SUMMARY

This chapter presents an overview of some of the most cutting-edge practices within current architectural practice, including transfer technology, full-scale prototyping, and CATIA processes. In relation to the DBS, transfer technology allows for interdisciplinary collaboration so the field of architecture can benefit from the successful methods of other industries. Full-scale prototyping allows students to see detail assemblies at full-size and to test their design ideas. The electronic model puts the architect in control of the building project. This study illustrates these methods in order to inspire DBS faculty to incorporate the rapidly changing technology into their learning objectives, thus better preparing students for practice.

REFERENCES

Cocke, A. (2000). The Business of Complex Curves," *Architecture*, December 2000.
Eisenman, P. (1992). Visions Unfolding: Architecture in the Age of Electronic Media, https://fatemehnasrollahi.wordpress.com/2010/10/28/peter-eisenman-%e2%80%9cvisions-unfolding-architecture-in-the-age-of-electronic-media%e2%80%9d/.
Kieran, S. and Timberlake, J. (2003). *Refabricating Architecture*. New York: McGraw Hill.
Lindsey, B. (2001). *Digital Gehry*. Basel: Birkhauser.
Novitski, B. J. (1992, January). "New Frontiers in CAD," *Architecture*, 81(1), 103+
Rice, P. (1993). *An Engineer Imagines*. London: Artemis.

Art of Making

Jim Burton and William Carpenter

INTRODUCTION

This chapter is about the art of making and haptic cognition. It is important for designers, industrial designers, and architects to learn about the inherent characters of materials and assembly similar to methods used in fine arts education such as sculpture. By studying their artistic side of making, designers can become students of craft and emphasize quality, simplicity, and cultural expression.

The design build studio is certainly inspired by the act of making. Artistic education, particularly in sculpture, has been influenced by the materials the students work with. In Architecture the Art of Making and experimentation has been greatly influenced by American ingenuity and in turn by the Bauhaus and its global impact. Artistic training often centers in working with the material they work with, learning about how to work with the materials in an additive or subtractive way. In contrast Architects often learn with a removed process of representation in paper, model, or computer drawing form.

It is important to understand the process of making and how it impacts and inspires local, regional, and international cultures. The act of making should not be confused with assembling. The act of making is comprised of conceiving, experimenting, and constructing. Making is telling a story, revealing who we are at that time. It requires a direct engagement with the materials and tools to explore an outcome.[1] The art of making can be either an unselfconscious process when focused on materials and connections, or when focused on symbols or sensation, the art of making can have more meaning than a mere building. With an open mind and patience we can become more aware of how a design build education process may tie in with different types of "making" that relate to artistic expression.

SCALING UP

The Wassily chair by Breuer was inspired from early Bauhaus thesis work, which inspired a skeletal structure that Mies van der Rohe would use in his furniture design and steel grid structures. The new process of continuous steel tubing that evaded welding flaws was merged with Eisengarn, a nineteenth-century wax-coated thread material. The integrity of this chair design has created an iconic, timeless, and functional expression which continues to be produced to this day.

We will scale from line and surface through object and space while appreciating a process of the shared artists featured here.

Art of Making

FIGURE 0.3.1
Wright Brothers prototyping, 1908.

FIGURE 0.3.2
The Wassily chair with tubular steel and Eisengarn by Breuer 1925.

Source: www.shutterstock.com/image-photo/bilbao-spainaugust-8-2021-club-chair-2220487063

xli

■ Art of Making

FIGURE 0.3.3
Tom Nakashima, artist known for developing multiple layers of collage often revealing a surprise palimpsest detail. This full-size first responders magazine image is featured in "Westwood Nocturne" in the next section.

FIGURE 0.3.4
"Westwood Nocturne" by Tom Nakashima.

SURFACE PROCESS: GRID, WEAVE, COLLAGE, AND THE BEGINNINGS OF SURPRISE IN MAKING

Mies Van Der Rohe would "draw to think" working to unhide the grid and build a stage for the dynamic modern existence of people and movement. Artist Tom Nakashima works with imagery, collage, and grid structures open to bonus discoveries that only the process of making can reveal beyond predetermination. His work in social protest and the sublime create an appreciation of time and scale as the works are often ten feet tall creating a backdrop of space and texture. Orchard trees find new use as pollination encampments after their life of apple production is outgrown.

ARTIST AND FILMMAKER

David Lynch defies classification in his design; he brings his positive energy and rigor with daily transcendental meditation, preparing for discovery of a mix of ideas that the materials help dictate in their tectonic elemental expression. The well-known filmmaker trained first as a painter and has expanded his list of works to drawing, music, photography, and now light sculptures and lamp design.

The resin, wood, metal, plaster, power cord, and switch are elements he shapes as intended for each part while always reminding us what the materials are with their limits. This honesty shows the malleable stretching, twisting, and curving of resin in contrast with space-framing metal lattice or visual "scaffolding" in the more surreal shapes. These compositions are born from a place that inspired Lynch's early *Boy Lights Fire*, a mixed media masterwork.

The *Table Top Lamp* of 2022 may have been a more deductive design process as an essential, objective lamp reinforced by the materiality of each element—a cold-rolled steel

FIGURE 0.3.5
David Lynch, *Table Top Lamp*.

■ Art of Making

sub structure, a plaster form, a handmade subtlety, and a minimal resin screen for ambient color and light. A true masterwork that reflects his daily meditations informing a reductionist intuition of haptic cognition and simultaneity. This stillness allows for designing and making to occur in the same flow of action.

UPCYCLING

Fashion designer Eleanor Trask uses spray foam to evoke ancient bone-like structures that emphasize the human figure. The frozen-in-time pieces offer an unconventional use for this foam-building product.

Artist Martin Puryear has enjoyed the design build process, seen in the previous section in his New York studio. He has thrived with continuing education and experimentation in 2D and 3D design. His research and artistic sharing has expanded across continents, which reinforces his appreciation for how culture and place can influence his ideas. "My education, such as it was, taught me how to teach myself, and in that sense it continues right up to the present." Martin enjoys collaborating with engineers and specialists when working with new materials and larger scales. Martin finds that the essential difference between design and building is "the difference between thinking and doing."

STORM KING SCULPTURE

A new work designed by Puryear is under construction after complex analysis and planning. The original form carved of wood led to several studies, and the final model was scanned to create a 3D digital file to support a series of project drawings—design drawings to visualize the sculpture and problem-solve its details; fabrication drawings for the wooden formwork (e.g., for the arch) and the wooden guidework (e.g., for the steel), and construction drawings (e.g., for the foundations).

The wooden formwork and steel guidework were CNC cut and assembled on site. A great deal of customization was carried out on the wooden formwork by the team led by Lara Davis of Limaçon Design. This included laying lathe and inserting the fiber-reinforced cement tubes.

The half-scale mock-up we just completed (segments 4 and 5) allowed us to confirm that we will be able to construct the segments 4 through 9 without inside centering or formwork, by using a method borrowed from so-called "Nubian Vaulting."

The first three segments will be constructed over a more conventional supporting formwork, probably made of wood, but once the brickwork courses reach a certain angle (at the fourth segment), bricks can be laid to lean against previously laid courses, with no need for interior support.

We'll be laying brick inside and outside the curved form, and the cavity between the inner and outer brick walls will be filled with a layer of concrete grout reinforced by a shaped rebar grid, which will also act as a guide for controlling the overall form.[2]

FIGURE 0.3.6
Spray foam design fashion exhibit.

FIGURE 0.3.7
Spray foam dress by Eleanor Trask.

■ Art of Making

FIGURE 0.3.8
Martin Puryear in his New York Studio.

FIGURE 0.3.9
Masons creating a vault with earth bricks using the Nubian Vault method.

Art of Making

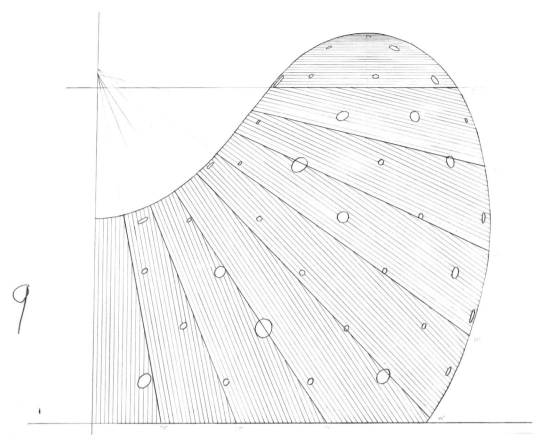

FIGURE 0.3.10
A side elevation drawing, showing how the masonry courses change from vertical at the arched opening, gradually transitioning through nine segments and culminating in a horizontally based dome at the top.

FIGURE 0.3.11
The original scale model with brick detailing was done with 13 segments before testing and landing on 9 as a final solution.

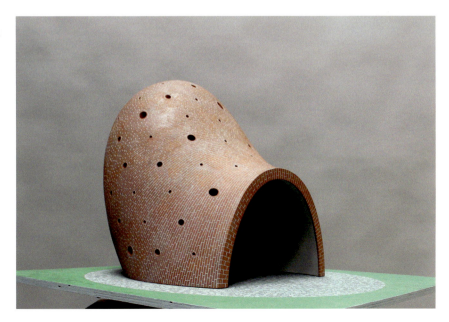

xlvii

■ Art of Making

FIGURE 0.3.12
Formwork used for segments 1–3 insert.

Art of Making

FIGURE 0.3.13
Process detail.

xlix

■ Art of Making

FIGURE 0.3.14
The team packing structural grout between brick layers.

FIGURE 0.3.15
Connecting with the site is an essential part of the structure and the pilgrimage process of the Storm King Art Center.

Davis shares how they made the mock-up to test the concept:

> The form finding for the original form was done in Martin's studio by carving from a block of wood. Several studies were done, and then the final wood model was scanned to create a 3D digital file. This file was then used to develop a whole host of project drawings—design

drawings to visualize the sculpture and problem-solve its details, fabrication drawings for the wooden formwork (e.g. for the arch) and the wooden guidework (e.g. for the steel), and construction drawings (e.g. for the foundations).

The foundations were built to spec by Storm King. The wooden formwork and steel guidework were CNC cut and assembled on site. Then there was a great deal of customization carried out on the wooden formwork for the arch by us, including laying lathe and inserting the fiber reinforced cement tubes. KC Fabrications has custom bent and welded all of the stainless steel rebar over the wooden guidework.[3]

Puryear was inspired by his experience in Mali photographing the Nubian Vault method.

GEORGE AND MIRA NAKASHIMA—FURNITURE AND A CAMPUS OF DESIGN BUILD EXPERIMENTS

After having spent seven years in Asia, with its tradition of fine craftsmanship, I felt I should take a survey trip from Seattle to California to witness firsthand what was considered the best of modern American architecture. The work of Frank Lloyd Wright was especially disappointing to me, although the forms used were interesting and the results were causing a certain excitement in the architectural world. I found the structure and the bones of the building somehow inadequate, however, and the workmanship shoddy. I felt that I must find a new vocation, something that I could coordinate from beginning to end. I decided to follow woodworking as my life's work.[4]

Lara Davis studied the work of George Nakashima at Golconde, appreciating the collision of master craftsmanship in wood and in masonry and how that has left its mark on

FIGURE 0.3.16
Conoid studio interior.

■ Art of Making

FIGURE 0.3.17
Interior bresolie fins.

Golconde. She speaks about the collision of master craftsmanship in wood and in masonry and how that has left its mark on Golconde. This perspective draws on my experience as a masonry craftsperson, with Golconde, with Georges Nakashima's work, and with the project with Martin Puryear. "In particular with Golconde, I believe that it is Georges Nakashima's sensitivity to the craft of wood that influenced the design of the concrete shuttering—and that is what made this building so special."[5]

George Nakashima worked for Antonin Raymond as an architect learning how important craft and tectonics were in design and construction. As he decided to become a furniture maker, he developed an experimental campus of buildings over time, some of which have been recognized as masterworks in architecture.

Mira Nakashima, the daughter of George, describes her transitions in education and an appreciation of materials which helped her find her path as a designer and maker. Here are the questions to consider:

How did your education prepare you for your work over the years?

I am glad that my parents allowed me to attend a private high school named Solebury which got me into Harvard/Radcliffe college. They also encouraged me to take "architectural sciences" a basic design course which helped develop my artistic tendencies but unfortunately did not prepare me for graduate school in architecture in Japan! However, the atelier system at Waseda University was a great learning experience and all of my classmates helped me not only understand the Japanese language and customs, but taught me how to draft, make scale models and to collaborate on projects we were assigned. When I returned to new hope to work with my father in 1970, both the drafting and collaboration skills came in handy. The assertiveness training classes and independent thinking, however, did not lead to harmonious interaction with my parents and working with them developed my sense of humility.

In your work; what is the difference between designing and building?

Designing to me means thinking out form and function and expressing that resolution in a visual way. Designing in my world is usually done in two dimensions on paper; building is done in three dimensions, mostly in wood.

Art of Making

We very rarely make mockups or scale models at Nakashima's, and rely on past precedents as a way of training our eyes and hands to create contemporary objects. Building means understanding the structure and joinery and being able to execute them in a precise manner, along with developing the woodworker's eye to recognize proportion in three dimensions which the designers may or may not have expressed through drawings.

How do materials affect your ideas and designs?

Materials are how we begin, each with their own range of possibilities; with wood, it already has its own form and direction which we need to study and listen to as we select various pieces for different functions, which often determine a design different from what has come before. Our material, then, is our muse, not just an inanimate substance to be molded in our hands.

Would you say the buildings on your factory campus were built as experiments or as fully developed ideas or a little bit of both, either in whole or in pieces?

The early buildings from the 1940s were very much built of necessity, as efficiently and inexpensively as possible, protecting inhabitants from the cold north winds yet allowing the sunshine in from the south, especially in the winter; cross-ventilation through sliding windows and doors allowed air movement even in the hot summer months. In 1956, my father became fascinated with the capabilities of thin warped shells and built the first hyperbolic paraboloid shells on the property which still stand, intact and functional, to this day. In 1957, he built a mock-up for the conoid studio in plywood which was intended as a "break room" but was taken over for chair assembly; in 1958–59, he designed and built the conoid studio with a thin shell reinforced concrete conoidal roof, which has never been done before or since. In 1960, he designed and built a free-form swimming pool and an open-ended barrel-vault plywood roof pool house, again facing south to welcome the warmth of the sun. In 1967, he built another thin-shell plywood hyperbolic paraboloid roof on concrete block and masonry

FIGURE 0.3.18
Elk Run Ridge floor plan.

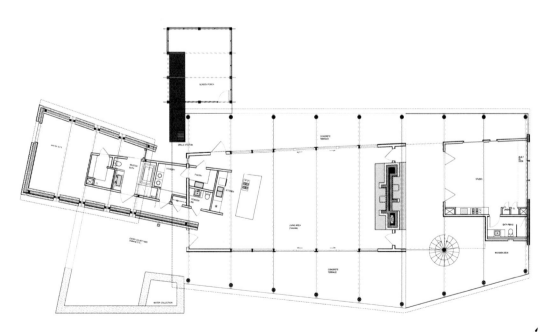

■ Art of Making

walls as a gallery for his friend Ben Shahn. \When one of the nearby trees dropped a branch which punctured the roof, we performed some repairs, but it still stands as a testament to Nakashima's understanding of engineering as well as building.[6]

MIRA NAKASHIMA

COLLABORATION ARCHITECT and ARTISTS
Design, Build, and Teaching With On-site Emersion
Making and Tactics as Part of a Whole Nakashima, Carter + Burton Architecture, Richard Lew and Helvetica Design Kitchen and Bathroom Core With Wood Basket Weave, Concrete, and Metal Work Elk Run Ridge

FIGURE 0.3.19
Nakashima shelving shop drawing.

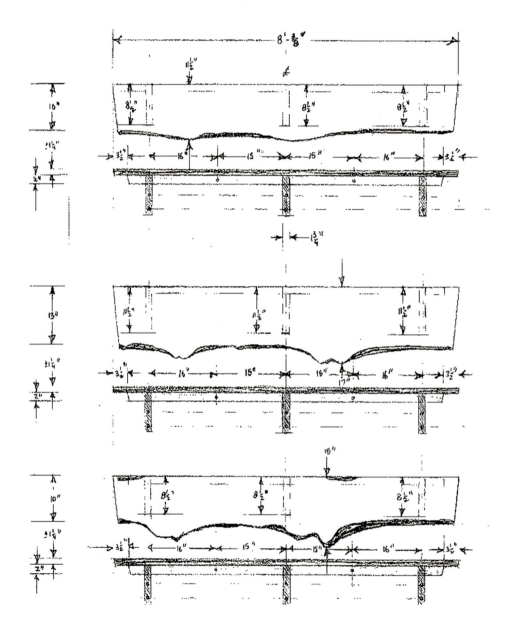

Art of Making

FIGURE 0.3.20
Open space with walnut kitchen core and Nakashima furniture.

Elk Run Ridge, a collaboration with Carter + Burton Architecture PLC and the works of Mira Nakashima and George Nakashima.

FIGURE 0.3.21
Kitchen with custom vent pipes and Nakashima shelves and stools.

Custom vent pipes designed by Burton form a contrast of machined to crafted surroundings, including Nakashima shelving and furniture design.

■ Art of Making

FIGURE 0.3.22 Bent weave walnut core and stone gravity wall hall.

FIGURE 0.3.23 Custom fir front door and corten steel roof catchment beyond.

Bent weave walnut boards made with ¼" veneer form the kitchen bathroom linkage core crafted by Helvetica Design. The entry pivot door by Helvetica is an organic engineering masterpiece which holds steady against heavy winds while being manageable for all ages with a custom antler handle.

Other Carter + Burton collaborations of making include this white concrete reflecting pool. Richard Lew and Jim Burton developed this bird bath concept with fiberoptic constellations. On the interior the design continues with matching concrete and cantilevered white kitchen element to relate from inside to outside. Lew worked with the concrete and resin panels to establish quadrants within the intersecting geometries that allow for the open plan to define spaces within spaces.

The white concrete water feature used sand from Alabama and includes fiberoptics. The drip edge was handcrafted on-site for the infinity release to a linear feature inspired by the river in the next section.

FIGURE 0.3.24
White concrete reflecting pool by Richard Lew.

■ Art of Making

FIGURE 0.3.25
Concrete and cantilevered white kitchen element relating inside to outside.

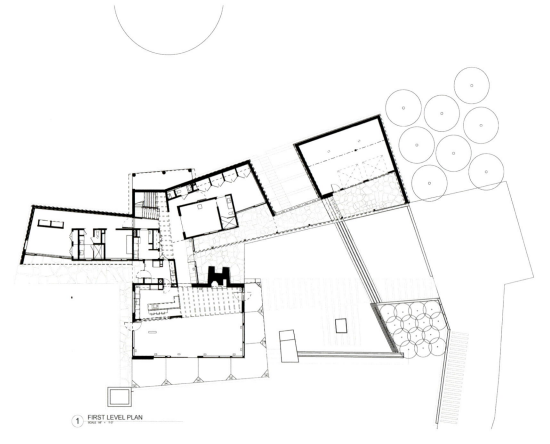

FIGURE 0.3.26
River House site design collaboration with Gregg Bleam Landscape Architect.

FIGURE 0.3.27
River House infinity edge plaza with corten steel firepit by Richard Lew.

CONCLUSION

Beauty, function, and meaning combined will be preserved and cared for when a culture shows an appreciation for an authentic and rigorous built expression. By studying this artistic side of making, we become students of history, as we learn how the materiality may function or last in a place. Process and the journey of concept through completed work will more than likely always provide surprises to the maker, and when open to them, a richness in the work is enhanced.

NOTES

1 Kennesaw State University Focus Studio from Welty's focus studio design build philosophy.
2 Martin Puryear.
3 Lara Davis.
4 Nakashima, G. (1981). *The Soul of a Tree: A Woodworker's Reflections.* Tokyo: Kodansha International, page 69.
5 Lara Davis.
6 Mira Nakashima, the daughter of George Nakashima.

1
PEDAGOGICAL MODELS

Design-build Program at KSU

William Carpenter, Arief Setiawan, and Christopher Welty

The history of our institution informed the pedagogy of our architecture program. Indeed, our institution started as a polytechnic school. Indeed, it has gone through changes in its more than 70 years of history. The institution started as the Southern Tech in 1947. In 1986, it morphed into the Southern College of Technology. The school changed into a polytechnic school as Southern Polytechnic State in 1996. Eventually, the polytechnic school was merged into Kennesaw State University in 2015. Throughout these changes, however, the core or the pedagogy of the school revolve around the emphasis on technical school. This position reflects the social, cultural, and economic contexts of our state.

Historically and geographically, the state of Georgia was a part of the nation in which agriculture was the primary economic sector. Crops such as cotton was the main contributor of the economy of the state. However, around the beginning of the twentieth century, the economy of state started to turn into the industrial sector, and it kept growing in subsequent decades. By the mid 1940s, the state had more than 600 new industries. This process of industrialization changed the characteristics of the state. One of the impacts was the need for a workforce with knowledge and skills that would fit with demands in the industrial sector. To meet these needs, the education sectors moved to accommodate them and establishing schools that trained engineers and technicians. One of these schools was the Southern Tech, which was founded in 1947 in Marietta, Georgia. The town itself was an example of the socioeconomic transformation of the state. Originated as a small rural town just outside Atlanta, it changed into one of the major industrial centers in the state. World War II accelerated the industrialization of the area, as Marietta housed a production facility for Bell Aircraft. Constructed in 1943 in less than a year, this aircraft plant was the site for the manufacturing and fabrication of the B-29 bomber. By the end of the Second World War, the B-29 production facility was the single largest private employer in the state. With the size of its main building, which was six times of a football field, it reflected its prominence. It was strategically located near the Marietta Naval Air Station.

The Southern Tech was established and developed within this context at the site of the former bomber manufacturing plant. This context proved to be very advantageous for the new institution. It took over facilities and equipment from the Marietta Air Bade and Bell Bomber Plant. These facilities ranged from advanced laboratories to welding and machine shop. Students and military personals used these facilities for their education and training. With these advantages, the school from the beginning developed its pedagogy as highly interdisciplinary around the rapidly changing cutting-edge technology. This pedagogy demonstrated a synergy of education and industry. It aimed to educate and train technicians who could bridge and connect research-trained engineers with craftsmen. Faculty and top industry specialists developed courses jointly, facilitated by the availability of laboratory equipment. The school established its characteristics as an education built around interdisciplinary approach and entrepreneurship. These characteristics distinguished the school from other institutions that focused on academia. It allowed Southern Tech to educate graduates that met the demands of industry.

The School of Architecture in our institution was established in 1989–90 and received its full accreditation in the fall quarter of 1995. The initial spirit of Southern Tech to train technicians informed the development of the school as it inspired to address the need for a "technician" in architecture who could bring together design and construction. However, it was also in tune with the interdisciplinary mindset of the institution, as the vision of the architecture program to house under one roof disciplines in art, humanities, engineering, and construction. In this setting, our pedagogy places a premium in nurturing knowledge and skills in constructing and assembling a building together in logical and feasible manners. This emphasis runs parallel with fostering the understanding and abilities to conceptualize design. It intends to bridge the gap between academic research, architectural design, and construction industry.

Given that background, hands-on curriculum has always informed the pedagogy of our architecture program to achieve the vision to combine theory with practice in a collaborative and integrated manner. This mindset informed not only our design studios but also other courses across the curriculum. The program hired practicing architects as faculty to bridge academia and industry. The school also established partnerships with other institutions and exchange programs with a view on the vision of collaborative and integration of academia and industry. In order to support this position, the architecture department has invested heavily on facilities and infrastructure for fabrications, including shops, tools, and machineries. Crucial for our facilities is the recruitment of skilled staffs to manage and run them.

In the history of design pedagogy, hands-on curriculum is a well-established practice. Indeed, one of the legacies of the Bauhaus was its pedagogy that was built around the notion of "learning by doing" in its multiple shops. In education in general, learning by doing echoed the pragmatism philosophy of John Dewey, who emphasized experience as the center of a learning process. Along this line, Salama and Wilkinson mapped four main approaches in the history of design education, including academic, engineer to technological, craftsmen-builder, and social scientist approaches.[1] The academic approach privileged the primacy of formal principles, and end goal was to satisfy the aesthetics aspects. The curriculum emphasized compositional theory and principles of formal design. The obvious example of this approach was the pedagogy of the Ecole-des-Beaux-Arts, whose education focused on training design in abstract manners following established formal principles. Design pedagogy in the traditions of craftsmen-builder and engineer-technological evolved from practice and traditions in building trades, in which advances in technology supplemented the engineer-technological approach. Vocational training was a crucial part in these approaches. The Bauhaus was a prime historical example of this approach, in which its workshops played a central role in the education process, down to the division of its students and instructors into apprentice, journeyman, and master. The social scientist approaches grounded itself in the studies of users and their behavior as the driver in design-generation. These approaches reflected opposite views in design. Design in the fold of the Ecole tradition was an abstract and intellectual activity, detached from actual practices of making and constructing buildings. The craftsmen-builders and engineers emphasized on utilitarian and structural concerns, supported by the ability to apply scientific principles in design processes. They also differ in detachment, abstraction, and critical distance.

The pedagogy of hands-on, learning by doing of the Bauhaus provided the starting point for the lineage of the design/build program in architecture school in the United States. Richard Hayes has illustrated a brief history of this program.[2] He noted some of the antecedent of the emergence of this program, besides the Bauhaus who came to America through the Black Mountain College in North Carolina. Dewey's pragmatism was a philosophical reference. In practice, Booker T. Washington directed students to design and construct buildings at Tuskegee Normal and Industrial Institute as a part of the pedagogical approach to develop skills and self-respect among the students. Frank Lloyd Wright set up the pedagogy at his Taliesin based on the apprenticeship system, that included on-site labor. The first design-build program in the country was The First-Year Building Project at Yale School of Architecture in 1966–67 that was a part of its graduate program. Directed by Kent Bloomer, Herbert Newman, and Charles Moore, this program emerged out of activism and volunteerism to address the social and economic problem as a part of the War of Poverty in President Lyndon B. Johnson's Great Society. In the initial stage, students from this program constructed community facilities in rural Appalachia, including community centers, a health clinic, and a recreation center. This program continued until today, morphing into the Vlock Building Project, which was required for all graduate students. In 1970s, they constructed recreational structures in and around New Haven, while in the 1980s focused on affordable housing in the same area and eventually partnering with nonprofit organization such as Habitat for Humanity. Obviously, the most well-known design-build program is the Rural Studio at Auburn University, which was established in 1992 by Samuel Mockbee and Dennis K. Ruth. The goal of this program was to bring design as a humanistic efforts to the poorest counties in Alabama. It consisted of a semester elective course for second-year students and a year-long thesis course for fifth-year students. Hayes noted that common features of this program included a course divided into design and construction phase; partnership with community group or nonprofit organization, volunteers, efforts to raise funds to support the program.

OUR FOUNDATION OF DESIGN BUILD PEDAGOGY

Beginning Design Level

The notion of hands-on learning in our program is cultivated from the beginning design level. In this vein, the history and visions of our institution has led the author to develop a design pedagogy for the foundation studio that capitalized on the capabilities and assets of our program. Especially, the author developed studio projects and exercises based on the learning of some basic, introductory skills in the woodshops. In particular, these design projects sprung for techniques and methods of wood-carving and wood-joining. The ideas stemmed from the considerations that the knowledge of the staffs of our shops combined with our extensive facilities could be a perfect resources in developing some aspects of the pedagogy of the beginning design studios. Given the context of beginning design, our woodshop served as an appropriate introduction to the notion and practice of construction and fabrication. Analogous to a laboratory, the shop worked as a means to expose and train students on the habit and rigor of working with hands.

However, we were very aware that working in the shop could lead to privileging the development of technical skills in working with tools rather than nurturing skills and abilities

■ William Carpenter, Arief Setiawan, and Christopher Welty

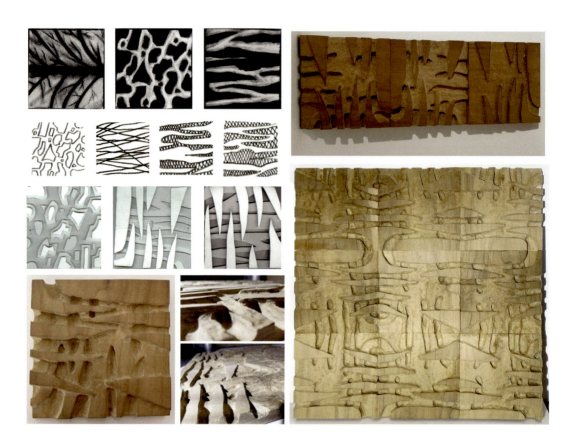

FIGURE 1.1.1
First-year studio, Artifacts and Constructions, Module 03—Texture and Carving Project, Sam Walden, student.

in design thinking. This mindset could condition students to approach design as a linear thinking and technical approach. We also saw the tendency among students and faculty to treat our shops and other fabrication facilities simply as a means to produce representations of design, such as models and other forms of representations. We wanted to nurture the habit of design thinking and design process as process of explorations and inquiries, in which every artifact, including models and drawings, is a means of experimentation rather than a representation of ideas. We constructed a pedagogy as an inquiry in developing and formulating design intent and generative principles based on constructing things. Underlying this approach is the notion of thinking-through-making. We drew a connection with Sennett's notion engaged material consciousness, in which experiences in hands-on working fed the mental process of reflections and imagination.[3] Hence, in these design problems, the act of making things served as the springboard for the design process and thinking.

We designed these projects into modules that spanned over the fall and spring semester of our first-year studios. This strategy came out of the considerations that it would take longer time for students to learn and develop basic craftsmanship skills in woodworking. This slow pace, however, also offered possibilities to integrate other basic skills, such as diagramming and precision drawings, into these exercises with wood. These projects aimed at achieving multiple pedagogical goals, the first of which was obviously to learn to work with tools in the woodshop and to understand the nature of materials. This initial goal should lead to the next, which was nurturing and stimulating students to take techniques in working with tools, capabilities of tools, and properties of materials to inform their design thinking, processes, and decisions. In order to facilitate these goals, we set up design problems that emerged from basic techniques in carving and joining. Conceptually, carving related to design through subtraction, while joining fit into the notion of design through additions. Further, carving matched with the problem of surface and of planes as a space-defining element. Meanwhile, joining fed into the problem of assembling space-defining elements to create three-dimensional volumes. In developing these projects, we sought input and feedback from our staffs in the woodshop, and we developed syllabi and exercises with close coordination with them.

Through these design projects, we learned multifold aspects in which aspiring designers worked with constraints and opportunities afforded by materials, tools, techniques, and procedure. Constructing a wood artifact required thoughts and considerations on tools that were needed, the properties of different types of wood, the sequence of fabrication, and possibilities of the needs for supporting tools, such as jigs. It revealed a continuing dialogue between the designer with tools and materials, that ranged from imposition to acceptance to negotiations. Some students executed their task by forcing and imposing their design ideas on the materials and tools. On the other hand, some students developed their design by accepting the strengths and limitations of materials and tools. Some students negotiate their design ideas to suit the strengths and limitations of materials and tools. These various modes of dialogues between students and tools and materials demonstrated the agency of tools and of materials in the process. Hence, essentially, planning and executing the construction of the artifact were a design process in itself. This type of design process reflected the development of the ability to contextualize the procedural and technical skills and knowledge. Walter Benjamin's thoughts on the notion wisdom provide a metaphor for this ability.[4] Benjamin argued that a skilled storyteller would tell a story based on the contexts of his audience, reflecting his wisdom and level of craftsmanship.

PROJECTS: KSU DESIGN BUILD URBAN STUDIO:
CARPENTER DESIGN-BUILD

In 1993 Samuel Mockbee FAIA visited the KSU campus to deliver a lecture and work with Dr. William Carpenter FAIA to found the Urban Design Build Studio. Mockbee's advice to Dr. Carpenter was "stay put," which focused the studio efforts in Reynoldstown. A part of Atlanta that was a neighborhood which at the time had some of the highest rates of crime in the city. The neighborhood was formed by about 1,200 families, many who were former slaves who migrated to Atlanta to work in a cotton bag factory. The first projects involved urban planning and a community gospel and blues outdoor theater. These projects were all offered as part of a spring fourth-year design studio as part of the core curriculum.

Wheelbarrow Summer Theater

This project was conceived by a local architect, Joseph Amisano FAIA, who contacted Dr. Carpenter and KSU to form a long-term relationship with the community. The first project of the studio was a summer theater program which included a ticket booth tower, a stage and entry sequence made of 100 doors, which were hand painted by neighborhood children. The project raised funds for future Design Build projects and brought together over 8,000 people over the three-day festival. The materials were all donated, and the total budget for the projects was $3,300.

■ William Carpenter, Arief Setiawan, and Christopher Welty

FIGURE 1.1.2
Wheelbarrow Summer Theater design sketch.

FIGURE 1.1.3
Wheelbarrow Summer Theater, a place for celebration.

FIGURE 1.1.4
Wheelbarrow Summer Theater, with 100 donated doors painted by the community.

The project allowed 16 students to design the project in a collaborative method, where teams of four developed concepts, and the team itself chose the winning scheme. The entire team then presented the project to the community for review and comment. The class worked on site for five weeks to build the wooden tower, stage frame, and the entry sequence using the donated doors.

Mad Housers Homeless Shelter

The next project dealt with the prototype homeless shelter working with a local homeless advocacy group for a site in Reynoldstown. Like the Tiny House movement, this 40 square foot shelter created sleeping, cooking, and showering areas for the resident and could be built for $310. The first prototypes were built on KSU campus and involved student teams of four students for a ten-week quarter. The students volunteered with the Mad Housers to allow them to visit the large communities of homeless shelters in three locations around the city normally located on flood plain tracts near the interstate.

■ William Carpenter, Arief Setiawan, and Christopher Welty

FIGURE 1.1.5
Painted door of Wheelbarrow Summer Theater.

FIGURE 1.1.6
Mad Housers Homeless Shelter.

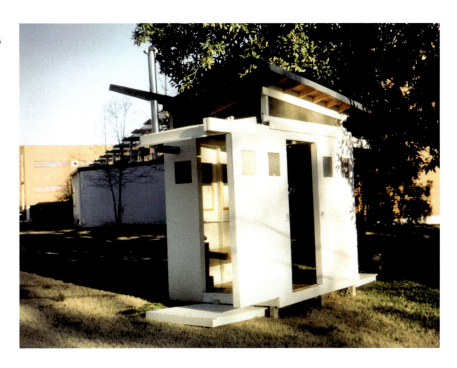

FIGURE 1.1.7
Mad Housers Homeless Shelter, build team. The start of the 2 × 4 exercise.

Reynoldstown Urban Parks

The next two projects were located on derelict sites in Reynoldstown. The first is the memorial garden, which was on the site of a junkyard and abandoned house. The project involved community charettes and many planning meetings, and it was led by a neighborhood leader, 89-year-old Ms. Mattie Robinson and her husband, Mr. Grady. The project program was for an outdoor chapel space, seating, garden trellises, and an entry path. Students cast concrete tiles with fossilized stamps of natural leaves and the neighborhood logo. The project budget was $6,500, and it was built over ten weeks during the normal three-day-a-week studio with afternoon times from one to six o'clock.

FIGURE 1.1.8
Ms. Mattie Robinson park bench.

Design-build Program at KSU

The project involved 14 students working to design the project in a period of three weeks, and the construction part of the project was the remainder of the semester with a dedication and final jury on site. The project received a major honor award from the local AIA competing against local practicing architectural firms. This project continues to be used as a memorial park, and neighbors, KSU students, and faculty still volunteer to clean up and maintain the park.

The Gateway Park was a project using the legacy of the KSU connection to the Dobbins and Lockeed Air Force base. This project involved prototyping and materials study. The project is located on a major artery of Atlanta connecting Little Five Points with East Atlanta. Most people did not know Reynoldstown existed, and the site for this project helps define the edge of the neighborhood. The Gateway Park involved working closely with a steel fabricator, Stein Steel, which is located two blocks away. Students worked on shop drawings and in the shop of this fabricator to assemble the parts of the steel trellis and learned folding, welding, and bolting techniques. Prototypes were also made in the shop at the KSU campus in the same shop the engineers at the Dobbins Air Force base used.

The park concept was to relate the steel pavilion to the existing railroad "roundhouse" that was once located near this site. The roundhouse allowed the locomotive to be turned around in place. The pavilion also related to a large electrical substation and translated it into a sculptural expression of growth and exuberance. Students worked with a local graffiti artist to paint the graffiti walls and carefully collaborated with a group of second-grade students who hand-painted tiles on the inner floors of the pavilion. This project won both a local and national AIA design awards and was built with over $300,000 of material donations, including the value of the site itself.

FIGURE 1.1.9
Ms. Mattie Robinson park entrance.

13

FIGURE 1.1.10
Reynoldstown Gateway Park.

FIGURE 1.1.11
Reynoldstown Gateway Park urban context. A mural by a local artist of the community and the build team.

Welty Design Build Studio

Café Design Build was a design build program proposed as a small-scale project sponsored by the KSU chapter of Freedom By Design. Proposed as a focused studio, the proposal built on a long history of design build within the Architecture Department at KSU. The act of making should not be confused with assembling. The act of making is comprised of conceiving and then constructing. Making is telling a story, revealing who we are at that time.

FIGURE 1.1.12
Café Design Build in the KSU Architecture Building atrium.

Whether low tech or high tech, you will learn more with the first thing you build bound by constraints such as weather, codes, and budget than almost anything else you learned in school. Recalling a time of the master builder, the studio focused on the main aspects of design build: design, construction, and management. Learning by doing, the students explored and experimented with the art and craft of architecture. Structured as a design build practice, the studio presented an educational model that reflects a comprehensive design build environment. The project followed the entire design and construction covering topics from design, systems selection, detailing, budgeting and procurement, scheduling, and construction.

The project brief outlined the moveable kiosk and envisioned as permanent home for their weekly bake sale fundraiser. The purpose of the kiosk is twofold, one as social mediator and two as philanthropic revenue stream. Design guidelines detailed a kiosk that must house all the bake sale components, be transportable and function self-sufficiently with no permanent connections to its site. All services should be self-contained, only utilizing and accessing existing infrastructure. It must provide storage for seating and tables when not in operation. As a full-scale installation, the project must be constructed to handle the forces incurred during transportation as well as those of everyday use.

An interesting transformation had occurred since the weekly bake sale begun. The space was transformed, moving from an informal gathering to social mediator activating the atrium space. When the bake sale is present, people stop, they linger, and they talk. The bake sale and future kiosk provide the catalyst for this interaction transforming space into place. As philanthropic arm, the venue provides a way to generate capital to further Freedom's projects.

FIGURE 1.1.13
Café Design Build in the open for business.

FIGURE 1.1.14
Café Design Build set up and ready for opening.

As a portable kiosk, the project typology provides some interesting complexities itself. Essentially the project is a permanent installation with a temporary site. This notion invokes a fundamental question, how does one design for a temporary site? What elements are fundamental to transform space? The addition of program complicates the inquiry. It has to function to work. This requires an investigation into systems and other fundamental questions, such as, how does it connect to the existing infrastructure? Maybe it creates its own energy. As a full-scale project, the kiosk is bound by the physical constraints such as weight and structure. Ideas of enclosure and skin complete the image, providing the container and security. Tectonic development requires an investigation into materials, connections, and the design decision that drive their use.

Embracing our history of applied learning the studio is extremely hands-on from the start. The studio methodology began with a series of design exercises intended to allow for experimentation, enhancing student creativity while exploring both aesthetic and technical criteria for creating architectural space. The pedagogical goal was to explore and experiment with architectural constructs, emphasizing materiality and constructability. The design research investigated the built, natural, and human environments, focusing on building a physical and social intervention informed by human behavior and tectonic development.

Simulating a small practice, the studio required both individual and collaborative work. Cooperation and communication were critical to successful studio completion, both individually and collectively. Studio exercise followed the entire life cycle of an architectural project from schematic design through construction. Each phase of the studio provides an intimate understanding of materials, their constructability and impact on design decisions providing a balance of research, experimentation, design, management, and construction.

■ William Carpenter, Arief Setiawan, and Christopher Welty

FIGURE 1.1.15
Café Design Build.

Tectonics, materiality, and constructability were at the center of each investigation. The studio will foster an environment that promoted collaboration and the integration of design and construction.

The final project was refined through a series of perspectives and models. Understanding the impacts of design decisions, the studio will have to develop a cost estimate, project schedule, and working budget to achieve their design. Material was fabricated in the woodshop and then erected outside the studio. Once completed, the kiosk was transported to the site location and became the property of the Architecture Program and Freedom by Design.

The Tactile Urbanism (TU) special elective led by Zamila Karimi carries on the long history of design build at KSU. Tactical Urbanism tackles social and spatial justice issues within our cities through the lens of architects as social agents of change by creatively disrupting the notion of normalcy around placemaking, shelter, and sustainable practices that directly impact citizen-users in our cities. The class seeks to develop a discourse on how design contributes to the material production of space, urban furniture, playscapes, and shelter that promote social interactions and playful encounters.

The city serves as the experimental ground to test ideas using inexpensive short-term tactics as playful provocations that appeal to the needs of multiple groups of people with diverse backgrounds. Tactical Urbanism, Guerilla Urbanism, Streets Alive, and Parking Day have become annual events in many large cities. Such events can bring real-life opportunities to design build pedagogy in the classroom for meaningful social engagement and community building, thus expanding the role of education as a participatory practice-based design research and fabrication lab. Open to upper-level students, the course engages real-life issues, which allow students to put into practice what they have learned.

Design-build Program at KSU

FIGURE 1.1.16
Café Design Build details.

FIGURE 1.1.17
Tactile Urbanism ideation review one, with community partners.

19

■ William Carpenter, Arief Setiawan, and Christopher Welty

FIGURE 1.1.18
Tactile Urbanism ideation review one, exploring ideas with community partners.

The process follows strict rigor: designing, iterating, testing scalar mock-ups, construction/fabrication, and final installation in a physical setting to test the project's efficacy.

Through the tactic of the design charrette, the process starts, resulting in a collective design response that goes through refinement to agree upon the final design that is buildable on a one-to-one scale. During design development, scalar models are developed at various scales to explore materiality, assembly, and portability. Once a fabrication strategy is agreed upon and a prototype developed and tested with all the kinks sorted out, the class is ready to start the one-on-one fabrication. This process is an invaluable lesson for students as everyone works towards one goal: building and deploying the project on-site. A thorough project management strategy with timelines, material procurement, shop time, finishing, and on-site assembly/installation in place for an efficient outcome is agreed upon by the team. The test is the project's constructability in a collaborative setting, engaging students in multiple roles as an atelier.

The process is fast-paced, with committed students straddling between practice and production, engaging community volunteers in fabrication tasks. Deployment of these projects within the public realm in performative settings, where chance encounters and social interactions nurture community building provides readings of the success of these projects. Understanding the nature of a design build project requires a certain level of intellectual rigor, the practical know-how of both materiality and fabrication capabilities within a strict timeline, and excellent organization and interpersonal skills. This approach seeks to engage pedagogy on many levels—theory, design, practice, constructability, and deployment—weaving all aspects of architectural practice into one elective class.

Design-build Program at KSU

FIGURE 1.1.19
Digital fabrication process, creation of the parts.

■ William Carpenter, Arief Setiawan, and Christopher Welty

FIGURE 1.1.20
Woodshop part preparation.

TU 2022 student project, as a case study, will illustrate how design build as an elective can be structured for specific outcomes with the curriculum. The Fibonacci Nook is an outdoor reading area derived from the Fibonacci curve and its proportions to respond to the KSU Math Club's programmatic needs. The concept is to interrogate the notion of a wall as a multifunctional device to integrate seating, storage, and collaborative spaces at varying heights. The design is a modular system as a kit of parts; each piece is systematically numbered to make the fabrication and assembly process manageable. Based on six modules, the arrangement can work in unison as a spiral form that responds to the rectangular site context with pine trees or can be customized into new configurations. The simple construction of stacking horizontal profiles with spacers and threaded rod makes the assembly simple and easy to transport in a flatbed pickup truck. The colorful edges are painted bright to create a playful atmosphere. They also invite students and passersby to engage and interact with math books integrated into the installation. As the project moves into the fabrication phase, the class organizes as a design build lab/atelier, with students dividing tasks into multiple work streams from material takeoffs and acquisitions to delivery, CNC digital fabrication, sanding, painting, staining, and assembly. Each member works within a team and individually to see the project through. Project management tactics such as lean boards are used to manage workflows in a continuous chain where each member picks up tasks where others left off as an assembly line. Upper-level thesis students take on leadership roles to manage the project's complexity, engage team leads for specific jobs, and organize timelines.

Design-build Program at KSU

FIGURE 1.1.21
Prototyping.

Tactical Urbanism and DIY tactics activate otherwise desolate areas within the university campus as social interactions generate around the colorful, provocative form. Such temporary design build projects are testing ground to spark imaginations to offer alternative readings of quotidian campus (public) spaces. Engaging students (the public) in the physical testing of ideas that can yield unique insights into the expectations of future users as discerning clients: truly participatory planning, in this case, goes beyond drawing on flip charts and maps as real-life experiences. Over the years, TU projects have been deployed at many events around the city. These projects are often sought after by city managers working to activate public spaces. There is also an interest in putting the Fibonacci Nook in front of an elementary school to promote social interactions and playful encounters.

23

■ William Carpenter, Arief Setiawan, and Christopher Welty

FIGURE 1.1.22
Tactical Urbanism 2022 design build team.

CONCLUSION

Creating an architecture school around the idea of design build has enormous advantages for students. They learn about aspects linked to practice that often include understanding workflow from design to fabrication and assembly, interaction with clients and the community. It provides an opportunity to connect with industry and prepares them to be young architects after graduation. Our pedagogical framework has been developed over the past 25 years in order to refine the community involvement process, design and construction methods, and the relation to the NAAB and university criteria.

The legacy of full-scale prototyping has been the hallmark of the studio, which has benefitted from the connection to the nearby aerospace industry and the burgeoning city of

Atlanta. As faculty, we are also examining the idea of component-based design build, where students can work on a specific component of a project and collaborate with other departments on campus for engineering and research input during the design process.

NOTES

1 Salama, A. and Wilkinson, N. (2007). "Introduction," in Salama, A. and Wilkinson, N., eds., *Design Studio Pedagogy: Horizons for Future*. Gateshead, UK: The Urban International Press, pp. 4–5.
2 Hayes, R. (2012). "Design/Build: Learning by Constructing," in Ockman, J. and Williamson, R., eds., *Architecture School: Three Centuries of Educating Architects in North America*. Washington, DC: ACSA and Cambridge, MA: The MIT Press.
3 Sennett, R. (2008). *The Craftsman*. New Haven, CT: Yale University Press.
4 Benjamin, W. (2007). *Illumination*, "The Storyteller," New York: Schocken Books.

Making to Construct Design Thinking

Arief Setiawan and Christopher Welty

At KSU, we developed a design pedagogy that explored materials, tools, and techniques. Our approaches to the design processes in our studio *problematized* techniques of observations, procedures in graphic representations, drawings and model-making techniques, and qualities of materials. We set up design problems based on these premises. Findings from these explorations served as the starting point for the problems of defining and organizing space and forms. Our focus is on studying ways in which designers transpose engagements with materials, techniques, and procedure to generate a design process. In a way, we linked the process of making things with the design thinking processes. It is essentially pedagogy based on learning by doing. Along the line of making thing, another fundamental aspect of our pedagogical approach is the primary importance of establishing basic components in the making process. These basic components would be limited in types, which provided constraints in the design process. It linked to the notion of standardization in design practice. Through establishing this constraint, we intended to instill the notion of rule-based design. We implemented our methods in design studios at different levels, from the beginning design to the final year of the architecture program.

Richard Sennett problematized the distinctions between animal laborans and homo faber that Hannah Arendt made.[1] In this scheme, the former described people who performed an act or produced things as the end goal. In doing so, their activities happened in mechanical and repetitive manners. In contrasts, the latter pointed to people who are concerned with thoughts and mental aspects that preceded and went into doing and making things. These aspects covered conceptual dimensions, including reasons, meanings, values, and consequences. Arendt's thought separated thinking from doing, with an implication that animal laborans lacked understanding of multitudes aspect of activities that they engaged. This view privileged homo faber over animal laborans, the distinctions between mental and physical activities, between thinking and making. The former was a subject who acted mechanically without many considerations of consequences and meanings of actions, while the latter was a thinking subject who laid out the conceptual basis of actions and their meanings. Mental activities and thinking preceded the act of making. It implied the distinction between those who plan activities and those who executed them. Sennett challenged these distinctions that place thinking as the precondition of doing, making, and performing. Instead, in his views, doing, making, and performing could inform the way we think and eventually yield knowledge. Instead of concepts in the first place, doing, making, and performing could form the foundations of our understanding and conceptual frame of our world. Further, he argued that doing, making, and performing could play a vital part in the development of knowledge. He noted that doing things had the potential to stimulate thinking and eventually yielded knowledge and consciousness.[2] As animal laborans strived to improve their work, these efforts would lead into improvements in the ways we did, made, and performed our tasks. In turn, this would form a habit that necessitated reflections and dialogue between what we did and what we thought. In other words, it set a dialogue between practice and thinking. In this argument, skills and concepts are informing each other. According to Sennett, these to-and-fro between our hands and our mind would happen under certain conditions.[3] The first notion is the understanding of skills as a form of knowledge that are acquired through bodily activities and physical and direct interactions with the material world. Further, they grew through repetitions of acts and material interactions. Along this line, challenges and difficulties that occurred in these repetitions prompted us to make efforts to comprehend them to find answers. In these efforts, we applied our verbal and visual facilities to make problems intelligible. These comprehensions of the problems could stimulate our imaginative faculty in efforts to improve the ways we did, made, or performed. In other word, it pointed to our grasps of procedure in doing things. Both repetitions and improvements of practice benefitted from sustained efforts. Hence, the developments of skills are a function of routine, rather than initial talents; motivation mattered more than talent. Developing skills depended on efforts put in the process, rather than potentials that a person might possess. Routines in doing, making, and performing shaped our experiences. Our efforts in developing and improving these experiences are our crafts of experience. A fundamental factor in developing our crafts is our comprehensions of procedure and forms of doing, making, and performing, which Sennett called as the techniques of experience. Our engagement with the crafts and techniques of experience would transform not only our faculty but also things or situations that we worked on.

In line with the craft of experience, Sennett argued that humans tended to be drawn to transformations of things or conditions.[4] Further, he classified three types of transformations that humans could impart: metamorphosis, traces, and anthropomorphism. Metamorphosis, or changes of forms, could happen through the process of evolution, such as evolutions of our everyday appliances and habitations. Changes of forms could also be a result of conjoining of multiple elements, such as our discovery of metal alloy. The third type of metamorphosis is the domain shift, in which humans applied knowledge and procedure of one problem to another realm. Sennett talked about our ancestors who learned about orthogonal joining of vertical and horizontal fiber in weaving, which they then transposed to construct wooden joints. Over time, they applied the principle of orthogonal joining on a much larger scale in organizing layouts of human settlements following the grid order. Humans are also interested in transformation caused by traces of our activities. Further, we have the capacity to attach values when we transformed things or conditions, hence anthropomorphizing the transformations.

An architectural example that resonated with these transformations is the work of the French architect Jean Prouve. As Dahmisch explained, Prouve's design process started from observations and understanding of fabrications and manufacturing of metal building components, including cutting, bending, and folding of metal sheet to fabricate building components. He also explored techniques to assemble these metal components. Prouve's design of houses and other structure stemmed from his understanding of building elements and their assembly techniques. Prouve learned how to construct elements and connect them, and this knowledge would inform the design of his structures. In Dahmsich's view, Prouve's contribution is to think of a building starting from the elements that reveal its generative principles.[5] Dahmisch made an analogy to the distinctions between engineers and bricoleur.[6] Engineers approached their tasks by developing the plans, from the overall to the details, before executing them. It is a top-down and comprehensive approach and provided an illustration to the privileging of homo faber over animal laborans. In contrast, a bricoleur started from anything that they could lay their hands on, a practician who picked up things that he or she encountered and constructed an artifact based on these found materials. Their process stemmed from figuring out ways to work with these constraints, including finding best ways to assemble them. This is an incremental and bottom-up approach, a process that yielded from the craft of experience.

Among other things, the theory of experiential learning explains the cognitive process of learning by doing. As Kolb argued, experiential learning posited that humans acquired knowledge through experiences.[7] He explained that our cognitive faculty developed through a repeated cycle of experience, observation and reflection, abstraction, and experimentations. Like the discussion previously, our engagements with the real world and our tasks shaped our experiences. We observed what we encountered and what we did, which could prompt to our reflections. Cognitively, we developed the ability to distill findings from observations and reflections, forming conceptual understanding. Hence, it is a process of abstraction of our experiences. We tended to apply these conceptual understanding in our subsequent practice, hence experimentations. In turn, these experimentations formed the beginning of the next cycle of our cognitive process. Experiential learning is similar to a type of problem-solving approach, that is, heuristic thinking.[8] In this context, the problem-solving activities proceeded without prior knowledge of the efficacy of the procedure being applied. Activities happened through a sequence, in which each sequence is determined by the result of prior acts. This is very apt with design process, in which designers never knew whether their design moves would yield to expected results.

The issue, in this vein, was to make that process intelligible, that is, methodical and teachable. Hence, it was the problem of exposition of the technique of experience. Dewey argued for a pedagogy that would incorporate stimulating senses, including through physical activities, besides developing intellectual aptitudes. His pedagogy aimed to achieve a balance between practical and academic learning. This approach was often labelled as pragmatism. In his view, pragmatism would develop the craft of experience, that is, the way in which we could develop qualities of experiences. In his argument, experiences should not be just passing phenomena but something that could be arrested and studied to improve ourselves. At the heart of this argument was the notion of the techniques of experience. According to him, it was necessary to grasp the form and procedure of experiences, to make it intelligible. This intelligibility would be conditions that would make experiences worthy for us.[9]

In mapping learning by doing in design pedagogy, Ashraf Salama classified four historical model of design pedagogy.[10] They are the academic, the craft, the engineer, and the social science models. The academic model placed the primacy on instilling the understanding of formal and conceptual aspects designs, such as the idea of beauty based on proportions and geometry and theories of compositions. In contrast, the craft model strived to develop the aptitude in trades of constructing building as the gateway into architectural design. With the scientific development, the engineer model emerged, following the same approach as the craft model, supplemented with the integrations of technology and scientific principles in design. The social science model came later, as design process was seen to be based on the scientific understanding of users' behaviors and experiences of buildings. Salama also traced modern design pedagogy from the Ecole-des-Beaux Art, the Vkhutemas, and the Bauhaus.[11] The Ecole-des-Beaux Art was the embodiment of the academic model and the setup of design education based on master-apprentice set up. On the other hand, the Vkhutemas represented the beginning of a design pedagogy based on the craft and engineer models, in which they embraced contemporary materials and techniques along with rational thinking in efforts to formulate novel design principles and approaches.[12] Similarly, the Bauhaus also developed design pedagogy based on engagement with materials and techniques as the starting point of design processes.

Salama continued his survey of design pedagogy to map contemporary models. He identified ten pedagogical models that emerged from the late 1960s to the mid-1990s.[13] One of these models is the Concept-test Model, that evolved from the considerations of learning as a developmental process that connected conjecture and testing argued by Jean Piaget.[14] In this model, a design project consisted of a series of small design problems. It treated drawings and models to test and evaluate these design problems in each exercise. In this vein, each problem is an exercise in making, testing, and analyzing. The form-generation strategies emerged from the findings of these analysis. The learning process proceeded in an incremental fashion, in which each part contributes to the understanding the whole design process. Another model is the analogical model that was developed in the University of Cincinnati by Gordon Simmons from 1978 till 1990s.[15] Simmons developed this model based on Peter Collins' ideas that a design process followed a path of an eclectic process of selection and rejection of possible solutions. In this line of thought, for Simmons, design is an intuitive hypothesis that is rationalized through the process. In his survey, the trends of architectural design pedagogy from the late 1990s till mid 2010s showed the growth of those models, one of which was the integration of critical inquiry and empirical approach.[16] In this line of thought, Mitchell argued for a discipline-specific design thinking based on inductive methods and practical inquiry.[17] In this model, students would develop the abilities to distill abstract principles from doing, making, and performing through the analytical process. These findings illustrate the long lineage of hands-on learning as a pedagogical model in architectural design education. This model placed experimentations of techniques and materials to develop design aptitude, instead of applying skills in doing and making simply to manifest design concepts.[18] Salama also documented the emerging and shifting approach from the late 1990s till the mid 2010s, which emphasized critical inquiry and process-oriented design. He pointed to an argument in Kevin Mitchell's book on a design pedagogy based in inductive method. This teaching method promoted emphasis on independent investigation and strong interaction. The aim is to nurture students to discover the way abstract principles have been applied or embedded in phenomena.[19] In this line of thought, Salama discussed a model of learning-by-making and heuristics thinking. An example of this approach from Ryan Smith proposes a design process that started from construction of an artifact. The studio revolves around unpacking this artifact through multiple architectural means. Smith based his approach on Peter Zumthor's argument that a design process should start from "physical, objective and sensuous examination of architecture, its material and its form."[20]

This heuristic model relates to the emergence of design-built studio and learning by making. As Jara has outlined, the heuristic emerged from the study of Peter Rowe, borrowed from a concept in mathematics, in which he views design as a problem-solving activity.[21] In essence, the heuristic model referred to a way of directing experimentation. In this model, precedents or technical knowledge were analyzed and then tested and evaluated. Findings acquired from this testing formed the design knowledge. The nature of learning by doing, experimenting, and exploring made heuristic approach a common practice in studio teaching.

However, it also drew criticism, one of which was the difficulty to deal with the fact that each solution in a design process was simply one possibility out of many. In the end, the heuristic model tended to be a way to rationalize a solution.

FIRST AND THIRD YEAR STUDIOS

In this context, we develop our design pedagogy following the notion of learning by doing and the historical idea of studio as a laboratory. As a background, in terms of rules in design, we separated generative rules from operative rules. Generative rules are rules that emerged in the form-making process. These rules tend to be case specific, emerging from analysis, observations, and findings from the sequence of exercises. On the other hand, operative rules referred to rules associated with procedure and techniques in a design process. These encompassed from tenets in ordering space and forms to procedure in drawing and model-making. Instilling the rigor in the operative rules is very crucial for us as they form the scaffold in developing the foundational skills and aptitudes. However, we push our students to go beyond following operative rules into problematizing these rules as a starting point in developing their generative rules. In this line of thought, this related to the differences between methodical and axiomatic thinking.[22] The former referred to a thought process that is guided by a set of established rules and principles. Applying and repeating operative rules is an example of this thinking. On the other hand, axiomatic thinking questioned these

FIGURE 1.2.1
First year studio, Artifacts and Constructions, Module 01—Observations, Kim Bach, student.

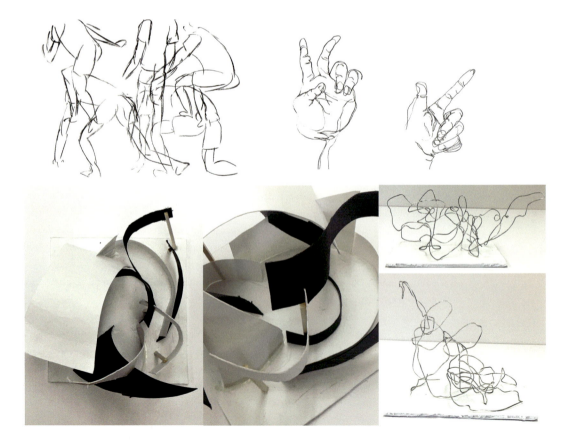

very rules. Asking "what if" questions and critically reflecting on experiences would lead to discoveries of ways in form-generations.

The beginning-design component spanned two studios over two semesters, consisting of a series of interconnected modules that eventually led to designs of a habitable structure with increasing scales and complexities. In this context, besides learning skills in drawing, drafting, and model-making, students also learned to work in our woodshop. Faculty and staff introduced them to some basic skills in working with wood, mainly with carving and constructing basic wood joinery. In a way, they related to design by subtractions and additions. The intent of this learning setup is for students to learn to work with opportunities offered by and limitations of materials and tools. Through the sequence of observing, drawing, making models, analyzing, and designing in a cyclical fashion, students learned to identify and articulate basic elements and to speculate and formulate rules that connected these basic elements. In turn, these findings served as the starting point in the form-finding process in generating a design.

The first modules in the sequence focused on observations, which introduced students to techniques in seeing and to document findings through drawings. Drawing types include free-hand drawings and measured drawings, that is, orthographic and axonometric projections. In a way, this module also introduced students to the notion of abstraction and methods of extracting information. However, drawings are not the end goal of the exercise. Instead, the charge asked students to turn their drawings into models. In essence, the exercise charged students to translate a three-dimensional world into two-dimensional representations and then back to three-dimensional artifacts. The emphasis of the modules was space-making rather than form-making. Graphic analyses through diagramming served as a tool in these design processes, in which it served as a scaffold for understanding and representations. Diagramming introduces the notion morphology by identifying or extracting the formal structure. It included the understanding of geometry and terminology, including alignment, proximity, modularity, and similarity. The transformation from two- into three-dimensional proceeded as a process in morphological transformations. Rules emerged from actions in transformations in the morphological studies. Students started to discover by themselves space-defining elements, hence abstract principles of space-making. Engagement with objects furthered the notion of self-discovery of formal properties and structures. However, these modules posed challenges including the difficulties in distancing from pre-conceived conceptions, such as the name of an object and mimetic representations. Overcoming these challenges allowed students to improve significantly in their designing and drawing skills. These processes allowed us to introduce vocabularies of spatial properties and conditions, which stimulated students to start conceptualizing space. Repetition and recursive setup proved to be very crucial in developing design cognitions.

The next module charged students to transform observational drawings into a design of wood panels. Similarly, the intent is to abstract observational drawings through diagrams that articulate elements and rules. These findings served as a starting point to develop elements and rules, hence parameters, in fabricating carved wood panels. The exercise started from a tile, from which students extended into three tiles along the horizontal axis. The third part asked students to expand the tiles into a panel that consisted of nine tiles. Students expanded and transformed their original ideas into larger artifacts, following their diagrams as the basic rules. The modules created dialogues between geometry, ordering principles, tools, and materials. With regards to woodshop exercises, the joinery parts of the module induced students

■ Arief Setiawan and Christopher Welty

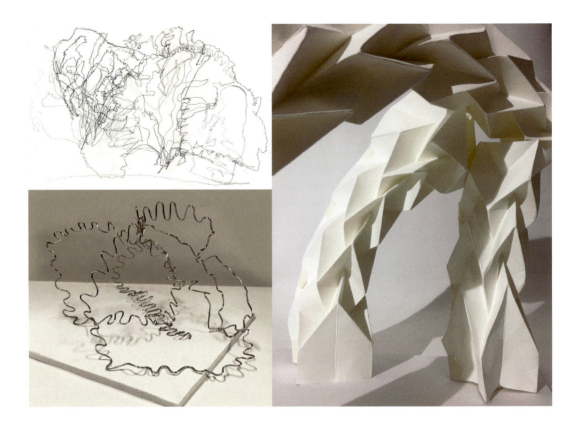

FIGURE 1.2.2

First year studio, Artifacts and Constructions, Module 01—Observations, student work, Aby Akridge, Kathryn Folger.

to construct basic flat and corner wood joints. In turn, they practice constructing flat panels and cube-shaped artifacts based on these techniques. Along a similar trajectory as the carving exercises, they started with constructing a small artifact, which they use as a starting point to fabricate larger artifacts. The hands-on exercises in the woodshop offered a scaffold for the design inquiries, giving students directions in studying the ways properties of materials and capacities of tools to inform design process and decisions. Hence, design responses emerged from the dialogue with the agency of tools and materials. Developing basic skills in handling tools and materials, which were crucial in setting up the stage for experimentations, required a significant amount of time, which led to the slow pace in exercises on texture, carving, and joineries. However, these slow paces offered opportunities for longer observations and reflections of challenges stemmed from tools and materials. Two possible avenues in dealing with challenges included working with or fighting against them.[23] In this vein, constraints and limitations became design opportunities.

The final module of each semester integrated learning experiences from each module to construct a personal space in the fall semester and a multi-person space in the spring semester. The design brief called students to start from orthographic and axonometric drawings and models from the subsequent module. It directed students to investigate formal structure from these drawings and modules to inform initial design responses. Similarly, the spring studio asked students to integrate their explorations of joints, flat panels, and volumetric artifacts into a multi-person space. Overall, the setup introduced students to multilayered design problems. The underlying premise in the constant transformation from three- to two- and back to three-dimensional, in which constructing drawings and models occupied a central

Making to Construct Design Thinking

FIGURE 1.2.3
First year studio, Artifacts and Constructions, Module 01—Observations, Kim Bach, student.

FIGURE 1.2.4
First year studio, Artifacts and Constructions, Module 03—Texture and Carving Project, Kim Bach, student.

33

■ Arief Setiawan and Christopher Welty

FIGURE 1.2.5
First year studio, Artifacts and Constructions, Module 04—Joinery Project, Ashlyn Wiege, student.

FIGURE 1.2.6
First year studio, Artifacts and Constructions, Module 04—Joinery Project, Tim Gatto, student.

34

Making to Construct Design Thinking

role. Another layer was the notion of elements and rules, which refer to the relationship between parts and the whole. On top of those was ways these transformations generated spatial effects.

Third-Year Studio

The pedagogical approach follows a similar process of learning by doing and the idea of the studio as laboratory. Third-year spring studio addresses issues of sustainability in the built environment. Students study how passive systems can be introduced into buildings to be heated and cooled. In Atlanta solar shading becomes one of the largest concerns. Over the semester students use this knowledge to develop a mid-rise project in the urban context.

Studio investigations centered on making a way to construct design thinking, introducing tools, both digital and manual, for design documentation and fabrication. Though we use kinetic mechanisms in everyday life, it was assumed that these students had never directly or intentionally played with kinetic systems. In the first exercise, prototyping precedent, students used precedent projects to identify formal structures and mechanisms for movement. Initial research focused on diagraming the movement systems understanding the transformation and impact of scale. Small artifacts were constructed to test the ideas. Fabrication methods ranged from traditional tools in the woodshop to digital equipment of laser cutting and 3D printing. These artifacts became the primary thinking devices and idea generators.

FIGURE 1.2.7
Kinetic facade studies for solar shading—Stephanie Bulga.

■ Arief Setiawan and Christopher Welty

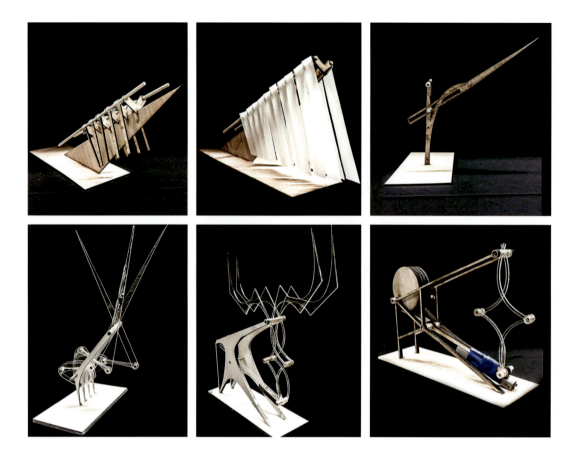

FIGURE 1.2.8
Kinetic facade studies for solar shading—Noah Beiber.

As the students researched kinetics, they continued to advance and fabricated their ideas. Photographic documentation was used to capture the design solutions in addition to the physical prototypes. The graphics allowed student to understand the relationships while the physical models allowed an understanding of the transformations. In the dianthus blooming facade, the skin of the facade is derived from the simplified abstraction of the bending movement of the dianthus flower. The system proposed an integrated and interactive mechanism based on a push-and-pull movement translated into a twist movement. The mechanism is broken into two parts, part one is a retractable twisting motion and part two is the skin. Final design solutions were fabricated into 24 × 24" panels.

Ideally when designing a facade, we want a combination of inspiration and function. In fragmented flux the kinetic facade is a combination of these ideals where the construct breaks up the mundane wall and celebrates the structure and inner mechanics. Creating a facade that breaks up the geometric shards through the circular motion of the gears. As the facade opens and closes, it creates a feeling of tension for what seems like an impending collision and a sense of relief as the delicate panels slide past one another. Through its multiple combinations of enclosure, it offers the opportunity in the play of light but also the potential for photovoltaics to represent the black panels.

One skin system studied the track system of the "solar wings" in the Apple Store design by Foster + Partners to develop a kinetic enclosure that will allow the building's facade to open and close without a double skin system. Using a radial enclosure created a facade system

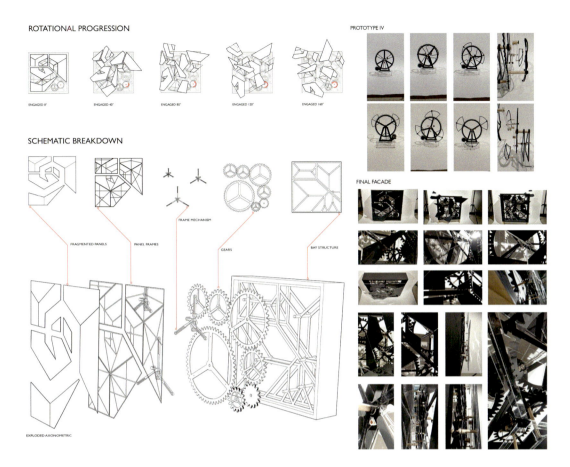

FIGURE 1.2.9
Kinetic facade studies for solar shading—Devon Sams.

that can pivot to close the building envelope. The module panels can repeat across the exterior of the building or vary in sizes depending on the program and desired lighting exposer.

Through a mid-rise typology, the studio challenged students to investigate the connection between kinetics and a building enclosure. The pedagogical approach linked to doing and making established a design problem that centered on prototyping. Students worked through making. Drawings and diagrams provide the bases for fabrication, while the material selection and systems of connection had measurable consequences on the prototype outcomes. The project focused on understanding kinetic systems as the basis for developing a design solution for prototyping a building enclosure to be more responsive to the changes of environmental conditions throughout the day and the seasons.

CONCLUDING NOTES

Unexpected results from doing and making, hence working with tools, materials, and techniques, demonstrated the values of experimentations. They led to self-discovery of well-established abstract principles in design, such as geometry and order. Further, this self-discovery formed personalized understanding of design process and thinking. Self-discovered abstract principles, combined with associative acts, such as the use of analogies and metaphor, formed the path in constructing design decisions. These abstract principles guided the formal, scalar,

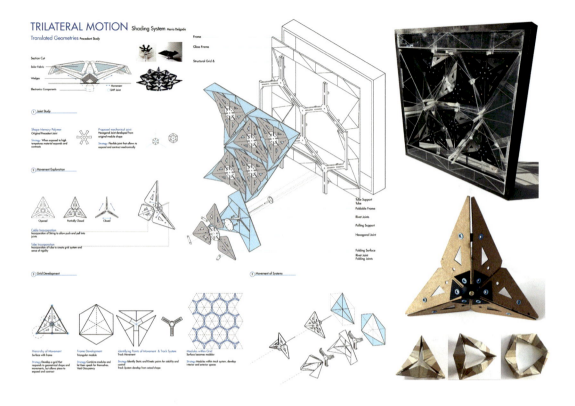

FIGURE 1.2.10
Kinetic facade studies for solar shading—Maria Delgado.

and dimensional transformation of the formal structure throughout the design process. Making small-scale study models allowed students to discover techniques of space-making and spatial organization. The associative acts using words that describe spatial and formal properties allowed them to explore possible ideas about space.

Aristotle classified the forms of knowledge into episteme, techne, and praxis. The first, episteme, referred to the pure knowledge of things and phenomena, while techne pointed to knowledge of the making of things. The last, praxis, described knowledge on how to do or to act. Reflecting on this distinction, our pedagogy of thinking-through-making is a form of praxis, that is, inquiring of ways a designer translates intuitive, conceptual ideas to technically competent constructions. As praxis, our pedagogy intends to empower students to develop a design methodology that intersect knowledge of making thing, or techne, with pure knowledge about beauty or good design episteme *[2015 NCBDS Beginning to End: Revisiting the Foundation]*.

NOTES

1 Sennett, R. (2008). *The Craftsman*. New Haven, CT: Yale University Press, pp. 7–9.
2 Ibid., pp. 10–11.
3 Ibid.
4 Ibid., pp. 119–146.
5 Damisch, H. (2016). *Noah's Ark: Essays on Architecture*. Cambridge, MA: The MIT Press, p. 238.
6 Ibid., pp. 231–246.

7 Kolb, A. and Kolb, D. (2014). The Kolb Learning Style Inventory 4.0: A Comprehensive Guide to the Theory, Psychometrics, Research on Validity and Educational Application, pp. 6–7.
8 Rowe, P. (1991). *Design Thinking*. Cambridge, MA: The MIT Press, p. 70.
9 Sennett, R. (2008). *The Craftsman*. New Haven, CT: Yale University Press.
10 Salama, A. and Wilkinson, N. (2007). "Introduction," in Salama, A. and Wilkinson, N., eds., *Design Studio Pedagogy: Horizons for Future*. Gateshead, UK: The Urban International Press, pp. 4–5.
11 Salama, A. (2015). *Spatial Design Education: New Directions for Pedagogy in Architecture and Beyond*. New York: Ashgate (Kindle ed.), pp. 78–86.
12 Cooke, C. (1989). "The Development of the Constructivist Architects' Design Method," in Papadakis, A., Cooke, C., and Benjamin, A., eds., *Deconstruction: Omnibus Volume*. New York: Rizzoli, pp. 20–35.
13 Salama, A. (2015). *Spatial Design Education: New Directions for Pedagogy in Architecture and Beyond*. New York: Ashgate (Kindle ed.), pp. 141–162.
14 Ibid., pp. 152–156. This model was, developed by Stefani Ledewitz at Carnegie Melon since 1985.
15 Ibid., pp. 144–145.
16 Ibid., pp. 202–204.
17 Ibid., p. 202.
18 Ibid., p. 277. An example that Salama cited was the teaching of Jeff Haase from OSU, Department of Industrial, Interior, and Visual Communication Design. Haase points out that through this model, students also contribute in producing knowledge, and they became more well-rounded, equipped with conceptual and physical aptitudes.
19 Ibid., p. 202.
20 Ibid., p. 207.
21 Jara, C. (2014). "Verbal Literacy in the Design Process: Enthusiasm and Reservation," in Beyond Architecture: New Intersections and Connections, Proceedings of the ARCC/EAAE 2014 International Conference on Architectural Research, University of Hawaii at Manoa, Hawaii, pp. 41–47.
22 Setiawan, A. (2010). *Modernity in Architecture in Relation to Context*, Ph.D. Dissertation, Atlanta, Georgia Institute of Technology, p. 235.
23 Sennett, R. (2008). *The Craftsman*. New Haven, CT: Yale University Press.

Folding Research Into Teaching

Joseph Choma

Folding can be a mechanical deformation of a material, a mathematical abstraction, a structural logic or a mechanism to create art. Within the context of this research, paper folding and foldable structures are explored. Although many researchers dismiss the material properties of paper, "paper folding" inherently suggests materiality. This research exploits the fibrous material as a nontrivial constraint. Therefore, numerical-based simulations are considered subservient to physical models and fabrication-based design experiments. That said, this research does begin to illuminate some of the computation and governing rules behind folding.

Although origami is an ancient art form, the earliest known example of paper folding within the formal education of a designer was not introduced until the 1920s. In 1927 and 1928, within Josef Albers' preliminary course at the Bauhaus, students explored paper folding as a means to learn about design as an iterative, reflective, and rigorous process. Josef Albers said, "The best education is one's own experience. Experimenting surpasses studying. To start out by 'playing' develops courage, leads in a natural manner to an inventive way of building and furthers the pedagogically equally important facility of discovery" (Albers, 1969). When looking at the student work in Albers' course, there is a clear systematic rigor—executed through constraints, rules, and variations. One way to understand Albers' thinking is by looking at his own artistic work—his numerous serial paintings which explore the "interaction of color." Within this body of work, there is an intense "scientific" discipline with constants and variables. For example, in the series *Homage to the Square*, through hundreds of paintings for over 25 years, Albers explores the same geometric constraints of four squares nested inside each other but vary the use of color within those bounds (Albers, 1975). When looking at just a few old photographs from his preliminary course at the Bauhaus, we see extraordinary paper models (Wingler, 1969). There is a hyperbolic paraboloid and the earliest known example of curved-crease folding. Additionally, one of the models photographed closely resembles a Miura-Ori crease pattern—named after the astrophysicist Koryo Miura in 1980 (Demaine and Demaine, 2015). These exuberant and impressive paper models were not only novel designs but have inspired mathematical open problems and research inquiries within the intellectual discourse of folding. They are truly objects to think with and were invented through design-based rigor.

NOT JUST ORIGAMI

This research would like to make a distinction between the term "origami" and foldable structures. Traditionally, origami is dominantly composed of hidden under tucked folds, which is neither an efficient use of material nor ideal for resisting structural loads. However, once

FIGURE 1.3.1
Folded fiberglass vault.

■ Joseph Choma

FIGURE 1.3.2
Looking up at the inner ceiling of the folded fiberglass vault.

a folded geometry has a specific orientation to gravity and is considered to have material thickness with the intent of carrying loads, it is no longer "just origami" but a foldable structure. Although this research won't empirically calculate or test a folded geometry's structural performance, it considers folded geometries within the context of architectural structural elements.

The word "structure" may relate to how a building stands up. However, beneath the literal technicalities of structural engineering are ideological positions. Fred Angerer conveniently simplifies structural logic to three general types: solid, skeletal, and surface (Angerer, 1961). Solid structures can be traced back to caves and pyramids composed of mass. Another primitive form of human inhabitation is the tent. This structural typology is composed of members covered (or clad) with a skin. Angerer would call this a skeletal system because of the discrete elements used to support the space. Surface structures are drastically different than the other two. "With surface construction the external form coincides with the internal form" (Angerer, 1961). Similar to the idea of inhabiting an eggshell, the surface thickness is minimal, and the geometry of the structure is the space. This is arguably the most "pure" of the three structural systems because of the simplicity and interrelated dialogue between form, structure, and space. Domes and vaults are just two architectural examples of surface structures.

Foldable structures are a unique type of surface structure, which incorporate discontinuities (discrete edges or creases) into a continuous system. This research is motivated by the poetic desire to create "honest structures" through folding, where the folds are structural and not ornamental. As Rudolf Schwarz writes, "If we define truth as pure expression, we may then say that shell construction is the most truthful of all building forms, since the shell expresses space more closely" (Schwarz, 1947).

Conceptually, ideas of honesty and purity resonate with a range of engineers, architects, designers, and artists. At a more foundational level, the idea is rooted in modernist thinking. Within a small square pamphlet book titled *Good Design*, there is a section where Bruno

FIGURE 1.3.3
Side profile of the folded fiberglass cone.

■ Joseph Choma

Munari describes an orange in detail to explain modernism. "An orange, therefore, is a perfect object, in which the absolute coherence of form, use, consumption is found. Even the color is exactly right. If it were blue, it would be wrong" (Munari, 1963). In other words, every aspect of the orange is contributing to some kind of performance—nothing is extraneous or ornamental. Each part is serving its own function while being in direct dialogue with another part (Choma, 2018a). As Josef Albers would say, "Adding two elements must result in more than just the sum of those elements" (Albers, 1969). Similarly, every crease must contribute to the foldable structure.

FOLD-INSPIRED STRUCTURES

Within the field of architecture, we think we have a whole discourse dedicated to foldable structures. However, most structures we label as "folded" are not folded at all but are fold-inspired. For example, in 1923, Eugène Freyssinet designed and engineered two identical aircraft hangars at Orly Aiport in Paris. These are considered the first long-span, folded structures (Šekularac, Ivanovic-Šekularac and Cikic-Tovarovic, 2012). Although Freyssinet's innovative structural technique was directly linked to the development of reinforced concrete, the structure was not literally folded like the way we think of folding paper. This research does not intend to dismiss the historical significance of the aircraft hangars but questions how they are typologically labeled. In general, Freyssinet demonstrated a

> mastery of moving formwork for the casting of in-situ concrete. These 91 meter-wide, 61-meter-high vaults were each built in two stages. The first stage consisted of 17-meter-high springing, cast in place as an integral part of the reinforced foundations on either side of the hangar. The fully 'folded' and partly glazed concrete shell arch cast above this springing was built by adding one V shaped rib at a time.
>
> (Frampton and Futagawa, 1983)

FIGURE 1.3.4
Looking inside the folded fiberglass cone.

Folding Research Into Teaching

Similar to the approach taken here, the material logic, method of construction, and structural system are holistically incorporated into this research. However, this research seeks to literally fold materials—like paper folding—at the scale of architecture.

The geometry of Freyssinet's hangars closely resembles the shape of earlier shell structures, such as the barrel vault. Later fold-inspired structures started to diverge from the continuous surfaces of traditional shell structures by introducing diagonal folds into the system. This led to the commonly used folded plate structures, which are composed of flat planes that are interconnected at some dihedral angle. Folded plate structures are sometimes preferable to other shell structures because of their simplified manufacturing process. With advancements in construction techniques, folded plate structures have been built out of a variety of materials: concrete, steel, wood, and plastic. Architectural details also continue to be developed and refined (Lebée, 2015). However, most contemporary folded structures look surprisingly similar (if not identical) to those outlined in Heinrich Engel's *Tragsysteme/Structure Systems* (Engel, 1967). Of course, there are rare exceptions to this generalization, such as Heatherwick Studio's *Paternoster Vents* in London from 2002. Within that project, two folded towers emerge out of the ground in a public square near St. Paul's Cathedral in London. Each tower is composed of 63 identical isosceles triangles of stainless steel sheets welded together. The surface is then glass-bead blasted to give the faceted geometry a softer quality. These elegant mirrored forms activate the urban void, while pragmatically contributing to the adjacent building's cooling system. Heatherwick's project is aesthetically elegant but not literally folded.

When looking at Engel's beautifully illustrated book more closely, the book's strengths and shortcomings become quite apparent. Each structural logic is first introduced at a conceptual level through stress distribution and span capacity. Then, a catalog of design variations is presented to inform and inspire. His chapter on "Surface-Active Structure Systems" dedicates more than 20 pages to folded plate structures and presents a collection of variations of structural designs through incremental changes. Therefore, individuals can easily understand Engel's thought process, but it is challenging to develop your own design

FIGURE 1.3.5
Detail of the folded fiberglass cube.

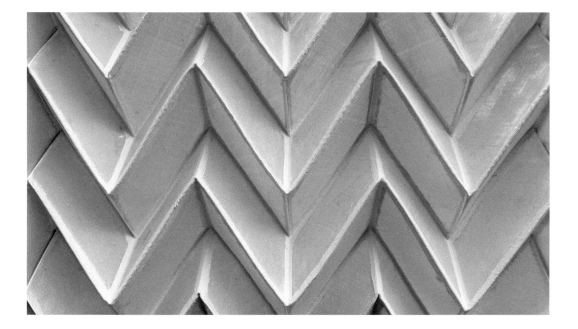

45

without adopting his literal framework. Furthermore, we can see that the structures within the book were intended to be built with an assembly of discrete planar elements. This is obvious because there are no crease patterns documented. A crease pattern is the graphical instruction which specifies the location of mountain and valley folds. With this diagram an individual can recreate a folded geometry with precision. However, the crease pattern is also a lens that allows an individual to design their own folded geometries. It is important to understand the relationships between two-dimensional crease patterns and three-dimensional folded geometries. In contrast to Engel, Paul Jackson's *Folding Techniques for Designers: From Sheet to Form* provides a clear introduction to crease patterns and paper folding but does not discuss structural constraints. It provides a foundation to design with paper folding but not a foundation to design foldable structures through paper folding (Jackson, 2011). This research attempts to fill part of the gap between Engel and Jackson.

MAKING TO LEARN AND LEARNING TO MAKE

In the 1930s and 1940s, Josef Albers continued to teach folding at the Black Mountain College (Harris, 2002). Some photographs from 1936 and 1937 document paper models that look very similar to the earlier exercises taught at the Bauhaus. In particular, there is another paper model which looks to be composed of a series of concentric circles. However, not all of the work was derivative of the prior student work. Arguably, one student model of significant importance is a crease pattern composed of sine curves that reflect and repeat where each crease "kisses" the other at the apex. Two ends of the folded sheet are then connected together to form a tube or cylinder-like geometry (Koschitz, 2016). This begins to suggest a specific architectural element, a column. In 1950, Albers took up the appointment as chairman of the design department at Yale University. In addition to teaching at Yale, Albers continued to teach at a variety of universities around the world. When teaching at the Hochschule für Gestaltung, Ulm, in 1953, he is photographed holding a much larger paper model composed

FIGURE 1.3.6
Exterior photograph of the folded fiberglass A-frame.

Folding Research Into Teaching

of concentric circles. In another archival photograph, there is a student folding a large column-like model across a table that is longer than the wingspan of that student's arms (Spitz, 2021). These photographs suggest a growing interest in scaling up these folded paper models.

In the late 1960s at the École Nationale Supérieure des Beaux-Arts, folding continued to be taught, but with a different primary learning objective. There was a clear transition from Albers' artistic abstraction to develop fabrication-driven assemblies at full-scale. These exercises were referred to as *Géométrie Constructive* (Emmerich, 1970). Many of the small-scale study models were tested through a strict combinatorial logic. Sometimes the same model was produced through different frameworks. In one instance, a folded plate structure was physically modelled twice, once out of paper (surface) and once out of dowels (wireframe/skeleton). The text that documented each study was written in an overly objective manner. Each task that was completed was recorded like a scientific logbook, without any emotional or conceptual poetry attached. "Topology" and "morphology" were just a couple of the new words added to the vocabulary of an architect. One team used corrugated cardboard to translate their paper models into two outdoor installations. Although this pedagogical approach was not entirely new, it does mark a cultural shift in the education of an architect. Overall, a common theme was the translation of representational abstractions into large "tectonic" physical artifacts—which can be experienced at the human scale. In other words, how do we record and reproduce something within a different set of constraints? This was right around the same time the computer was on the verge of being incorporated into architectural practice (Barnett, 1965).

In the 1970s, similar design studios began to be taught in the USA. For instance, the first year studio taught by Glen Small and Ahde Lahti at Cal Poly Pomona in 1971 also

FIGURE 1.3.7
Interior photograph of the folded fiberglass A-frame.

47

■ Joseph Choma

explored foldable structures at an inhabitable scale. The premise of the studio was to design a community for a three-day campout in the dunes at Pismo Beach. The students created small scale models and then large temporary dwellings out of corrugated cardboard. The structures were designed to be inexpensive, lightweight, flat-packable, and deployable. Unlike the École Nationale Supérieure des Beaux-Arts, the studio was motivated by "what makes a community function and to teach [them] how to plan with nature, man and machine" (MacMasters, 1971). They also looked at an ancient Indian fishing village as a precedent. It looks as though the folded geometries were literally derived from the material constraints and the desire to create something structural that could withstand the winds of the site. Although they only used corrugated cardboard, there is something compelling about the simplicity of the fabrication of these lightweight deployable structures. How can we bring these qualities back into more permanent foldable structures?

FIGURE 1.3.8
Folded fiberglass cube.

Over the past 20 years, there have been numerous intellectual contributions within the mathematical abstraction of folding, such as "geometric folding algorithms" (Demaine and O'Rourke, 2007). There have also been major advancements in the computational simulation of curved crease folding (Rabinovich et al., 2019). However, much of those advancements have not influenced the field of architecture directly. Most of those contributions ignore materiality, sheet thickness, and gravity—which are fundamental to the built environment. Other folding-related research does focus on construction-based architectural constraints. Some of that research explores prefabricating concrete elements (Studio Vacchini Architetti, 2019), perforating metal sheet materials (Raducanu et al., 2016), or connecting discrete planar elements (Buri et al., 2011). My research seeks to find new alternative means and methods of construction for foldable structures and materials. How can we stay true and pure to the folding logic even when we scale up?

PAPER FOLDING TO FOLDABLE COMPOSITES

Paper is a fibrous material and surface, not completely different from fiber-reinforced polymer (FRP). This research develops a technique to fold fiberglass—like folding paper by hand—at the architectural scale. Within this research, pliable fiberglass sheets are called "foldable composites."

The concept of foldable composites is straightforward. Take a dry fiber-reinforcement fabric, mask off seams to create fold points, infuse the unmasked fabric with resin, and cure the resin. This results in a composite laminate with uncured, soft seams that allow the entire structure to be folded for easy transport and installation on site. After the entire laminate is installed, the dry seams can be infused with resin to solidify the whole structure (Choma, 2018b).

Key features of the fabrication technique include the potential for numerous variations, no fasteners or molds, decrease in manufacturing costs through a reduction in production time and zero material waste, high portability and flat-packing capabilities, and the possibility to design stronger lightweight structures.

FIGURE 1.3.9
Photograph of the four deployable shelters.

Joseph Choma

With the recent inclusion of FRP construction in the International Building Code (IBC), textile-based composites are now recognized as viable building materials (International Code Council, 2015). Additionally, the Architectural Division of the American Composites Manufacturers Association (ACMA) has produced guidelines and recommended practices for fiber-reinforced-polymer architectural products (Kreysler et al., 2016). Major advances in fire retardant performance suggests that FRP will likely become more widely used in architectural applications. Currently, the IBC and ACMA guides dominantly focus on FRP as cladding systems. This research predicts that FRP might have potential applications in lightweight, long-span, deployable structures and stay-in-place formwork for concrete casting. Potentially, this could be a first step to elevate the material beyond decorative cladding (secondary component) and to structural applications (primary building material).

RESEARCH THROUGH TEACHING AND TEACHING THROUGH RESEARCH

In the fall 2021, I taught a design studio at Clemson University which explored deployable shelters for disaster relief with foldable composites. Instead of a typical design studio, we embraced the pedagogical approach of research through teaching and teaching through research—where my students and I collaborated on an applied research project.

The design research studio was split into four parts. First, we analyzed the existing state of deployable shelters for disaster relief. We discovered a significant gap between lightweight tents and more permanent dwellings made with a kit of parts. In particular, people usually ended up living in tents significantly longer than originally anticipated. How can we begin to fill this gap? Additionally, other approaches to shelter—such as containers—are often left behind and can be difficult to retrofit. How can we use folding as a means to design shelters that can be flat-packed, deployed, and flat-packed again? How can foldable structures be retrofitted into part of a permanent structure—such as a stay-in-place formwork for concrete casting? These questions motivated our research inquiry.

Secondly, we explored the geometric constraints of foldable structures through four frameworks: arches, saddles, vaults, and tessellations—each through both straight and curved creases. This was followed by an introduction to my patented fabrication technique, which allows fiberglass to fold like paper.

Lastly, the studio developed four design strategies (vault, cone, cube, and A-frame) while simultaneously exploring four different focused research agendas (ground anchors, integration of apertures, self-folding hinges, and material calibrations).

Each of the half-scale prototypes took five days for four people to fabricate. All of the shelters were made from one continuous flat crease pattern. In other words, a large single flat sheet of fiberglass was folded by hand into an inhabitable shelter. As a material constraint, each team of four students was limited to 232 sq ft of fiberglass. These foldable structures begin to suggest a possible future for deployable shelters for disaster relief.

REFERENCES

Albers, J. (1969). Creative Education. In H. M. Wingler (Editor), *The Bauhaus: Weimar, Dessau, Berlin, Chicago* (pp. 142–143). Cambridge, MA: MIT Press.
Albers, J. (1975). *Interaction of Color*. New Haven, CT: Yale University Press.
Angerer, F. (1961). *Surface Structures in Building: Structure and Form*. London: Alec Tiranti.

Barnett, J. (1965, January). Will the Computer Change the Practice of Architecture? *Architectural Record*, 143–150.

Buri, H. U., Stotz, I., & Weinand, Y. (2011). Curved Folded Plate Timber Structures. In *Proceedings of the IABSE-IASS Symposium: Taller, Longer, Lighter*.

Choma, J. (2018a). *Études for Architects*. New York: Routledge.

Choma, J. (2018b). Foldable Composites for Architectural Applications. In R. J. Lang, M. Bolitho, & Z. You (Editors), *Origami 7 Volume 1: Design, Education, History, and Science* (pp. 135–150). St Albans: Tarquin Publishing.

Demaine, E. D., & Demaine, M. L. (2015, May 15). History of Curved Origami Sculpture. Retrieved May 10, 2018, from http://erikdemaine.org/curved/history/

Demaine, E. D., & O'Rourke, J. (2007). *Geometric Folding Algorithms: Linkages, Origami, Polyhedra*. Cambridge: Cambridge University Press.

Emmerich, D. G. (1970). *Exercices de Géométrie Constructive: Travaux Détudiants*. Paris: Presse du Centre de Recherche dUrbanisme.

Engel, H. (1967). *Tragsysteme/Structure Systems*. Stuttgart: Deutsche Verlags-Anstalt.

Frampton, K., & Futagawa, Y. (1983). *Modern Architecture 1851–1945*. New York: Rizzoli.

Harris, M. E. (2002). *The Arts at Black Mountain College*. Cambridge, MA: The MIT Press.

International Code Council. (2015). *International Building Code*. Falls Church, VA: International Code Council.

Jackson, P. (2011). *Folding Techniques for Designers: From Sheet to Form*. London: Laurence King Publishing.

Koschitz, D. (2016). Design with Curved Creases: Digital and Analog Constraints. In S. Adriaenssens, F. Gramazio, M. Kohler, A. Menges, & M. Pauly (Editors), *Advances in Architectural Geometry 2016* (pp. 82–103). Zürich: vdf Hochschulverlag AG.

Kreysler, W., Dembsey, N., & Steffen, R. (2016). *Guidelines and Recommended Practices for Fiber-Reinforced-Polymer Architectural Products*. Arlington, VA: American Composites Manufacturers Association.

Lebée, A. (2015). From Folds to Structures: A Review. *International Journal of Space Structures*, 30(2), 55–74.

MacMasters, D. (1971, July 25). Design Lab in the Dunes. *Los Angeles Times HOME*, 16–20.

Munari, B. (1963). *Good Design*. Milan: All'insegna Del Pesce D'oro.

Rabinovich, M., Hoffmann, T., & Sorkine-Hornung, O. (2019). Modeling Curved Folding with Freeform Deformations. *ACM Transactions on Graphics*, 38(6), 1–12.

Raducanu, V. A., Cojocaru, V. D., & Raducanu, D. (2016). Structural Architectural Elements Made of Curved Folded Sheet Metal. In A. Herneoja, T. Österlund, & P. Markkanen (Editors), *Complexity & Simplicity: Proceedings of the 34th International Conference on Education and Research in Computer Aided Architectural Design in Europe*, 2 (pp. 409–416). Brussels: eCAADe.

Schwarz, R. (1947). *Vom Bau der Kirche*. Heidelberg: Verlag Anton Pustet.

Sekularac, N., Ivanovic-Sekularac, J., & Cikic-Tovarovic, J. (2012). Folded Structures in Modern Architecture. *Facta Universitatis—Series: Architecture and Civil Engineering*, 10(1), 1–16.

Spitz, R. (2021). *Hans G. Conrad: Interaction of Albers*. Cologne: Walther Koenig.

Studio Vacchini Architetti. (2019). Sports Education and Training Centre Mülimatt in Brugg/Windisch, CH. In S. Hofmeister (Editor), *Sports Facilities: Leisure and Movement in Urban Space* (pp. 162–175). Munich: DETAIL.

Wingler, H. M. (1969). *The Bauhaus: Weimar, Dessau, Berlin, Chicago*. Cambridge, MA: The MIT Press.

Beyond (the) Building

Fabricating a Design Build Program on the
Arabian Peninsula

Michael Hughes

INTRODUCTION

The Design Build Initiative (DBI) at the American University of Sharjah presents an alternative approach to full-scale pedagogy crafted to transition from an individual interest to a shared, sustainable platform. As deployed, the initiative features a diverse faculty collective working within a supportive and resilient infrastructural framework structured to overcome burdens associated with excessive stress borne by individual instructors working in isolation.

Working together, participating faculty developed an integrated curricular model in a region unaccustomed to celebrating manual production. In this context, DBI seeks to empower students through direct engagement with the instruments of making highlighted by an inclusive and iterative attitude toward tools and processes. Projects undertaken since the initiative's inception in 2011 illustrate the attempt to distill lessons from traditional, upper-level design build studios and distribute them throughout the course sequence while leveraging both digital and analog fabrication methods.

THE CHALLENGE

Leading a design build studio is lonely. While the design build projects rely on an inherently collaborative process in which faculty work closely with 12 or more students, responsibility at all levels is ultimately borne alone by the design build instructor. The professor in charge is typically expected to cover all aspects related to client engagement, project acquisition, logistics, liability, administration, construction supervision, cheer-leading, pedagogy, and turn-key delivery. Compounding the isolation, this solo act is too often accompanied by a dearth of collegial support or even empathy. Counsel from peers with similar experiences is equally rare as it is not unusual for a school to have only one "DB" faculty member on staff. Sadly, design build teaching may even come with the added responsibility of defending the pedagogical and scholarly merits from prejudices voiced furtively or openly by faculty and administrative colleagues.

In his 2011 study Geoff Gjertson found that

> the primary challenge to programs is the lack of integration of design/build activities into the overall curriculum. Ultimately, a lack of integration and lack of institutional support can lead to the marginalization of both the design/build program and the involved faculty.
>
> (Gjertson, 2011)

The immediate association between individuals and a specific school (i.e., Steve Badanes at Univ. of Washington, Mary Hardin at Univ. of Arizona, or Rick Sommerfeld at Univ. of Colorado) speaks to the inherent, underlying singularity of the enterprise. Over time a few programs, notably Yale and the Rural Studio, have evolved some infrastructural scaffolding, but in the majority, quality outcomes succeed not because of a thoughtful, planned program infrastructure but "by various combinations of naiveté, ingenuity, interpersonal skill, deceit, leadership, risk taking, and wizardry possessed by the individual faculty leading the projects" (Hughes et al., 2019).

It is no wonder then that leading a design build studio is not only lonely but also physically and mentally exhausting. Gjertson notes that "the stresses upon faculty caused by excessive workloads, multiple roles, and project scope threaten structural collapse" (Gjertson, 2011). Faculty accept this responsibility, often repeatedly year after year, despite the numerous structural gaps separating normative university culture and design build pedagogy because it is incredibly rewarding. However, the embedded disjunction between load and support suggests that standard model is not compatible with long-term sustainability at the curricular level.

Ultimately, institutional practices honed to deliver normative curricula and traditional scholarship in an efficient manner present more numerous and insidious obstacles related to the academic calendar, teaching loads and institutional bureaucracy (Hughes et al., 2019). These burdens, familiar to most DB faculty, negatively affect program longevity as faculty burnout undermines regular course offerings and continuity. Dan Rockhill notes that "when I stagger away from these projects, I think '*There has got to be an easier way*'" (Kraus, 2017).

AN EASIER WAY V1.0: SHARED + SUSTAINABLE

After 15 years leading design build projects in the US, the search for Rockhill's "easier way" led to the head of department position at the American University of Sharjah (AUS) in the United Arab Emirates. As a young school without the weight of institutional tradition, the faculty at AUS were free to imagine and implement a holistic approach to design build in a region largely unaccustomed to haptic production. Instead of attempting to institute one new design build studio, a group of allied "makers" set to work designing a new vision of design build explicitly crafted to combat the most egregious symptoms undermining program sustainability and individual well-being.

The resulting Design Build Initiative (DBI) relies on a radical model of shared responsibility, curricular integration, and fluid teaching assignments. An existing cohort of four

FIGURE 1.4.1
FORM_work at the University of New Mexico in 1998. Faculty: M. Hughes.

Michael Hughes

faculty were soon joined by a series of new hires between 2011 and 2014 to create a team of eight to ten makers who animate both the five-year bachelor of architecture program and the four-year bachelor of interior design degree with a wide range of fabrication courses and design build projects. Collectively the participating faculty deliver projects that range from simple to complex delivered in workshops, seminars, and more traditional one- and two-semester design build studios.

Unique to this team-based approach, individual faculty members do not teach fabrication or DB courses continually, year after year or semester after semester. The relatively large number of fabrication-related faculty allows for a platoon system of substitutions that keep everyone fresh and engaged. In this way no individual faculty member has "ownership" of a particular course or project type. As a result, members of the DBI team are also fully integrated members of the faculty who regularly teach non-DB courses, thereby defusing internal department politics. In addition, the relatively large number of participating faculty provides for an unusual degree of diversity both in terms of project type/scope/scale, aesthetic predilections, and outcomes.

In the first ten years of the DBI (2011–21), ten different faculty have led design build studios, and 14 have offered required or elective fabrication courses. The wide range of courses and project types allows flexibility and options for faculty teaching while also providing an opportunity for junior faculty to build their capacity rather than being dropped into a complex project from the start. Completed projects have been recognized with three design build awards from the American Collegiate Schools of Architecture (ACSA). Notably, each of these three award-winning projects was led by a different faculty member or faculty team.

CULTURAL CONTEXT

Beginning with the discovery of oil in the mid-twentieth century, vernacular craft traditions native to the Arabian Peninsula have been in decline (Sarnecky, 2012). Today the UAE exists within a contemporary social and cultural context that views manual labor with derision. The founding dean of the college, Martin Giesen, notes,

> One obstacle we face is that school curricula in the UAE and the upbringing of youngsters today rarely include the making of things. How many ever used a shovel to dig up a flower bed or whittle away with a knife at a piece of wood? Most student work in the College of Architecture, Art and Design (CAAD) results in objects rather than in written work.... Conditions in the UAE and the MENA region are particularly challenging when it comes to incorporating practical aspects in higher education: Disciplinary boundaries discourage the mixing of theory and practice. Manual work is often looked upon as being below status. Gender roles are entrenched. Architecture is often misunderstood as exterior aesthetics.
>
> (Giesen, 2021)

In this context digital fabrication facilitates the introduction to full-scale learning as students arrive at the university with a preexisting facility for electronic media and software. Predisposed to technology accessed through keyboard or mouse-based interface modeling software and CNC tools provide a smooth, familiar, if not seamless transition to material fabrication. In contrast, hand drawing with traditional tools (i.e., pen and pencil) is largely unfamiliar and

Beyond (the) Building

often intimidating, as are the loud, fast-moving analog tools that require a closer proximity between hand, material, and sharp blades or bits.

INFRASTRUCTURE

As faculty worked to envision a new curriculum, the campus facilities department was completing a scheduled refurbishment of the building that included an extraordinary investment in new labs stocked with an extensive array of digital and analog tools. Large well-appointed labs devoted to ceramics, wood, and metal were located directly adjacent to labs housing the latest CNC equipment. Multiple small laser cutters and 3D printers facilitated product design and modeling, while two Kuka robots, two 3-axis CNC routers, and a large metal-capable CNC laser cutter provided capacity to create large, building-scale components. The diverse array of equipment in close proximity contributes to the hybrid approach to fabrication evident in much of the subsequent production (Figure 1.4.2).

Combined with the arrival of a new department head with firsthand experience juggling the logistic and administrative challenges associated with design build, the new labs and tooling provided much of the foundation necessary to support the new program. However, even with students and faculty donating labor, full-scale projects require significant financial resources. In North America, grants and entrepreneurial fundraising often compliment the budgets provided by nonprofit partners; suffice it to say that in the Middle East, charity operates differently. In response, the department applied for and received $80,000 in annual support from the provost's "Special Initiative Funding" grant program. In addition to providing an internal source of funding for design build projects, the grant supports faculty training, guest speakers and skill-building workshops.

College faculty interested in developing new skills related to utilizing equipment available in the school's wood, metal, and digital fabrication labs can apply for a "Skillset Development Grant" that has ranged from $1,500 to $5,000. All skill levels, from beginner to advanced, are encouraged to apply. In this way new faculty are encouraged and invited to participate in the fabrication curriculum, while existing team members are encouraged to develop or hone capacity. In a typical year, the grant funding supports one "prototyping" studio (one semester), one interior design DB studio (one semester), and one architecture DB studio, a week-long metal fabrication workshop, a guest lectures, one final review critic, and two Skillset Development Grants.

FIGURE 1.4.2
Digital fabrication labs at the American University of Sharjah.

55

■ Michael Hughes

IMPLEMENTATION

The Design Build Initiative relies on an incremental and multifaceted curricular approach designed to increase student and program capacity over time. The curriculum features short exercises and workshops embedded in required studio and lecture courses at the introductory level, while a coordinated series of material fabrication (a.k.a. analog) and digital fabrication electives provide incremental steps to fabrication proficiency (Figure 1.4.3). The segregation between analog and digital begins to blur in advanced seminars, while the upper-level design build studios almost invariably avoid polemical approaches to the means of production even if a particular digital or analog method is privileged within a particular project.

In a tradition dating to the Bauhaus, small but full-scale furniture projects laid the foundation for a new tradition of making at AUS. The history of furniture making at the school predates the Design Build Initiative and can be traced to the arrival of Bill Sarnecky in 2006. Working in a makeshift, modestly equipped shop, Sarnecky relied upon his own graduate school experience on the analog FORM_work design build project (Figure 1.4.1) as well as experience in digital fabricated projects with Pugh + Scarpa to extend the young school's (est. 1997) existing tradition of model making into the first sustained engagement with full-scale work. Over the next six years, increasing student capacity fueled by competitive ambition culminated in a selection of exquisitely crafted student work being exhibited at the 2012 Milan Furniture Fair and featured in *Wallpaper* magazine (Figure 1.4.4). Subsequently,

FIGURE 1.4.3
Student work completed in ARC237 Introduction to Material Fabrication (center) and ARC233 Introduction to Digital Fabrication (left and right). ARC237 Faculty: D. Chavez, ARC233 Faculty: G. Spaw.

FIGURE 1.4.4
Student work completed in ARC335 Furniture Design. Faculty: B. Sarnecky.

architect and furniture maker Daniel Chavez joined the faculty to guide the establishment of a three-part sequence of introductory, intermediate, and advanced furniture courses.

Since 2013 projects evolved to include medium- to large-scale installations occupying underused spaces internal to the College of Architecture, Art, and Design. The Display Wall, created in a fifth year options studio led by Prof. Sarnecky, exhibits the school's growing capacity for fine detailing and ambitious form-making enabled by a combination of analog and digital tools while introducing site-specific context (floor, wall, ceiling), material tolerance, extended programmatic requirements, security, glazing, electricity, and challenging environmental conditions (Figure 1.4.5). The complex forms house integrated benches and display shelves that rely on a three-axis CNC router, while a more conventional batten structure negotiates between the less-than-plumb walls and the precision of the furniture-grade panels.

A parallel sequence of installation projects specific to the Interior Design students was introduced in 2015. Unique among Interior Design curricula in both North America and the Middle East, the unprecedented program integrates a required one-semester design build studio in the fall of the fourth year (Figure 1.4.6). Inaugurated by Prof. Chavez and now taught by Prof. Ammar Kalo, the studio builds upon the design and construction of a light fixture embedded in the required second-year color and light course as well as the furniture and fabrication electives, which are open to all students in the department.

FIGURE 1.4.5
Tarkeeb Display Wall, AUS, 2013. AIA Middle East Honor Award. Faculty: B. Sarnecky.

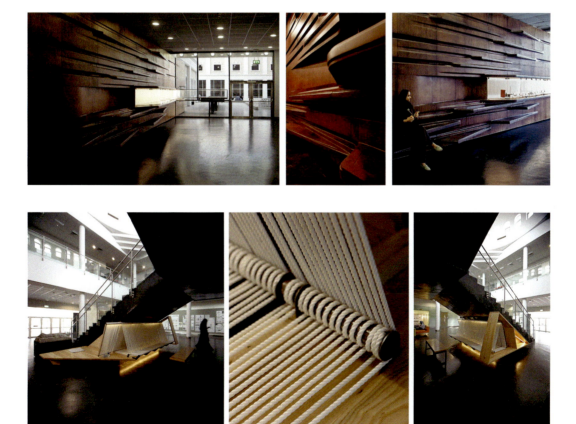

FIGURE 1.4.6
Khaima: Theatre Under Stairs, AUS ID DB, 2017. AIA Middle East Honor Award. Faculty: D. Chavez.

In addition, faculty have developed a range of single-semester speculative studios focused on prototyping with a specific tool or material process. The hybrid format provides for in-depth engagement not typically possible in a fabrication seminar while also balancing an immersive experience with a more manageable set of logistic challenges for the lead faculty. Emily Baker utilized the prototyping studio to investigate innovative material systems for acoustic mediation while preserving visual transparency (Baker, 2015). In this case these prototyping experiments informed the subsequent Audi-Fab design build project that resulted in a large screen assembly crafted to insulate a quiet study space adjacent to the rambunctious first-year studio (Figure 1.4.7).

FIGURE 1.4.7
Audi-Fab, AUS, 2014.
ACSA DB Award.
Faculty: E. Baker.

Beyond (the) Building

The 2015 prototyping studio led by Ammar Kalo engaged reusable formwork capable of producing a range of non-repeating concrete panels. While digital fabrication techniques have the potential to automate processes and increase material efficiency, there are very few examples that produce complex highly textured concrete surfaces without requiring countless hours of explicit modeling and CNC milling (Figure 1.4.8). The investigation focused on analog methods informed by digital design to develop complex and textured molds made of fabric, wax, and sand (Kalo, 2017).

More recently the portfolio of projects has expanded in terms of type and scope to include outdoor pavilions sited on campus and beyond. The AVM Pavilion led by Ken Tracy exploited the potential of a metal CNC laser cutting to create a lightweight, monocoque shade structure on campus (Figure 1.4.9). The project translated the form of a native flower,

FIGURE 1.4.8
Audi-Fab, AUS, 2014. ACSA DB Award. Faculty: E. Baker.

FIGURE 1.4.9
Soft States Prototyping Studio, AUS, 2015. Faculty: A. Kalo.

Dipcadi serotinum, into a full-scale 30 square meter pavilion. The process relied on both heuristic prototyping and parametric design tools to derive the form, from the global massing to the individual panel units, while considering the real-life material constraints of working with digitally cut and manually folded sheet metal (Tracy et al., 2021).

The first foray beyond campus, *Neonomads* constitutes a series of design build studios taught by Patrick Rhodes and Greg Spaw over three years that investigate prototypical, off-grid desert survival shelters deployed in the Arabian desert as research stations for local environmental scientists (Figure 1.4.10). Focused on weight-saving to enable mobility and ease deployability, the projects exploited analog MIG and TIG aluminum welding alongside digital fabrication tools for aluminum tube bending and the fabrication of jigs to facilitate assembly (Rhodes et al., 2021).

Proto-architectural projects inclusive of mechanical systems and weather enclosure represent the most ambitious production to date. Led by Bill Sarnecky and myself, the *Tarkeeb Gatehouse and Garden* replaced an old, small (one square meter) guard booth adjacent to the college with a new approach to campus infrastructure focused on mediating the harsh local environment through the provision of shade and human comfort (Figure 1.4.11). The

FIGURE 1.4.10
AVM Pavilion, AUS, 2017. Faculty: K. Tracy.

FIGURE 1.4.11
Neonomads, AUS, 2018–2020. ACSA DB Award. Faculty: P. Rhodes and G. Spaw.

project featured a hybrid approach to fabrication that combined digital and analog processes. For example, individual components defined through a series of computational studies and formed with a CNC-plasma cutter were assembled with traditional welding processes to provide seating, visibility, and signage within the normative steel bar-grate that shades the interiors. Similarly, the curved wood volume features components cut on a CNC router and then laminated and finished manually using clamps, glue, screws, and ample amounts of sandpaper.

AN EASIER, EASIER WAY V2.0: INSTITUTIONAL ENGAGEMENT

Over the last ten years the Design Build Initiative evolved to exemplify an "easier way" to conduct full-scale pedagogy. Working from a broad, holistic perspective, the faculty team successfully addressed many of the "five issues and challenges" that Vincent Canizaro found, "present, to varying degrees in all" design build programs (Canizaro, 2012). Collegial and administrative resistance, equipment and facilities, and quality of work have all been addressed to a great degree. Associate professor of architecture and AUS alumnus Faysal Tabbarah observes that

FIGURE 1.4.12
Tarkeeb Gatehouse and Garden, AUS, 2019. ACSA DB Award. Faculty: B. Sarnecky and M. Hughes.

a wide range of faculty members, particularly junior faculty, have been provided with the teaching assignments, budget and guidance necessary to begin or expand their fabrication-based scholarship. Amongst all the successes, perhaps most surprising has been the high degree of collegiality and lack of negative politics amongst faculty participants.

(F. Tabbarah, pers. comm.)

Stress still exists, but participating faculty now have a supportive network of like-minded, empathetic colleagues. At the same time, the quality of the outcomes has been vetted through significant peer-review scholarship and awards. Internally the department administration has provided consistent support for the program to expand throughout the curriculum and even beyond architecture. Current Dean Varkki Pallathucheril observed that

> the impact of the initiative has extended beyond the Architecture program to reenergize our previously struggling Interior Design program. Through this transformative initiative, a nascent tradition of making has become fundamental to the identity of the department and the college.
> (V. Pallathucheril, pers. comm.)

That said, an even easier way is within sight if obstacles related to the ongoing lack of support residing beyond the department can be overcome. Funding support has been steady, but calcified attitudes in the upper administration on issues ranging from teaching load calculations to administrative assistance to internal bureaucracy block the path. The multilayered chain of command common to academia requires visible and vocal advocacy from dean to provost to chancellor such that campus planning, the facilities department, and the chief operating officer work proactively to enable rather than obstruct. Sustaining and extending the success achieved in the first ten years will require cultivating more consistent and supportive partnerships at the institutional level. The easier way is not necessarily a shorter path, but the journey is better together.

REFERENCES

Baker, E. (2015). Audi-Fab Design Build. In *2015 ACSA Design Build Award: ACSA 103rd Annual Meeting, Toronto*. Washington, DC: ACSA.

Canizaro, V. (2012). Design-Build in Architectural Education: Motivations, Practices, Challenges, Successes and Failures. *International Journal of Architectural Research*, 6(3), 20–36.

Giesen, M. (2021). The Early Years of CAAD: Seeking the Rightful Place. Manuscript in preparation.

Gjertson, G. (2011). House Divided: Challenges to Design/Build from Within. In *ACSA: Fall Conference: Local Identities/Global Challenges, Houston* (pp. 23–35). Washington, DC: ACSA.

Hughes, M., Baker, E., Sommerfeld, R., & Zell, M. (2019). Potemkin Fabrications: Administrative Gymnastics, Messy Boundaries, and the Alternative Facts That Enable Design-Build Pedagogy. In *ACSA Fall Conference: Less Talk | More Action, Stanford* (pp. 122–126). Washington, DC: ACSA.

Kalo, A. (2017). Soft States: Experimental, Highly-Textured Concrete Architectural Panels. In *Poster presented at the ACSA 2017, Detroit*. Washington, DC: ACSA.

Kraus, C. (2017). *Designbuild Education*. New York: Routledge.

Rhodes, P., Spaw, G., & Al Qassimi, L. (2021). A Perfect Failure: Speculation, Risk, and Beginning Again through Design-Build. *Journal of Architectural Education*, 75(1), 115–120.

Sarnecky, W. (2012). Building a Material Culture in Dubai. *Journal of Architectural Education*, 65(2), 80–88.

Tracy, K., Jandaghimeibodi, M., Aleem, S., Gupta, R., & Tan, Y. (2021). AVM Pavilion: A Bio-Inspired Integrative Design Project. In *CAAD Futures 2021 Conference: Design Imperatives*. Los Angeles, CA, United States.

2
EXPERIMENTAL METHODS

Studio 804, Inc.

Dan Rockhill

INTRODUCTION

I operate Studio 804 as a not-for-profit corporation. The studio is available as an option for graduate students in their last year of studies for their first professional degree, the master of architecture degree. I have an affiliation agreement with the University of Kansas and am not subsidized by them for my projects and therefore operate entirely independent of the university and the school of architecture. We produce mostly residential buildings but also have done six commercial buildings, starting and completing one every year and have for the last 27 years. Over the course of the last 16 years all of our buildings have been LEED Platinum. I do this to make the students that I share the Studio 804 experience with better architects. I'm not doing it to make them builders. Over the course of the nine months I spend with them, working all day every day for six days a week, we touch upon most aspects of designing and building from initial ideas to permits and site excavation, concrete work, right up through the roofing. We do everything and subcontract little to nothing. This also includes the mechanical, electric, and plumbing as well as all the finishes. We're a one-stop shop, and the experience is transformative for every one of them as they all learn a lot about building but also themselves in the process.

I only have them for this one single experience, and so I prefer to select the work we undertake based on how much it will contribute to their future. Because of that, I have been hesitant to embrace anything that deviates from the basics of the way we typically build. I purposely stick to the standard framed wall systems that are the backbone of the industry. As an example, it is for this reason I don't do structural insulated panels (SIPs), and I'm currently keeping cementitious 3D construction printing (3DCP) at arm's length. I think the fully immersive experience like I describe has no comparison to other systems produced in a factory and installed by others while students watch.

EXPERIENTIAL LEARNING

The entire design build experience, at least the way I do it, is predicated on the students having to figure things out on their own under my direction. My methods rarely include bringing someone in that shows them how to do something. This includes but is not limited to boyfriends, girlfriends, fathers, and mothers and people in the trades. I think understanding layout and the implications of getting off layout is an integral part of the building experience. Learning a method of building that begins with a system is important to young people just entering the industry. Sips and 3DCP has its place just not at the expense of

■ Dan Rockhill

FIGURE 2.1.1
519 Indiana Street view from the street. We pinched the design of the house in on the lower level to work with the neighboring properties that were built on the lot lines without a setback. This helped minimize the impact of the tight site. We placed the primary living spaces on the upper level with a mechanical room, bathroom, two bedrooms, and a generous entry foyer on the lower level.

a person learning the most ubiquitous technique of building that drives the way the vast majority of buildings have been and will continue to be constructed. For a long time, I have treated digital fabrication with the same caution, and even now I only use digital fabrication when I feel there would be no reasonable alternative. Someone who understands this is the Finnish architect, author, and philosopher Juhani Pallasmaa. His works and writings have always inspired me. ("The use of the computer has broken the sensual and tactile connection between imagination and the object of design.")[1]

Experiential learning is the process of learning by doing and then reflecting upon this action to apply it to new problems. I see this method of teaching as particularly applicable to architecture. Students are challenged to creatively solve interrelated concrete problems, and each decision creates a new set of interrelated problems to be addressed. There are limitations to teaching in a classroom, and this type of learning is best served in an apprenticeship-like situation. To quote Peter Buchanan, integrated thinking can be more successfully taught

> by letting the student work with someone who has mastered the skills, who knows how to think with his/her fingers and mind, drawing on both conscious skills and what has become unconscious bodily knowledge, so integrating head, hand and heart.[2]

I have contributed to the invitation from the authors to share with the reader what I do only after overcoming my hesitancy for several reasons other than just the loss of a little experiential learning. According to a 2016 report by the World Economic Forum, nearly 500,000 jobs will be compromised in the construction industry alone by 2020.

66

I haven't followed up on this prediction, but my guess is it was probably close to that number in the end. In short, the ethics of automation is troublesome; how many people will we put out of work? I know we will drive down the costs and make construction safer, but is it really necessary if we are reducing jobs for people and employing robots in their place?

Just recently, I've had help overcoming my anxiety about robots and digital fabrication after a recent article in the *New Yorker* by Jane Hu on May 18, 2022, titled, "The Problem with Blaming Robots for Taking Our Jobs." She references two recent books that suggest that we shouldn't believe the hype. She shares that

> Both books cite a range of writing on automation, positive and critical, to present a different view of our moment. The future might have fewer jobs, but it probably won't be because of robots. In fact, we are living not so much in the dawn of peak automation as in something like its long, drawn-out twilight.

What we have done digitally has met very specific needs for Studio 804 and solved problems that were significant enough that we would not have been able to do the work if we did not have the CNC router available to us to do it with, and as a result, we would have had to abandon the idea all together.

DIGITAL FABRICATION OF FOUR SCREENS AND TWO COUNTERTOPS

We seized upon the idea of using perforated screens to help modulate the light in our most recent residential project of 2022. We were working on a site in the older part of the city and were delighted to have found a vacant lot close to our vibrant downtown and only blocks from our river trail loop that forms a circular route 27 miles around the city. The only problem was it was in an established older neighborhood that was built up long before zoning controls were in place. Both adjacent houses were built almost directly on the property lines, which visually pinched our 50-foot-wide lot and crowded the first-floor plan, especially when the driveway to the garage and 5-foot side setbacks of our new work were met. We became enamored of the idea that we could push the upper level out over the lower first level and put the main living area on the second floor. We strengthened that concept when each of the second-level endcaps were glazed with floor-to-ceiling glass with walkout balconies, which enhanced the 24-foot building width of the open plan but also created the need to have some privacy between the living area and master bedroom suite.

The way to help filter the beautiful light coming from the east in the mornings and west on the evenings would be by filtering the light with perforated doors, or screens. The screens and perforations were made easily on our school's CNC router. We used black diamond Richlite (an incredibly durable, extremely versatile, and highly sustainable material made from resin-infused paper), which was 1.25 inches think, so it had some weight to it; at roughly four feet wide and nine feet tall, it weighed just a little under 300 pounds. Even after the perforations, they each weighed in at just under 200 pounds and fortunately still within the weight capacity of the recessed cavity sliders. The recessed sliders enhanced the look of the minimal presence of the doors and walls, black and white.

■ Dan Rockhill

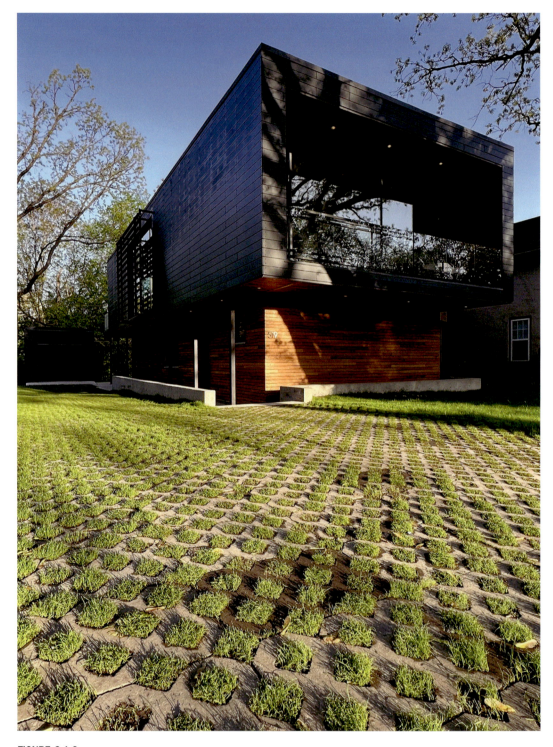

FIGURE 2.1.2
519 Indiana Street view from the street.

Studio 804, Inc.

FIGURE 2.1.3
519 Indiana Street south elevation composite.

FIGURE 2.1.4
The interior of the second level looking past the stairwell to the black screens separating the master bedroom suite. The core is a walk-in closet and bathroom separated by a similar set of screens that contributes to the effect of the filtered light. An eight-foot-long hallway separates them on both sides.

FIGURE 2.1.5
Interior looking to stairwell with screens to main bedroom beyond.

■ Dan Rockhill

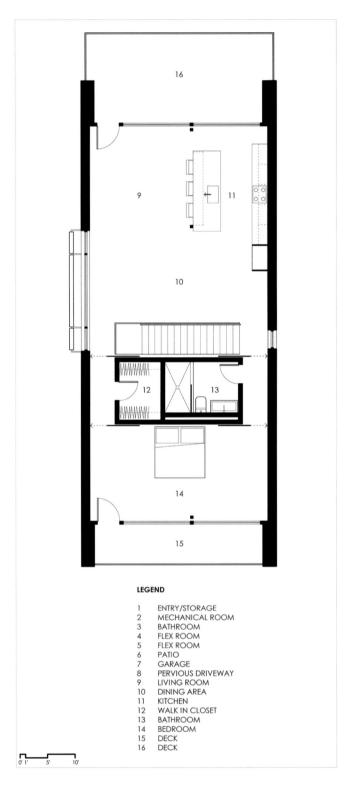

FIGURE 2.1.6
Second-level floor plan.

Studio 804, Inc.

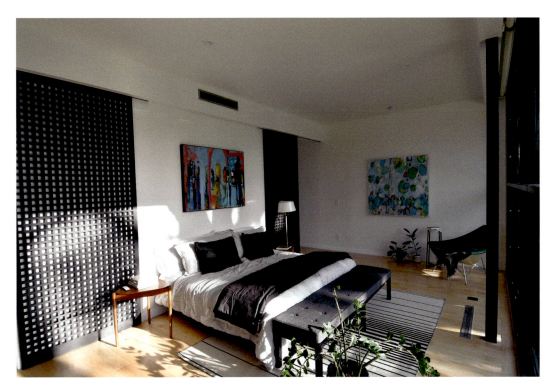

FIGURE 2.1.7
The master bedroom as screened from the living and dining area. The screens are open in the photo and can be closed easily with the cavity slider system.

FIGURE 2.1.8
We produce a small mock-up to help head off any possible problems before milling the expensive Richlite.

■ Dan Rockhill

FIGURE 2.1.9
Interior looking through bedroom to coconut chair.

Studio 804, Inc.

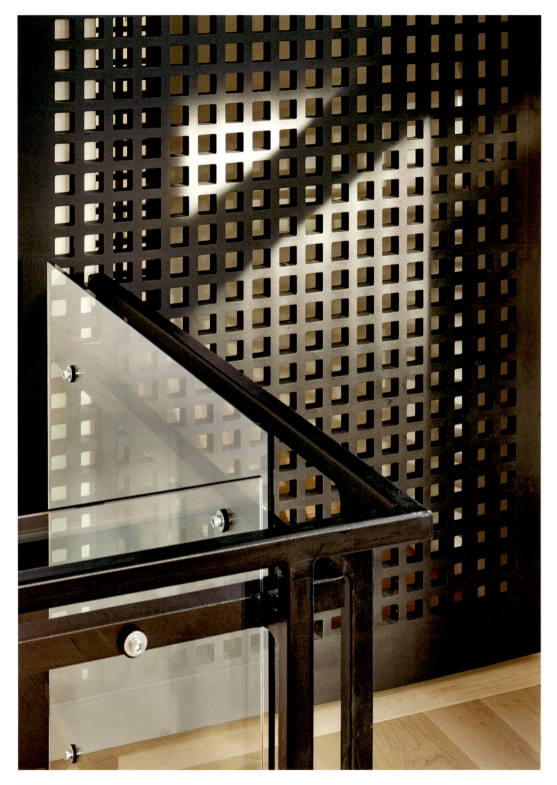

FIGURE 2.1.10
Interior milled screen made from Richlite.

■ Dan Rockhill

FIGURE 2.1.11
Interior layering of space with screens.

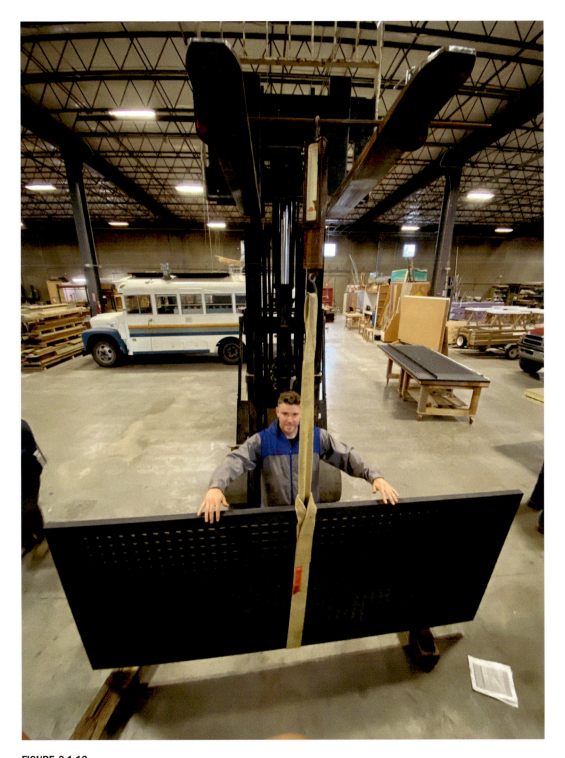

FIGURE 2.1.12
Weighing the Richlite after milling to confirm we are within the specific weight the sliders can support.

We found another use for the CNC router in the same project, which was to cut out the precise openings we needed in the Richlite kitchen counters for the cooktop and under-counter mounted sink. The CNC created these easily, and other than being careful to clamp splints to the countertop pieces to move them, it was a big help to the process to have the

FIGURE 2.1.13
Our CNC router made the production of the screens easy, and without it, we would not have been able to do the screens to achieve the quality we found desirable.

FIGURE 2.1.14
The sink and cooktop openings in the Richlite were also produced with the CNC Router. We clamp a steel stiff back to each long narrow edge to avoid stressing the material while moving it.

FIGURE 2.1.15
The finish cutout for the cooktop.

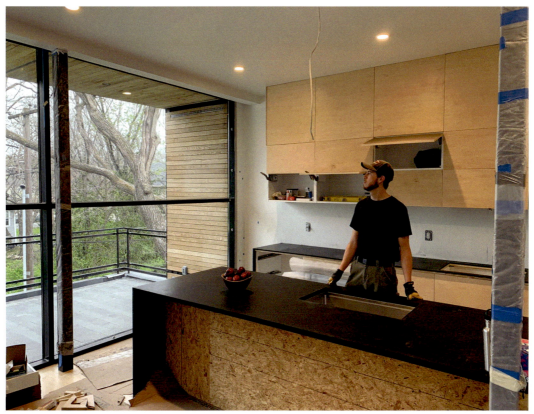

FIGURE 2.1.16
The kitchen countertop on the island will contain the sink, and the one along the wall is for the cooktop.

Dan Rockhill

router available to us. Having cut countertops in the past with either a jigsaw or circular saw, the router left the finished edges clean and ready for finish sanding as opposed to the rougher cuts from any other saw.

NOTES

1 Pallasmaa, J. (2009). *The Thinking Hand*. New York: John Wiley & Sons Ltd, p. 65.
2 Buchanan, P. (2012). "The Big Rethink Part 9: Rethinking Architectural Education," *The Architectural Review*, September 28.

Virginia Tech

Jim Burton and William Carpenter

Virginia Tech has a long legacy of experimental making as an integral part of design education. Material and technological innovation have been foregrounded in the pedagogy as a land grant university that provides research-based programs and resources for the state of Virginia and its residents.

In its early development being founded in 1872, the school's pedagogy focused on classical principles and historical models. As an Ecole des Beaux Arts pedagogy, there was an emphasis on drawing, rendering, and elements such as hierarchy, symmetry, historical precedent, and geometry were emphasized.

As the program developed and technological innovations emerged, an interest in engineering and aeronautical, nautical and automobile design would grow out of the American can-do spirit and Ford factory era, based on a better world for a growing world population. Prefabrication prototyping and mass production would infuse many early engineering and design studies.

As the Bauhaus model sought to overturn the Ecole pedagogies, Charles Burchard, Black Mountain College, and Walter Gropius would all help inform the curriculum. The Blue Book became a centerpiece of this special program.

Charles Burchard, while teaching at Black Mountain College in North Carolina in 1948 and 1949, met and worked with Walter Gropius, Josef Albers, John Cage, Buckminster Fuller, and other Bauhaus emigres. Self-directed learning and a range of inspiring professors to inspire student learning became an early focus. In 1965 Dean Burchard invited Olivio Ferrari to help write the Blue Book that year and form a new Bauhaus-inspired pedagogy.

Olivio Ferrari, the Blue Book, and design schools converging formed a multidisciplinary approach along with urban planning. This approach led to a program that would spawn a top design build program where students take ideas to complete product fabrication and delivery as built work in place, which includes shipping and return or built in permanent place. Ferrari brought a group of students and faculty from Auburn University. He also created a connection with architecture in Switzerland and Italy that continues to this day.

■ Jim Burton and William Carpenter

FIGURE 2.2.1
Virginia Tech FutureHAUS, Solar Decathlon Design Build in Time Square, NYC.

FIGURE 2.2.2
The Church of San Giovanni Battista in Mogno, Switzerland by Mario Botta.

FIGURE 2.2.3
The Thermal Baths in Vals, designed by Peter Zumthor.

■ Jim Burton and William Carpenter

FIGURE 2.2.4
The Biosphere in Montreal located at Parc Jean-Drapeau designed by Buckmaster Fuller.

FIGURE 2.2.5
Anni Albers at the Bauhaus, Haiku Ark Panels.

BAUHAUS INFLUENCE ON THE SCHOOL'S PEDAGOGY

The Bauhaus was made up of a diverse group of minds and skills creating a wider range of influence and longevity that is still influential and evolving today.

The abstract approach inspired by Cage may have contributed to a program that is not based on grades and outcomes but instead is inspired by experimentation, failure, and surprise after thorough and rigorous efforts and studies.

Italian architect and professor Olivio Ferrari was trained at the Huchschule fur Gestaltung in Ulm and worked under Max Bill teaching at ETH in Zurich and then Auburn, where he taught before a mass exodus of professors provided an opportunity for Ferrari to join Charles Burchard and to create the program that would continue to flourish to this day.

Visiting professors would continue to foster the diverse and creative process that has made the school one of the top design build schools

Fuller brought his tensegrity lab to Blacksburg that was a design build hands-on charrette. His Standard of Living Package prefab module house of 1947 looks like the inspiration for many Solar Decathlon shaped projects to come in the distant future.

In 1966 Lucy and Olivio Ferrari introduced The Architecture Europe Study Abroad Program and opened up a pipeline of Swiss professors who would teach the students in Switzerland and in Virginia. Swiss professors Hunziger, Botta, and others came out of a "Swiss Essentialist" movement that has spawned talent like Peter Zumthor.

The Swiss influence came from many talents on the faculty. Full-time faculty included Olivio Ferrari, Herbert Kramel, and Markus Breitschmid. Intermittent and repeat visiting instructors included Lucy Ferrari, Rudy Hunziker, Karl Flaig, Emil Rysler, Lorenz Moser, Peter Disch, and Fritz Schwarz. Gene Egger, an early Auburn transfer, continued the program as a professor exposing students to historic and modern European architecture and professors.

DESIGN BUILD

The rigor of design and making things was enriched by the abstract visionaries of Black Mountain College like the Albers, Fuller, de Kooning, and Cage, each one bringing their own strengths in a wide net of design. This design and making system was the early version of the design build education process.

We will see the evolution of a design build leadership in Virginia Tech that has translated its roots in engineering through the Bauhaus filter through this land grant institution where almost unlimited space allowed for large- and small-scale experiments. Assembly/making and experimenting in material form has enhanced a no-fear spirit and has created global successes with public design build and multidisciplinary approaches.

The early years at Virginia Tech brought postwar progress, conservation of materials, and an essentialist's approach to engineer-based design. In 1955 Homer Hurst came to teach at Virginia Tech to help establish a structures laboratory in agricultural engineering. He became very interested in the performance of buildings both from a structural perspective as well as thermal performance. Hurst is particularly well-known for using nominal dimensioned lumber by using one-inch-by-one-inch wood structural elements.

The collaborative focus of Hurst and German-born George Stern on pole-type structures resulted in some of the first experimental buildings at the Environmental Systems Laboratory.

Jim Burton and William Carpenter

These structures were typically tested to failure, repaired, and then occupied as permanent laboratory facilities. One of the bays of the pole structure lab was converted to become Stern's pallet testing facility and has been used by the Design Build Studio.

Small-scale student-based work

- 1971 Robert Dunay and Jay Stoekel designed an information center for the National Forest Service with bathroom module and office modules with fiberglass, prefab aluminum foam sandwich panels.
- 1973 Kenneth Blankenship master's program mass-produced patient bedroom working with 1/3 scale models.

Medium-scale collaborations

- 1976 Bill Sevebeckee, Bill Schillig, and Robert created the Hodge Prototype Day Care Center with Unistrut metal frame and Fiberglass pods.

Large-scale school-based collaborations

- 1984 Jim Riley student and Gary Day faculty developed Biaxial CMU modules.
- 1987 Research and Demonstration Facility. Davis and Shubert with Bill Galloway designed the CAUS RDF with biaxial block and space frame roof.[1]

A design competition was held with the 50-year celebration featuring a thesis of experimentation. Future Architecture by Professor Dennis Jones and his theories on a Sky Scraper system that builds itself and maintains itself. This Matrix-like concept shows that the professors can inspire and test the students, and the students will in turn test the professors, to continue back and forth.

The school also took advantage of visiting American professors sharing new thoughts from around the country. The best example of this was an important small-scale design build studio run by Shelley Martin called the Cone Studio inspired by visiting Mississippi State university professor Chris Risher. Risher had taught with Ferrari at Auburn for one year after graduating from that program. He had lectured at Virginia Tech and had returned after running a storied design build concrete door studio at Harvard. The Cone Studio had students working with chainsaws and crafting essential forms out of wood. This tabletop experience created a grassroots energy as students felt the weight and gravity of form while discussing perception and beauty.

In the Design Library Building, there are two digital fabrication labs that are surrounded in glass, allowing a full view of machinery and prototyping left for all to see even when the lab is quiet. Industrial design and architecture blur the lines for form and skin when using these scalable systems.

Working with larger budgets and prototypes has shown exponential growth in the program both in scale, complexity of systems, and in community engagement.

Keith and Marie Zawistowski's third-year architecture studio designed and constructed the amphitheater for the town of Clifton Forge, Virginia, and a Covington Farmers Market.

Campuses-design build at Blacksburg campus and the WAAC early design build.

FIGURE 2.2.6
Experimenting with the new digital equipment.

FIGURE 2.2.7
Masonic Amphitheatre open to the community.

■ Jim Burton and William Carpenter

BLACKSBURG PROTOTYPING AND CASE STUDIES

The Design Build program has worked with a range of formats, including accessing the Environmental Systems Laboratory, building experimental buildings on campus (The Inner College), and building prefabricated structures in lab spaces for shipping (Solar Decathlon).

The Solar Decathlon entries featured the School of Architecture and Design and an interdisciplinary team of architects and engineers.

Industrial Design, Interior Design, and Landscape Architecture; the Department of Building Construction; the College of Engineering; and the College of Business were part of the team creating a diversity of mindsets to learn from. Ultimately bringing these projects to a successful conclusion creates the most memorable college experience and forms a confidence that can be taken into the professional world.

Remote Design Build Format

The benefit of the expansive remote agrarian-based campus has created visual separation from the core campus for design build experiment labs. Testing ideas without fear of ruining a cohesive campus sense of place. This has led to prototyping at a remote systems lab with interior and exterior work spaces.

Experimental Structures

In the early years not all of the building experimentation was relegated to the Environmental Systems Laboratory. There was plenty of model prototyping and full-scale exploration taking place on campus at both the Architecture Annex and Cowgill Hall. One such experiment was a 28-foot-diameter geodesic dome constructed outside of the architecture annex.

Buckminster Fuller was popular at many of the campuses across the United States, if not the world, because of his enlightened vision. Buckminster Fuller offered insightful solutions at both the personal and global scale to some of our most challenging issues facing society at the time.

As the spirit and history of the interdisciplinary program has evolved and celebrated the LumenHAUS and FutureHAUS, both have been exhibited on the main campus in Blacksburg as finished products. The LumenHAUS could become a study in maintenance as the elements have begun to show how materials can begin to stress.

FIGURE 2.2.8
2002 Solar Decatholon (left), 2005 Solar Decatholon (right).

International experience has been featured as an important aspect of the modern Virginia Tech program. The Studio Residency program through Virginia Tech's Steger Center for International Scholarship (formerly Center for European Studies and Architecture—CESA) at the Villa Maderni in Riva San Vitale, Switzerland.

Historic structures locally and within short travel distance are available to an immersive experience. The students witness high-quality urban planning and detailed design in a world where land is limited, and every square inch has been developed and maintained over generations as only essential qualities remain as durability, functionality, flexibility, and beauty become the unspoken rule that has defined a true sense of place. Sketching is an essential process to capture details and materiality, which sparks ideas for design build investigations.

The Washington-Alexandria Architecture Center (WAAC) has served as an urban extension of the Virginia Tech School of Architecture + Design and was run by Jahn Holt from its start in 1980 to 2016. The current director is Susan Piedmont-Palladino. The center focuses on site-specific and urban interventions mixed in with the urban campus experience. The center also provides exposure to travel and construction sites for similar experiences as the travel abroad provides both in contrast to the rural small-town experience that Blacksburg has provided. Witnessing local urban construction and worksite management was part of the wholistic process that is important for students to understand. Some essential design build projects have included stair designs, furniture, and full-scale details. The school is exposed to Washington, DC, area architects for guest lecturing and visiting professors. Some students find part-time or full-time work for architecture firms while living in the Alexandria area and taking classes.

Case Studies and Feature Projects
- **LumenHAUS**—European Solar Decathlon winner
- **FutureHAUS**—Middle East Solar Decathlon winner
- **Masonic Amphitheatre**—Clifton Forge, Virginia
- **Observation Tower Radford, Virginia**—Community engagement and interdisciplinary material studies

LumenHAUS 2009 Solar Decathlon focused on standardization while celebrating its digitally fabricated sliding shade scrims. Students tested modeled schemes and voted on the best design to develop after studying the sun patterns with the models on campus. The solar systems are integrated into the design in a modest way as the students delve into commercial-grade materials for a residential structure. This was an early net zero study as the system could feed excess electricity back into the grid.

FutureHAUS is a prototype design based on the Solar Decathlon model and beyond. With the leadership as FutureHAUS program director of Joseph Wheeler, AIA, co-director of the Center for Design Research, and Bobby Vance, project manager of the Center for Design Research, a generational success story was born in the evolving design product FutureHAUS.

FutureHAUS Dubai explores the process of prefabrication to deliver modular structures that integrate smart technologies, energy-efficient systems, and new materials. Factory-produced, energy-positive smart home. The goal is to not only invent the future of housing with the integration of smart technologies but also invent the future of how they will be built.

■ Jim Burton and William Carpenter

FIGURE 2.2.9
LumenHAUS, digital fabrication cut the grid of perforations on the solar shading screens.

FIGURE 2.2.10
LumenHAUS digitally fabricated solar screen.

FIGURE 2.2.11
Early FutureHAUS prototype in the studio testing the spaces.

FIGURE 2.2.12
Illuminated FutureHAUS facade at night.

■ Jim Burton and William Carpenter

FIGURE 2.2.13
The front with fabricated screen reflecting tin the sun.

"In recent years, innovations in digital technologies have revolutionized the way we live, work, and build. The presence of technology in everyday life has become so ingrained that it would be impossible to function today without it. We have fully embraced the expectation of convenience that high performance technology offers. Cutting-edge technology has quickly been integrated into the design and manufacturing of high-performance products like aircrafts and automobiles. The construction industry, by contrast, has been slow if not resistant to change its operations. With FutureHAUS Dubai, Virginia Tech is challenging the construction industry by demonstrating the utilization of advanced manufacturing processes to prototype an energy-positive, solar-powered smart home."[2]

The research is focused on two major concepts, a new way to build and a new way to live. A new way to build, FutureHAUS challenges the construction industry to adapt by looking toward innovative prefabrication and manufacturing concepts that allow for the incorporation of the smart technologies and improve the construction process. By contrast, conventional construction methods remain archaic, revolving around weather, time, contractors and subcontractor's schedules, and permits—almost always resulting in inefficiency, waste, lack of predictability, and poorly finished products. The team believes that the use of advanced prefabrication processes is the way of the future, and will ultimately be the vehicle to provide an architecture of the future.

Designed to be a part of a compact, spatially efficient plan, prefabricated modules or "cartridges" deliver strong details and technology to the site. This system is unique: not

Virginia Tech

FIGURE 2.2.14
Inside the courtyard protected from the sun by the fabricated screen.

panelized wall construction or big-box modular, but a series of transportable, compact smart modules that are plug-and-play. "With our concept, we propose to ship technology to the site, not space. With the efficient delivery of precision, pre-built components, the on-site assembly is fast, highly improving the quality of the final product and ultimately reducing cost through industrial efficiency. At its core, FutureHAUS is about industrializing the process of house construction. The process is in demand with future needs for the production of smarter, more efficient, and more affordable housing."[3]

A new way to live is a significant part of FutureHAUS research to explore the best ways to integrate new digital technologies into the home. The greatest discovery has been the ability to integrate concepts of aging-in-place and universal accessibility through vertical adjustability and multimodal controls. Whether child or adult, short or tall, disabled or not disabled, the home adjusts to fit the need of the user. The home can autonomously recognize the user through voice, height, or gait recognition, so when an individual enters a room or performs a task, the room or item adjusts itself for that user. The home uses artificial intelligence to save user profiles and adjust to their settings every time. The technology remains intuitive with one complete home interface and manual controls of touch, gesture, or voice.

FutureHAUS was a part of a research elective open to all of the university, undergraduate and graduate. The budget evolved over time. Most of the items were donated, but just over 1 million was raised in cash, and the gift in kind items were approximately 1.5 million in value. The FutureHAUS was under construction for about eight months from initial SIP delivery to shipping to Dubai.

FIGURE 2.2.15
Living area looking out through the front digitally fabricated screen.

Virginia Tech

FIGURE 2.2.16
3D printed bathroom sink with motorized adjustable height for accessibility.

FIGURE 2.2.17
Motorized adjustable height for accessibility, the digitally fabricated bathroom sink promotes inclusive design.

■ Jim Burton and William Carpenter

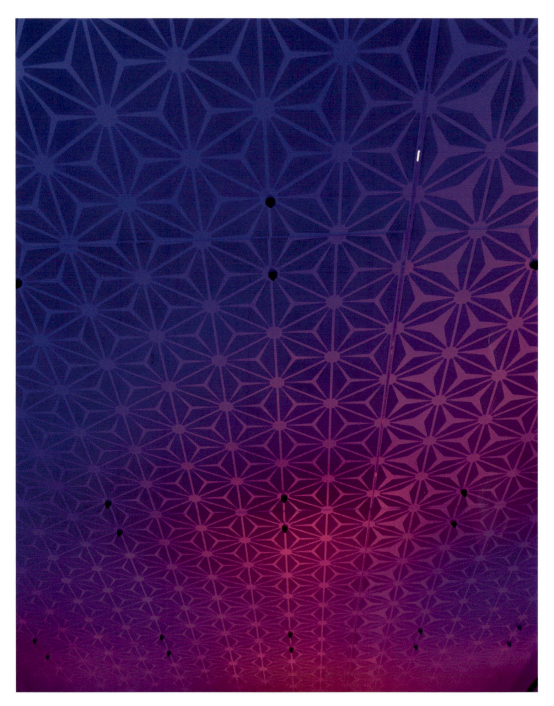

FIGURE 2.2.18
Ceiling detail with adjustable lighting, warm.

Virginia Tech

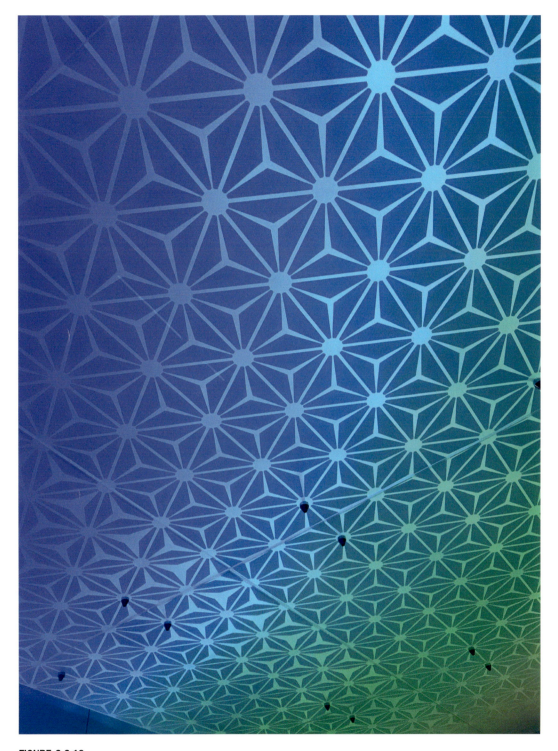

FIGURE 2.2.19
Ceiling detail with adjustable lighting, cool.

■ Jim Burton and William Carpenter

FIGURE 2.2.20
Digitally fabricated screen detail from the inside.

Virginia Tech

FIGURE 2.2.21
Digitally fabricated screen detail from the outside.

■ Jim Burton and William Carpenter

Sponsors may be found on the website www.FutureHAUS.tech. Notable students were Laurie Booth, student team leader, and Matt Erwin, lead engineer. Main sponsors were Dominion Energy, Kohler, Wood-Mode, and Dow-DuPont.

MASONIC AMPHITHEATRE, CLIFTON FORGE, VIRGINIA

Over the course of the 2011–12 academic year, students in Keith and Marie Zawistowski's third-year Architecture studio designed and constructed the amphitheater for the town of Clifton Forge, Virginia. The project consists of the complete redevelopment of a post-industrial brownfield into a public park and performance space. The idea driving the design is that the built elements are sculptural forms emerging out of the landscape of the park. The park is a series of extruded lawns and carved paths that knit the surrounding urban fabric into the site's circulation. The built elements include a stage with acoustic shell, a backstage with loading dock, green room and wings, a seating area, and a sound and lighting control booth. The ground plane is peeled up from the stage to create its shell. Steam-bent white oak walls curve to define secluded pockets offstage and intermediary zones of varying intimacy, allowing performers to slip in and out of audience view. The interior walls and ceiling of the shell are sculpted to naturally project acoustics toward the audience. Its interior is lined in CNC-routed composite panels with aluminum, zinc, titanium and stainless steel skins. The backstage area is conceived as a creek-side terrace: an intimate place for waiting performers or a casual place for social interaction. To this end, benches pull up from the deck to invite pause and crape myrtle trees push through its surface to provide shade. The rough-sawn white oak cladding dampens the noise of the rushing creek water, allowing it to resonate on the backstage terrace but muting it from the stage and audience. Wood benches provide cool summer seating for an audience of 200 in the sloping gravel orchestra. Staggered alignment allows for wheelchairs and folding chairs to be dispersed within the audience rather than

FIGURE 2.2.22

Masonic Amphitheatre, Clifton Forge, Virginia.

at the periphery. A central aisle, sliced diagonally through the benches, allows people to get in and out with minimal disturbance to their neighbors and accentuates a major pedestrian axis across the town. The elevated lawns provide overflow seating for an additional 800. Sound and lighting is controlled from a covered booth: an oak wedge, nested at the

FIGURE 2.2.23
The design/buildLAB setting up the cut run for the alpolic.

FIGURE 2.2.24
The design/buildLAB cutting alpolic, a smooth run.

■ Jim Burton and William Carpenter

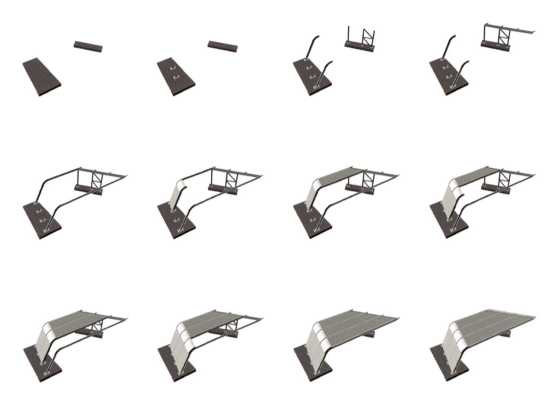

FIGURE 2.2.25
Drawing construction sequence.

FIGURE 2.2.26
Construction process, erecting the steel.

FIGURE 2.2.27
Construction process, still requires person power.

FIGURE 2.2.28
Construction process, large structural steel frame almost complete.

■ Jim Burton and William Carpenter

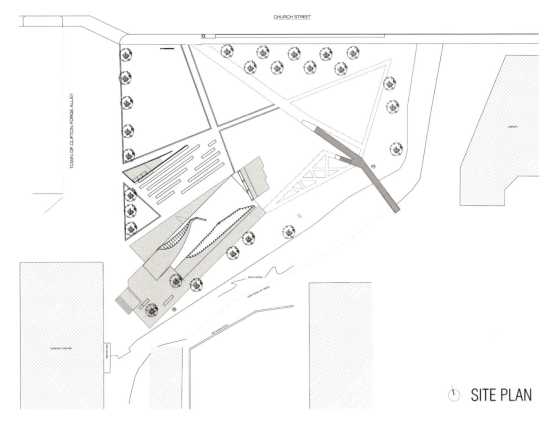

FIGURE 2.2.29
Masonic Amphitheatre, site plan.

FIGURE 2.2.30
The wood surface as playscape.

Virginia Tech

FIGURE 2.2.31
Side perspective at dusk.

corner of the seating area. Its shape and location provide maximum shelter for the control equipment with minimal impact on audience sight lines. The material pallet anchors the project in its context, while the timeless contours reflect the creativity and aspirations of a forward-thinking community.

Observation Tower, Radford, Virginia

In total, the NRTT design build project was included as part of seven courses across two colleges over a two-year period. The project engaged graduate and undergraduate students and faculty from the Departments of Architecture, Forestry, Wood Science, Sustainable Biomaterials, and Building Construction. Students from different majors were strategically paired at various project phases to challenge students "to speak the language of the other" and understand how discipline-specific knowledge can be effectively shared across project teams, among other key learning outcomes. As an example, architecture students engaged with sustainable biomaterial faculty to learn about forestry practices, and then followed that experience with hands-on engagement via the fabrication of hardwood CLT prototypes from raw material to finished product—planning, sawing, gluing, and pressing panels.

Faculty advisors Edward Becker and Kay Edge worked with faculty assistant Robert Riggs, student design team leader Kirt Hilker, and other graduate student team members.

"The random hole pattern in the wall panels was done digitally according to our drawings by SVHEC (Southern Virginia Higher Education Center). They also pressed and cut out the panels for us" (Kay Edge).

■ Jim Burton and William Carpenter

FIGURE 2.2.32
New River Train Observatory.

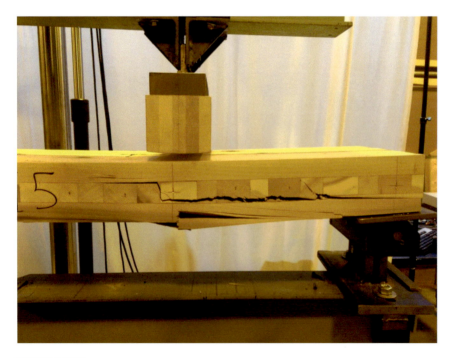

FIGURE 2.2.33
Structural test to failure of panel interlaminar shear strength.

104

The strength testing was done by Dan Hindman in the Department of Sustainable Biomaterials, which was instrumental in being granted a building permit since hardwood CLT panels are not ANSI rated.

CONCLUSIONS

Virginia Tech is one of the leading design build programs in the world. This is because of their rigorous design process and their emphasis on component-based design build studios. Digital Fabrication has more recently been foregrounded in their curriculum to more closely align with the research centers of their industrial partners.

Wholistic, deep, and wide knowledge based on experimentation and Pedagogy with a hands-on interdisciplinary approach has flourished. Fuller at Black Mountain College wrote of experimentation as "comprehensive design" and "total thinking." His tensegrity and space frame studies are part of the hands-on scaling down and scaling up research that turned individual efforts to group efforts scaling back up.

The wholistic approach helps students learn to self-motivate while accessing a range of professors and not being limited to the shrinking knowledge base of the traditional single professor. The electives are integrated as a way to expand the knowledge base of architect as citizen in an evolving technological world. The criticisms of the strict path that Joseph Albers has formed at the Black Mountain College is improved on with this feedback loop of experience. Burchard talks of this importance in his article, of how a wholistic knowledge based on experimentation and pedagogy with a hands-on interdisciplinary approach has flourished.

Site built work and prefabricated elements including a digitally fabricated LumenHAUS sliding screen wall and three generations of cassette modules have taken the FutureHAUS concept from a warehouse in rural Virginia to Times Square and Dubai. Design build has also been a small-scale single-source detail abstraction in materiality where making mistakes is encouraged as testing limits and sequence awareness.

As Virginia Tech assists in developing the new urban Amazon Campus, a new urban awareness in smart interventions may evolve of FutureHAUS modules or other but the school's mantra of studying a wide range of experience, knowledge, and a deep level of detailed understanding. The school introduces leaders in their field that practice in the professions studies, and they take on continued education with a passion as one of the top schools at all levels. The exciting Washington-Alexandria Center led by Susan Piedmont-Palladino offers the main campus an incubator prototypal which could evolve into a design build urban studio.

NOTES

1 Schubert, R. (2014). Associate Dean of Research, College of Architecture and Urban Studies, 50 Years of CAUS Research.
2 Vance, B (2023). Bobby Vance Principle at Vance Design Company, Lecturer at University of Virgina.
3 Ibid.

La Riviera Bistro

Gabriel Esquivel

DESCRIPTION

Commissioned by a local chef, La Riviera Bistro was a design build renovation project. The premise was to renovate the entry space of the restaurant; the scope included a new bar space, wall ornament, and a ceiling installation. Due to an extremely tight budget, the team developed innovative processes to reduce costs while achieving the desired atmosphere.

It was an ambitious project that included several fabrication techniques. The idea emerged from the bistro owner to create collaboration with Texas A&M University and donate the materials necessary for the project. The concept behind the project was to produce a new atmosphere more sensual and suitable for the type of food. Some of the sensibilities explored were pastries techniques like fondant, frosting, and cake ornamentation. The reason behind the research was to produce a series of sensations using materials and form or specific perceptions, sensations, and actions, basically interpreting wall, furniture, and ceiling surfaces as evoking sensations of frosting, fondant, and cake decoration.

The fabrication techniques were several, using CNC as the main resource from flip milling for the counter after a layout script, to Z-axis cutting for all the foam used on the walls. Finally, the ceiling combined two techniques. To fabricate the skeleton, the ceiling was split into seven smaller sections (A–G) and decomposed further using the software Lamina. The decision to use a wire mesh served two purposes: first, it allowed the maximum amount of light to permeate its skin, and second, the mesh provided a surface for the 4,000 flowers to be attached. The design began by folding pieces of pliable felt fabric into flowerlike forms. After several iterations, the team digitized the form and further refined the design on the computer. The finished model was exported as an STL file and sent to a lab in Mexico City that specializes in plastic injection molding.

The project took six months of fabrication, and it was installed in one week with great excitement from the community.

FABRICATION

Countertop

The bar uses three off-the-shelf cabinets as its base, each one measuring 60" long × 25" wide × 40" high. Additional 2 × 4s provided reinforcement against the heavy loads of the laminated countertop, front panels, and foam ornament. The countertop extends the full length of the bar to form one cohesive module out of the individual components. Designed not to compete with the other pieces, the countertop is a flat surface with a slight dip at one end

La Riviera Bistro

FIGURE 2.3.1
La Riviera Bistro Restaurant and Bakery, Bryan, Texas.

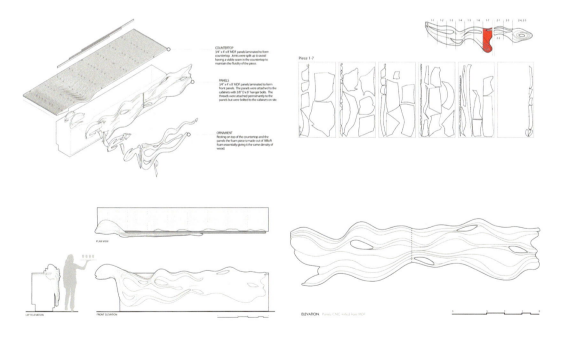

FIGURE 2.3.2
Presentation and fabrication drawings. Design Team: Gabriel Esquivel, Ky Coffman, Jeff Quantz, Dustin Mattiza, Heather Davis, Matt Miller, and Michael Tomaso.

to allow for the display of a dessert tray. Once we arrived at the final form, the model of the countertop was sectioned, and the pieces were nested together to reduce material waste during the milling process using a CNC router. The countertop is built entirely out of sheets of ¾" medium-density fiberboard (MDF). After cutting, the team laminated the pieces together, sanded them smoothly, and finished them with several coats of lacquer. The designers took a painstaking effort to retain the horizontality of the countertop by reducing the visibility of joints in the wood. They produced a template that spread the joints evenly across the length of the counter to eliminate a singular joint line that stopped the eye from moving along the entire length of the countertop.

Front Panels

Two 4' × 8' sheets of milled MDF attach to the front of the cabinets to create the facade of the bar. The panels attach to the cabinets using 6" long 3/8" diameter hanger bolts spaced out to distribute the weight across the whole structure. The panels can detach if the bar needs to be relocated.

Foam Ornament (Bar)

On the top of the countertop rests a golden ornament. The ornament needed to be extremely durable to resist damage due to its close proximity to guests. Therefore, the team chose an 18 lb polyurethane foam, which was both strong and easily formed. The piece had to be sectioned to fit within the 4" depth restriction caused by the length of the end mill on the CNC. After cutting, the pieces were glued together using epoxy and reinforced with metal

FIGURE 2.3.3
The bar countertop with wall ornament behind.

La Riviera Bistro

FIGURE 2.3.4
Bar front panel.

FIGURE 2.3.5
Bar installation.

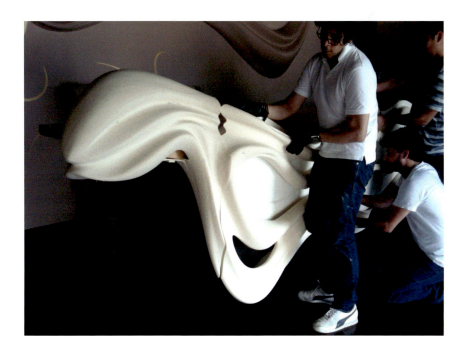

dowels. The entire piece went through several stages of sanding to remove any blemishes and was finished with a coat of golden car paint.

Foam Ornament (Wall)

The ornament on the wall was fashioned out of lighter 2 lb polyurethane foam in order to stay mounted to the wall, and also it was not within reach of guests coming in and out of the restaurant. The elaborate pieces were modeled in Maya and split to fit onto sheets of 4' × 8' × 4" blocks of foam. After several stages of sanding and coating with a compound to remove any blemishes, they were painted with golden car paint.

Ceiling Skeleton

The ceiling serves as an atmospheric installation blanketing the entire entry space. The light source is masked by a layer of translucent forms, which diffuses the light, casting an even glow over the entire space. To achieve this effect, a wire mesh forms the skeleton of the ceiling. The decision to use a wire mesh served two purposes: first, it allowed the maximum amount of light to permeate its skin, and second, the mesh provided a surface for the flowers to attach. The drawback of using the wire mesh came from trying to construct a double-curved surface out of planar sheets. To fabricate this, the ceiling was split into seven smaller sections (A–G) and decomposed further using the software Lamina. This software approximated the 3D geometry by generating a number of 2D parts. These parts were labeled, cut out, and joined together using a weaving technique to form the skeleton.

FIGURE 2.3.6 Wall ornament installation, created from polyurethane foam.

La Riviera Bistro

FIGURE 2.3.7
Wall ornament.

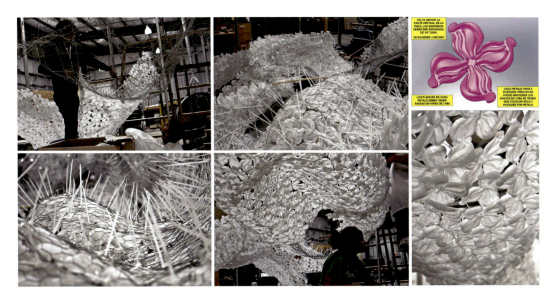

FIGURE 2.3.8
Development of the ceiling flowers.

111

■ Gabriel Esquivel

FIGURE 2.3.9
Details.

FIGURE 2.3.10
The bar, wall ornament, and ceiling flowers.

Flowers (Ornament)

There were 4,000 plastic-injection molded flowers that populated the skin of the wire mesh. The design began by folding pieces of pliable felt fabric into flowerlike forms. After several iterations, the team digitized the form and further refined the design on the computer. The finished model was exported as a stereolithography file (STL) and sent to a factory in Mexico City that specializes in plastic injection molding. The factory produced a cast from our model out of solid aluminum blocks. The cast is made up of an A-side and a B-side. The melted resin is forced into the two halves of the mold and pressed together under intense heat. This causes the plastic to harden quickly. The finished piece is ejected into a receptacle, and the process is repeated.

Practicing for Practice

Keith Zawistowski and Marie Zawistowski

FORWARD

Practicing for Practice is a critical survey of the evolution of the design/buildLAB, a two-semester studio in which architecture students collaborate with community leaders and industry experts to conceive and realize built works of architecture that are both educational and charitable in nature. This initiative was located at Virginia Tech until 2015, where it resulted in the construction of five community development projects over the course of five consecutive academic years. After which the program relocated to join the Laboratory of Excellence for Architecture, Environment, and Constructive Cultures ("LabEx AE&CC") at the National Architecture School in Grenoble, France ("L'École Nationale Supérieure d'Architecture de Grenoble"). As the program prepares its tenth project, we reflect on the context-specific evolutions that shifting continents has unlocked for the design/buildLAB. And in particular, how those evolutions might be universally relevant to design build education.

While French architecture schools have developed a rich history of experimenting with full scale mock-ups and prototypes, real-world, public-interest, student design build projects have been stifled by what were perceived to be complex regulation and contradictory legal interpretations. Breaking this jam required not only the political will to recast the legislative framework of the design/buildLAB but also the academic will to recast its pedagogical framework. Driven by these challenges, the design/buildLAB has come to favor the following:

- locally sourced, minimally transformed, natural materials over discounted, donated, or salvaged industrial products;
- vernacular form over global iconography;
- time-tested detailing over experimentation;
- mentorship over going-it-alone;
- professional-led student exchanges over student-led professional exchanges;
- assurability and insurability over protection from liability; and
- success over failure as the best teacher and ambassador.

THE REGULATORY FRAMEWORK

While the French architecture schools, notably Patrice Doat at Grenoble, have a history of full-scale pedagogical experiments that began in the early 1970s (note) and loosely parallel Charles Moore's pedagogical building projects at Yale (Caroline Maniaque D'A), the French regulatory framework has limited student design build to temporary experiments and prototypes.

Practicing for Practice

FIGURE 2.4.1
2022–23 design/buildLAB students and faculty celebrating the completion of their stone arch.

FIGURE 2.4.2
Maison Pour Tous ("House for All"), 2017–18 design/buildLAB student project in Four (38), France.

■ Keith Zawistowski and Marie Zawistowski

FIGURE 2.4.3
Maison de 24 Heures ("House in 24 Hours"). CRAterre/ENSAG 1986.

FIGURE 2.4.4
Lucy "Carpet" House, Mason's Bend, Hale County AL. Rural Studio 2001–2.

Practicing for Practice

In France like in North America, architecture and building are regulated professions that require experience, licensure, and insurance. In both contexts, a mix of building codes, building material and assembly standards, as well as zoning ordinances characterize, normalize, and standardize building in an effort to protect the health, safety, and welfare of the general public. The primary and significant differences between these two contexts are in review and enforcement frameworks. The specifics of these frameworks help explain the similarities and distinctions between the North American model of real-world, student-designed, student-built, often public-interest design build education and the French model of ephemeral experiments, mock-ups, and prototypes.

In North America, a building permit application addresses all aspects of regulatory conformity, including planning components such as zoning and accessibility, and structural components such as detailing and assembly types. Despite exceptions for residential buildings under a certain surface area, only a licensed, registered, and insured architect (or engineer) can prepare and submit the permit application. The application includes the building's construction documents. The local code official—a public employee—first reviews the credentials of professional who prepared the construction documents and then reviews the documents themselves for conformity with applicable codes and standards. Typically, a zoning officer or zoning board also reviews the project for conformity with applicable ordinances. Once conformity is established, a building permit is issued to the project owner or developer, and construction can begin by the owner or developer him/herself or by an appointed builder. While licensure and insurance are generally required of professional builders and contractors, in most states the mechanism of applicability is the value of the contract in question. This framework allows for unlicensed building of small projects, or even small pieces of big

FIGURE 2.4.5
Les Grands Ateliers ("The Big Workshops"). A platform for full-scale student design/build work shared by the French architecture schools. Villefontaine (38), France.

projects, when the contract value (not necessarily related to construction cost) falls below the threshold established by state law. Interestingly for charitable endeavors, this framework also allows for unlicensed nonprofessional volunteers to take part in large or small projects, assuming their contract has little to no financial consideration.

For small residential projects, when there is no legal requirement for a professional architect, students and even unlicensed teachers (or just about anyone) can design the project, prepare the construction documents, and submit the permit application. As projects expand in scale and complexity into the world where professional seals are required, teachers, if they happen to also be practicing architects, can maintain oversight and control over the production of their students' work and thus sign and seal the construction documents for their students' design build projects. (We will save the anomalies of sovereign immunity for state universities and unregulated localities for another time.) As design build projects pass from design to build, we find every mix and proportion of student volunteers, community volunteers, professional volunteers, and contracted professional tradesmen. But when students are doing the building, they are almost universally volunteers. Within this typical North American regulatory framework, it is plain to see, at least in part, why most design build programs have emerged around the realization of small residential projects and/or modest scale community service, volunteer-oriented public projects. Since Charles Moore began building with his Yale architecture students in the 1960s, design build in North America has become synonymous with service learning.

In France, a building permit application must similarly be signed by a licensed and registered architect, with two distinctions: building permit applications are restrained to planning conformity (zoning, project insertion, energy performance, accessibility, fire safety,

FIGURE 2.4.6
Maison Pour Tous students and artisan Timur Ersen installing prefabricated rammed earth interior walls.

Practicing for Practice

etc.) and are accordingly reviewed by planning commissions, and professional liability insurance is purchased per project rather than per term. A teacher who happens to also be a practicing architect can similarly sign a permit application, with the subtilty of negotiating who is responsible to cover the cost of the professional liability insurance for the project. Code review however takes place after the project has been permitted and is essentially the non-statutory domain of banks and insurers who rely on a uniformity in construction standards in order to measure and limit their exposure to risk. Owners or developers hire "control offices," private companies who independently certify conformity by authoring written opinions. While at first glance their private and advisory role might seem toothless,

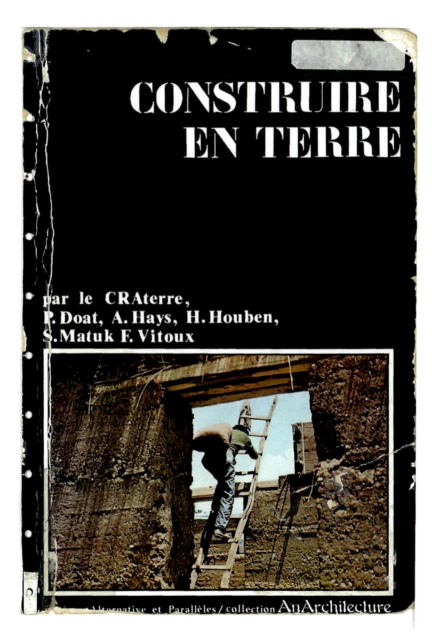

FIGURE 2.4.7
Construire en Terre ("Build in Earth") manual of earth construction, published by the CRAterre research team in 1979.

119

a control office's "unfavorable opinion" equates to no financing and no insurance. Even if a project is self-financed, no insurance equates to no public occupancy. Simply put, if the control office is unable to verify the professional credentials of the architect, engineers, and builders of a project, or the compliance of construction details to building codes, they cannot objectively offer a favorable opinion of it. While there exist some similar cutouts for self-built, self-financed small residential projects, design and building in France are effectively restricted to experienced, licensed professionals. Additionally, strong social safety nets, particularly in the domains of housing and public infrastructure, have limited the emergence of a culture of private volunteerism in those domains. And so, the North American model of students winging it to build charity projects for communities in need is all just a bit too "Wild West." Since its origins in the trade-guilds of the Middle Ages, through the Bauhaus in the 1920s, what has emerged instead has been a design build pedagogy predominantly centered on mentorship and focused on experimenting and prototyping affordable and environmentally sustainable building solutions, with the intent of demonstrating their viability for adoption by the professional sector.

THE PEDAGOGICAL FRAMEWORK

Unfortunately, the undesirable social stigma associated with the various construction trades—more often considered as lower-class actors of the building industry rather than respected craftsman of regarded knowhow—has generally prevented architects from thinking of the act of building as an integral part of the architectural discipline. This is due in part to a fundamental shift of the profession in the late 1800s to early 1900s, when it intentionally

FIGURE 2.4.8
Maison Pour Tous ("House for All"), 2017–18 design/buildLAB student project in Four (38), France.

Practicing for Practice

removed itself from the construction site in an effort to both differentiate itself from builders and to establish its authority in protecting the public interest. (note) This shift has had a lasting impact in academia, essentially removing the responsibility to teach the art of building. Through much of the 1900s and into the 2000s, architectural education has, despite a few notable exceptions, overwhelmingly revolved around the honing of theoretical concepts necessary to the development of creative sensibilities.

Today efforts are made across schools and around the world to reintroduce construction in ways that are not superficial. In Europe as in North America, design build education has immerged as a strategy to rebalance theoretical underpinning with technical aptitude (not to favor one or the other). Respected architectural theorists, such as Juhani Pallasmaa, have long argued that there is a valuable link between the careful actions of the hand and development of intellectual thought. (note) Indeed, the single most important premise of design build education is that student competence and confidence will advance exponentially by building themselves what they have conceived in abstraction. Questions of scale, tectonics, and materiality are easily apprehended and assimilated when experienced firsthand. Quite simply, a person does not approach design the same way once he or she acutely understands the concrete implications of a drawn line.

Despite sharing these foundational precepts, the context-specific regulatory frameworks in France and in North America have engendered very different peripheral learning outcomes.

FIGURE 2.4.9
Restaurant Scolaire ("Elementary School Dining Hall"), 2019–20 design/buildLAB student project in Bourgoin-Jallieu (38), France.

121

■ Keith Zawistowski and Marie Zawistowski

In France, the inability of students to build permanent structures outside of the academy has led to a reliance on collaborative teaching with trained professional craftsmen, and iterative prototyping has led to deep materials research such as the work of the CRATerre, a research laboratory at the Grenoble School which has effectively authored the codes for contemporary raw earth construction in France. Meanwhile in North America, the service-learning model has demonstrated that teaching collaboration and community engagement are indispensable components in the education of citizen-architects (note). Among the many latent values of immersive real-world learning is the opportunity to equip a generation of emerging professionals who wholeheartedly believe that architects can affect positive change on a grand scale.

FIGURE 2.4.10
Guild-trained stonecutter cutting complex curvature for the Restaurant Scolaire.

Practicing for Practice

THE LOGISTICAL FRAMEWORK

The idea to move the design/buildLAB to France after 2015 was a strategy to merge the strongest learning outcomes from both models. The rigor, discipline, and professionalization of the French model with the humanitarianism, scale, and complexity of the American model. The key to unlocking real-world student design build projects in France was in fact to reinterrogate the reasons for students to build in the first place, and whether the benefits of passing operational control of the build from the armatures to the professionals could be shaped such that the education of the students remained the primary driver of the projects.

The pedagogical model which has immerged is structured across two semesters and a summer in the first year of the two-year master's program. The fall is devoted to design. The

FIGURE 2.4.11
Students 3D scanning irregular stones using "Qlone" app.

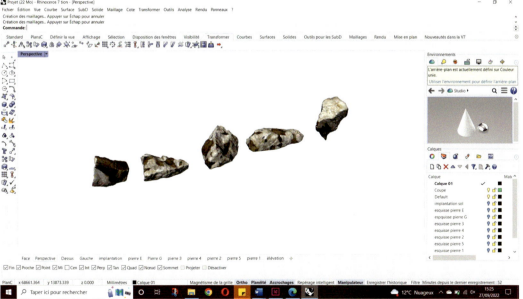

FIGURE 2.4.12
Point cloud files of scanned stones.

123

winter is devoted to permitting and prototyping, and construction starts in the spring. All master's students are required to undertake a two-month internship between their first and second years. Beyond the academic term, the project partners offer paid for-credit internships which fill this requirement.

In the design/buildLAB, projects are designed and built by teams of 20 to 25 students. After studying the project's physical and cultural context, researching precedents and working with the community to develop a detailed program, all students make individual design propositions. Through a series of studio pinups and community presentations, strong ideas are identified. The students iteratively merge these ideas, creating larger teams and fewer, more fully developed schemes. This process allows for multiple concepts, approaches, and solutions to be simultaneously explored, and for every student to contribute ideas to the discussion. It is imperative that no one scheme be "chosen." Rather, the result is a unified team who organically arrives at a single project for which there is consensus and community support. Short seminars from expert guests cover subjects from accessibility to BIM modeling. Civil, structural, and MEP engineers are hired to consult on the project as they would any other, with the exceptions that their clients are students, and part of their role is pedagogical, which is extremely valorizing to them. Typically, the building permit application is submitted around the time of the Winter Break. Because the permitting process can take up to three months, the students return from the holidays and divide themselves into smaller committees by construction trade to prepare the construction drawings and specifications, a process which is punctuated by stays at "Les Grands Ateliers" (The Big Workshops), a facility for architecture students and faculty to experiment and build protypes at full scale.

FIGURE 2.4.13
Stone arch constructed using irregular shaped quarry waste stones.

Because the projects are professionally built, the end user—always a community government—pays for the building. Public entities paying for buildings is of course subject to the laws of public financing, and so the students solicit bids for each trade. The key to the pedagogical model is that the first paragraph of the bid packages outlines the context of the project and binds bidders to each allow the students who designed the project to fold into their teams. The medieval trade guilds ("Les Compagnons du Devoir") still thrive in France, so the base of this kind of apprenticeship model takes shape fairly naturally. The unexpected treasure of this specific model is that unlike their typical apprentices, these architecture students designed the project. A profound richness unfolds as future architects valorize the discipline of architecture by regularly explaining the logic of their design decisions to the craftsmen, and craftsmen valorize their know-how by taking the time to share it with the students. As

FIGURE 2.4.14
A design/buildLAB student mechanically splitting large stones.

the owner of one masonry company put it with a smile, "My guys argue every morning over which ones get to work on the design/buildLAB projects."

Practice

Brian Mackay Lyons once shared with us the metaphor that if you want to become a really good skier, you don't just clip into a pair of skis and point downhill because you will only develop and repeat bad habits. Instead, you find the best skier you can, and you follow in their tracks until their movements become natural to you. (note)

Architectural education has been the subject of fierce debate for centuries, leading to major reforms, counterreforms, and countless approaches to pedagogy and curriculum. Continually driven by both socioeconomic context and the evolving aspirations of architects, the profession itself is ever-changing. The design/buildLAB was created as a direct response to the academy's increasing tendency to shroud the making of architecture in mystery[1] and to the resulting pressure that this tendency places on students to overintellectualize their work. In such instances, students, whose vocation as architects is to make a tangible impact on the world around them, often find themselves at a loss for a sense of meaning and purpose. Design build education is a counterbalance, providing students with the opportunity to practice for practice: to build from the "savoir" (knowledge), the "savoir-faire" (know-how), "savoir-être" (humanity) that has been accrued over generations.

FIGURE 2.4.15
Nomad Shelter 1 of 2 (Bus Stop Shelter). 2020–21 design/buildLAB student project in Villard de Lans (38), France.

Practicing for Practice

FIGURE 2.4.16
Nomad Shelter 2 of 2 (Bus Stop Shelter). 2020–21 design/buildLAB student project in Villard de Lans (38), France.

NOTE

1 Lyons, B.M. (2008). *Ghost: Building an Architectural Vision*. New York: Princeton Architectural Press.

Two Scales of Approach, Tulane's Design Build Programs

Byron J. Mouton and Emilie Taylor Welty

INTRODUCTION

Tulane's School of Architecture houses two long running design build programs, embracing the potential of design build pedagogy to educate professionals who can creatively manage complexity and transform their communities through design. This chapter outlines the school's flagship programs, URBANbuild + The Small Center for Collaborative Design, and discusses their pedagogical aims, logistics, and project outcomes. Started in 2005, Tulane's design build programs have produced over 45 projects ranging in scale and complexity from pavilions to houses to urban parks. URBANbuild is the annual housing program in which students design, permit, and construct affordable housing prototypes over the course of a full academic year in collaboration with a community nonprofit partner. Running parallel to URBANbuild is the work of Small Center, Tulane's community design center, where students work on projects with various agendas and less complexity in a single semester. Together the programs create an ethos of collaboration, creative problem solving, and understanding of tolerance both social and materially. The chapter looks at the opportunities and limitations of each program's approach through the lens of two recent research methods—URBANbuild iterations 14 through 16 and the Small Center's LOOP Pavilion.

URBANbuild + THE ALBERT AND TINA SMALL CENTER FOR COLLABORATIVE DESIGN

Tulane's School of Architecture houses two long-running design build programs, creating a culture of collaboration, professionalism, and a willingness to take on complex design challenges. Based in New Orleans, a city that's on the frontlines of many environmental and social challenges of our time, the design build programs have developed processes and pedagogies for transforming our communities through design. Started in 2005 the two programs, URBANbuild and Small Center, have produced over 45 projects ranging in scale and complexity from pavilions to houses to urban parks.

This chapter looks at the opportunities and limitations of each program's approach by outlining two recent research methods. URBANbuild is the annual housing program in which students design, permit, and construct affordable housing prototypes over the course of a full academic year in collaboration with a community nonprofit partner. Running parallel to URBANbuild is the work of Small Center, Tulane's community design center, where students work on projects with various agendas and less complexity in a single semester. Together the programs have honed their design processes and teaching methodology. Side by side, they

Two Scales of Approach, Tulane's Design Build Programs

FIGURE 2.5.1
New Orleans Context with Students Building.

complement each other and provide students opportunities to select from a range of design/build research studios that possess contrasting limitations of schedule, budget, and scope.

DESIGN BUILD HISTORY AT TULANE AND THE CONTEXT OF NEW ORLEANS

During the summer of 2005, a small group of students and faculty conceived a design build program to address the deteriorating conditions in many urban inner-city neighborhoods of New Orleans and to provide students with the opportunity to work collectively on the design, development, and construction of affordable housing prototypes. The goal was to provide families with affordable creative housing options while also aiming to make investment in struggling neighborhoods. Most importantly, the program offered students an opportunity to work with each other within the community.

Unexpectedly, in August of that same summer, New Orleans was struck by a catastrophic storm, Hurricane Katrina. The city was left 80 percent damaged with the population immediately reduced by one-third. Occupants of the city's most underprivileged areas struggled to return, which frayed the cultural, economic and social foundations of the city. Rebuilding became a critical task, and suddenly, design build efforts were challenged to explicitly address the imminent threat of water and the changing social demographics of a city struggling to survive.

Therefore, the school's design build initiatives quickly evolved as post-Katrina programs that address and investigate pre-Katrina problems. The research agenda relies on a comprehensive understanding of New Orleans as a city in a constant process of reconsidering and defining itself. The programs challenge designers to both respect and question the architectural history of New Orleans and redefine a contemporary vernacular. They are programs of optimism and investment.

INTRO TO THE URBANbuild PROGRAM—MISSION AND CONTEXTUAL RESPONSE

Since the summer of 2005, Tulane's URBANbuild program has realized a body of work in New Orleans comprising the efforts of student design and construction research, close faculty mentorship, and collaboration with local community partners, fabricators, and material suppliers. The program charges students with the task of developing responsible housing prototypes with reliance upon analysis of New Orleans' existing neighborhoods and the community's common cultural needs. In addition, students are asked to recognize the expectations and abilities of the region's workforce while striving to build upon and challenge available means in pursuit of progress.

In both the design studio and in the field, equal attention is given to conceptual contemplation and technical execution; reasons and methods are simultaneously considered. One design build project at a time, the program strives to build high-quality residences in underserved communities with an awareness of affordability. Particularly, the program has focused its efforts on transforming the Central City neighborhood of New Orleans, where 13 dwelling prototypes have been sited, with a fourteenth underway.

PROJECT SITES AND PROXIMITIES

New Orleans is a city of contrasts in adjacency. Rich and poor, black and white, left and right, high ground and low ground: these contrasts intermingle without a clear divide, and that allows for research to take place in fringe zones and make impact without being imposing. New Orleans neighborhoods are authentically old, and many of them are in desperate need of repair. Many of the inner-city urban blocks of New Orleans are typically home to a higher percentage of renters than homeowners. The city's urban fabric possesses many unique qualities and is a collection of struggling city blocks often existing alongside thriving ones. Some older neighborhoods are characterized by examples of historically significant housing types that have succumbed to blight; they are dense but pedestrian-friendly. Many older homes have a front porch or stoop that is often occupied as a stage for neighborly observation and conversation.

URBANbuild prototypes are envisioned with respect for the scale and character of the neighborhood; though, it's important not to confuse character with style. Careful attention is given to common components and qualities such as the inviting entry porch or stoop, interior volumes that are significant in height, design that makes the best possible use of natural light and air, exterior spaces for cooking and socializing—all of which are typical of New Orleans homes and lifestyle. The character of the older neighborhoods is sustained through the introduction of new homes that possess many of the qualities of old New Orleans architecture while offering progressive alternatives to the language of traditional housing. While the URBANbuild houses are in close proximity to each other, they are rarely side by side; they have intentionally been scattered and woven into the time-proven context of the city's urban density.

The new homes are fabricated using common and readily available materials and methods in a fresh way. Aiming to preserve positive qualities of street life and domesticity, they often borrow and reconsider common physical components of the context such as scale, size and pattern of windows, access to garden space, relationship to the street, and the importance of the front porch or stoop. The progressive homes bring new home buyers and investment to the neighborhood, and as the number of homeowners increases, greater value is placed in the maintenance of the community's public spaces. After years of commitment to a central local, a resulting sense of shared investment is surfacing. The URBANbuild program aims to prove that old and new structures can respectfully exist side by side; the distinction between preservation and progress is blurred.

PRESENTATION OF THE RESEARCH PROGRAM'S METHODS AND ITERATIVE PROCESS

Each design build cycle of the URBANbuild Program spans two semesters, starting with an empty lot in the underserved Central City Neighborhood of New Orleans. Most of the project sites have been acquired by our nonprofit partner, Neighborhood Housing Services of New Orleans (NHS). It is important to recognize that New Orleans is a small city, and collecting various lots within close proximity aids NHS in realizing its mission of working to coherently revitalize communities and neighborhoods.

The URBANbuild Program's relationship with the community is a significant aspect of the coursework. Every January, a group of students is welcomed by Central City neighbors who have watched the construction of prior homes and look forward to seeing a new residence surface. Introducing progressive, well-made projects into a struggling neighborhood provides a sense of support to community members. Neighbors form relationships with the students, and after 17 years of maintained presence in a single neighborhood, the return of student builders is annually anticipated and welcomed.

Beginning with the plot survey, a group of approximately 12 upper-level students begin the fall semester collaboratively developing design proposals tackling the problem of affordable single-family dwelling. The schemes are approximately 1,100 to 1,300 square feet in area with a construction budget of approximately $120 per square foot. Students begin by briefly working alone but are quickly paired with colleagues that share similar views. Proposals build upon analysis of previous program accomplishments, and students work at a very fast pace. Following midterm presentations, after contemplation and critical debate, they vote and select a favored strategy for construction.

Following that vote, during the latter half of the fall semester, students develop a set of construction documents for review by the municipal Office of Safety Permits, which aims to issue a building permit by the start of each spring semester. Students then construct the project during the 16 weeks of the spring term, between January and May. The mild winters of the region greatly aid in making this possible. With the exception of licensed MEP tradespeople, drywall hangers and sheet metal/roofing fabricators, students perform all of the work.

The spring semester fabrication team includes members of the previous semester's design studio, but new students are also welcomed. Therefore, taking advantage of fresh views provided by new colleagues, the spring construction experience is a continuation of the fall's design-research activities. The build process is a vehicle for further exploration, testing, and reconsideration of options. Students are expected to reflect upon design decisions of the previous fall term, challenge them, and perform on-site revisions at full scale—but at a very fast pace.

Recent Curricular Developments: Reduction in Scope/Increase in Scale of Thought

Single-family prototypes realized as units of proposed multifamily assemblies

Early URBANbuild prototypes (UB1–UB11) were always composed of three bedrooms and two baths; in response, two-story solutions were often required given the small size of the acquired "sub-standard" urban lots. That changed with Prototype 12.

Beginning with UB12, all prototypes have been developed as two-bedroom, two-bath, single-story strategies. Scope was reduced in pursuit of affordability, the appropriateness of scale, and in response to the limits of time and budget. However, the commitment to the development of single-level strategies offered opportunity for greater sectional exploration, and with prototypes UB12 and UB13, students introduced clerestory windows to the kit of parts. This vertical access to the sky, providing an abundance of light and air, proved to offer great relief to the compact spaces of the reduced project scope, and that strategy greatly influenced schemes to follow.

Following the conclusion of UB13, the idea of ever-evolving, iterative, prototyping surfaced as a method of sharing, conducting, and furthering research. In other words, the same schematic approach was repeated annually but with incremental improvements in every

FIGURE 2.5.2
Image of Prototype 12 on Streetscape.

FIGURE 2.5.3
Image of interior clerestory.

cycle. Expanding upon sectional qualities of UB12 and UB13, the following prototypes, UB14 through UB16, introduced interior courtyards to the mix—improving upon the qualities provided by the preceding clerestory schemes. However, the use of the courtyard strategy coupled with the elimination of all sidewall fenestrations immediately influenced an expansion in the scope of URBANbuild research and consideration.

Students quickly began to re-envision the "mostly" solid sidewalls of these long narrow schemes as party walls, leading to the development of multifamily townhouse strategies. While the tight annual schedule of the program does not provide time for the students to fabricate multifamily options, this increased range of research was simply realized through envisioning and fabricating "model" components of that larger program.

A commitment to the scale of a single-family residence must be maintained so that students can envision options, challenge alternatives, achieve resolution, and complete assembly within the timeframe of an academic year. It is critical that instructors provide students with achievable goals, and the recent prioritization of the "townhouse program" allows for expanded conversations related to the many topics of urban housing, planning, and scale. The program of the single-family residence coupled with its possible inclusion within a multifamily assembly is just beginning to greatly expand the content of the URBANbuild program's research, and currently program directors are in conversation with other departmental and city leaders working toward the realization of such assemblies at market rate and in collaboration with research initiatives.

■ Byron J. Mouton and Emilie Taylor Welty

FIGURE 2.5.4
The vertical spatial/clerestory qualities of post UB12 house.

INTRO TO ALBERT AND TINA SMALL CENTER FOR COLLABORATIVE DESIGN

Mission

Running parallel to URBANbuild at Tulane's School of Architecture is the Albert and Tina Small Center for Collaborative Design. The Small Center is the school's community design center with projects ranging from neighborhood planning and project visioning to design build.

The community design center began as an idea in early 2005 and in the wake of Hurricane Katrina quickly galvanized to address the issues, opportunities, and inequities exposed by the storm. While the moral and political content of design practice and our subversive role as educators contain questions we should have been asking all along, particularly in a city like New Orleans, full of inequity and "wicked problems" (footnote, see Denver 8), sometimes it takes a disaster to expose underlying structural inequities and force a collective reflection. The design and design build projects of the center have shifted from acute post-storm recovery to addressing ongoing needs and injustices in the community.

The center's mission is to advance community-driven ideas through collaboration, design education, and creative problem-solving. The work of Small Center is situated within a broader body of public interest design work that is focused on expanding access to design services and investigating how design can address social, economic, and environmental issues. Recent design build projects of the center include large public spaces such as Parasite skatepark built with and for the young people of the city and small bike-pulled apothecary carts that are used by artists and activists to advocate for prison abolition. Founded in 2005 as the Tulane City Center, in 16 years the center has completed over 100 projects and worked with over 700 students.

Comparison of Curricular Calendar/Schedule

Design build projects at Small Center primarily happen through one-semester studio work. Our design build studios pack a full project into one 15-week semester, from an initial conversation with the client/community partner to permitting and fabrication. The built projects have two major components, engagement with a community partner and their stakeholders, and making as part of the design, investigation, and project delivery process. The early weeks begin with iterative skill building exercises and expand to include experiments wherein students thoroughly research and understand materials, detailing, and fabrication methods. Students propose individual design responses and then are paired in increasingly larger teams each week. Within several weeks of intense design work and guidance from professors to navigate the opportunities allowed by code, material choices, and structural systems, the studio coalesces around a final design scheme. By midsemester a final scheme has been worked through, and full-scale mock-ups of materials and details begin. The last seven weeks of the studio are dedicated to construction of the project, which always includes on-site design work to resolve details or invent tools and jigs that make the final project possible.

The studios expose students to the coordination of construction at varying scales and the constraints of a budget and timeline. Students learn how to collaborate as a team and communicate with clients, subcontractors, and approving agencies. These small one-semester projects are our preferred approach to design build within an educational setting although it comes with strengths and drawbacks. One of the assets of the model is that a single group of students can see a project through from beginning to end and are forced to reckon with the full arc of design, consultants, approvals, and fabrication. With URBANbuild offering a two-semester design build sequence, this one-semester model is a compliment, allowing graduate students and those with limited curricular options the chance to participate in a full design build project. Additionally, the small project scale and lack of complexity (no sealed building envelope or systems) leaves more room for experimentation with materials, detail, and project delivery methods.

Byron J. Mouton and Emilie Taylor Welty

While this comprehensive experience has pedagogical strengths, the downside of the small timeline is that it necessitates a small project with less complexity than URBANbuild houses or other multi-semester design build projects with full MEP. As a result, students are not forced to contend with the implications of how to house and coordinate full building systems. Additionally, knowing a project has a short timeline forces us to choose projects and programs that are free of more complex approvals (as in historic districts approvals) or consultant coordination, which are hard to align with semester schedules and pedagogical aims.

Funding and Project Intake

A majority of Small Center projects begin with our yearly request for proposals (RFP). Targeted to the nonprofits and community-based organizations in New Orleans, the RFP involves an open call for project ideas and a jury consisting of past project partners, community members, faculty, and former students chose the projects TCC will work on for the year. This is a first step in ensuring that the work is grounded in an actual need or desire from our community and helps to build trust at the very onset of a project.

Design build projects are funded by third-party donations and grants, making the projects pro bono for our nonprofit partners. The typical project budget for a one-semester project is $12–14,000—which includes materials, consultants (often engineers and landscape architects), and subcontractors. Subcontractors vary depending on the project so that a project more digitally reliant might include work with a CNC plasma cutter, while others might involve powder coating or specialized products and aggregates.

FIGURE 2.5.5
LOOP Pavilion.

136

SAMPLE PROJECT OVERVIEW—LOOP PAVILION

The LOOP Pavilion is an example of a one-semester project with a simple program that allows for an expressive design response and a targeted research agenda for the design build team. Located in New Orleans' City Park, a large urban park, the pavilion is on a small island surrounded by lagoons. The site is dedicated to team building through ropes courses and is run by Louisiana Outdoors Outreach Program (LOOP), a nonprofit organization whose mission is to provide positive, life-changing outdoor experiences for children and youth in Greater New Orleans. The ropes course island site had no shade or seating for the youth who learned there, creating health and logistics challenges for the nonprofit running programs on site.

After engaging LOOP NOLA staff to assess their needs, the Small Center design build students designed a 250 square foot pavilion that incorporated seating into a large shade structure for teaching and gathering. The design was inspired by the tree canopy surrounding the challenge course and uses blank aluminum traffic signs as a modular, exterior grade unit to create an abstracted, high-performing canopy overhead. It took the design build team of 12 students and 2 teachers one semester (15 weeks, in a six-credit class) to design and build the project. The budget was $12,000.

This project's main innovation is a six-tabbed aluminum joint that holds the yield signs together with mechanical fasteners attaching them. The joint intentionally holds the signs apart to create a gap of light imitating the dappled light of the tree canopy. This joint also is flexible, which allowed the team to create an undulating complex curve with the roof form. In keeping with the context of the adjacent ropes course structure, the canopy is suspended with steel cable from a larger steel structure, which is hidden from underneath by the curving yield-sign fabric. This system has enough flexibility built into the connections to allow for complex shapes to form in the canopy, and while the overall form was modeled digitally and in physical models before installation, there were some on-site adjustments made during installation. The aluminum joints were prototyped and milled on a CNC mill and in the final structure connects over 500 yield signs.

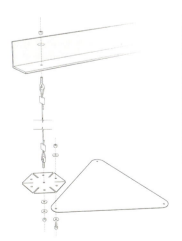  

FIGURE 2.5.6
Drawing and image of the joint detail.

Recent Curricular Developments: Tracking Impacts and Honing Research Agendas

Design build at Small Center varies greatly in content and research agendas because projects grow out of the request for proposals process. While the program for projects may change from an outdoor classroom at a farm to the renovation of a black-owned bookstore, the scale and systems complexity of the projects are smaller than that of URBANbuild. As a result, the body of work lacks the thematic cohesion of the program and makes tracking a similar dataset of impacts and post-occupancy outcomes more difficult. What the variety does offer is the chance to build coalitions across the city around projects, and it has given our team the opportunity to focus on engagement in the design process. Engagement with our partner organizations and their community/stakeholders is layered into each step of the design build studio's progression.

Additionally, the research agenda of each studio is related to the semester's project. A coastal pavilion with a low-maintenance requirement is a chance for a studio to dive deep into manipulating steel with CNC plasma technologies, while a farm focused on sustainability invites intensive research on sustainable materials and building practices. What we have developed in recent years is a pre-project questionnaire we use to guide a discussion with the project partner to identify research areas and pinpoint the goals and impacts we will track.

CONCLUSION

Tulane's School of Architecture offers multiple design build options rather than a singular curricular option. However, all options share a common trait: they are deeply embedded in the cultural and physical context of New Orleans. Students at Tulane can choose from a range of design/build research studios in support of their learning objectives and curricular timeline. Together the programs create an ethos of collaboration, creative problem solving, and understanding of tolerance, both socially and materially. In nearly 17 years of offering varying opportunities, we have prepared a generation of students for the profession, with an awareness of industry options available to them. We've also witnessed our projects transform neighborhoods, and our neighbors now understand design as a process and agent of change available to them.

Borboletta

Eric Goldemberg

Borboletta is a research project on the integration between microbiology, biodiversity, and architecture aimed at the construction of a new urban paradigm intended as an ecosystem rather than an artifice.

Its final realization will take place in the Italian pavilion at the Biennale 2021, curated by Alessandro Melis. The work results from an iterative design collaboration with Eric Goldemberg and Veronica Zalcberg of MONAD Studio and also includes Jumur Gokchepinar, who coordinates the integration between architecture and microbiology; Francesco Lipari, for biodiversity; and Jorge Cereghetti, for digital fabrication.

The success and interest of the media for this innovative project is proven by the invitation, followed by an award, to exhibit the first prototype of the Borboletta at the Buenos Aires Biennale (October 2019), among the most important architecture events in South America, then at the Pisa Biennale (November 2019), in its application version, and finally on display in Miami at Florida International University (March 2020), before reaching the final result expected for Venice (May 2021).

FIGURE 2.6.1 First prototype of the Borboletta at the Buenos Aires Biennale, October 2019.

■ Eric Goldemberg

BORBOLETTA IN BUENOS AIRES

Borboletta is a sonic installation with living organisms developed for the group exhibition FEEDback at the XVII Bienal Internacional de Arquitectura de Buenos Aires, curated by Eric Goldemberg.

Borboletta consists of four integrated entities representing the essential ingredients of a future-resilient ecosystem: a variable scaffolding structure which allows interaction with the human body, the sensoriality represented by the sonic integration (two 3D-printed guitars) and the Arduino feedback systems, the self-sufficient habitat oriented to the proliferation of biodiversity (bee spheres), and the climate responsivity of the system, through expansion and contraction of an acellular mass of creeping gelatinous protoplasm containing nuclei (slime mold).

This integration is the result of few years' cross-disciplinary and transgenerational research challenging the conventional relationship between artefact and nature. Here the research of Alessandro Melis/Heliopolis 21, Eric Goldemberg and Veronica Zalcberg/MONAD Studio, Francesco Lipari/Ofl, and Jumhur Gokchepinar/University of Portsmouth for the first time converge. The project also includes the collaboration with Jorge Cereghetti/UADE Labs in the construction of the CNC milled body of Borboletta and with William Carpenter on the creation of a music instrument.

The aforementioned research team believes that nature-facts, intended as a new axiomatic relationship between artefact and nature, can contribute to the construction of new ecologic paradigms for the positive development of the troposphere.

In Borboletta the interest in the field of climate sensitive design becomes an instrument to discuss the urban fabric and its relationship with the troposphere in order to transform the cities in virtuous open systems reacting to the climate change. Moreover, a radical spatial re-configuration of the built environment based on the Borboletta prototype can offer opportunities for the positive development/transformation of the current energy intensive metabolism into biomass power generation as well as for the conceptualization of

FIGURE 2.6.2
Music instruments designed by MONAD Studio | Eric Goldemberg + Veronica Zalcberg with William Carpenter and 3D-printed at FIU Miami Beach Urban Studios.

Borboletta

FIGURE 2.6.3
Borboletta prototype hybrid landscape generated by specific variations of the urban continuum.

a revolutionary biodiversity design. Borboletta is not an object, a unique and recognizable item. It is instead intended as a part of hybrid landscapes generated by specific variations of the urban continuum, also involving autopoietic processes aimed to the adaptation to extreme environmental conditions.

This is the first step of an ongoing research aimed at the construction of repeatable modules for a closed loop colonization of the urban sphere also aimed at terraforming.

Borboletta is therefore not a phenotype but a genetically modified chrysalis meant as an evolving organism, linking slime mold cell-farming to micro scale bee-topoi enabling eco systemic iterations, and questioning conventional artefact-nature dichotomies.

BORBOLETTA IN PISA

Borboletta has been used in this project as a biodiversity activator. The project presented is the future transformation of the Legoli landfill, in Peccioli, into an artificial lake intended as a place where art, technology, and sustainability are mixed in a story about the 30 years of resilience of the Peccioli phenomenon. The Borboletta installation, at the center of the lake, represents the synthesis of the cultural path and the virtuous model of Peccioli.

BORBOLETTA IN MIAMI/VENICE

The evolution of the project—whose name Borboletta refers metaphorically to the ephemeral, accelerated timeframe of a butterfly's life—is manifested in the culminating installation for Venice, developed previously through several iterations built for Buenos Aires, Pisa, and Miami, which embody the growth process envisioned to challenge the very notion of the perception of time and duration in architecture, as described by Henri Bergson:

> My own duration, such as I live it in the impatience of waiting, for example, serves to reveal other durations that beat to other rhythms, that differ in kind from mine. Duration is always the location and the environment of differences in kind; it is even their totality and multiplicity. There are no differences in kind except in duration—while space is nothing other than the location, the environment, the totality of differences in degree.

The morphology of the project aims to introject the multiplicitous timescales its rhythmical structure simultaneously supports and exhibits, allowing for a deep questioning of identity vis-à-vis duration. This intensification of the existential questions about how we perceive the environment in time is expressed via the objects contained in its vitrines, windows, and biomes (living insects, various marine organisms in different states of evolution, and coral-reef fossils).

The formal articulation of the support structure for Borboletta consists of a series of smoothly articulated unit-frames that proliferate in staccato, evoking the effect of perceptual rhythms that operate in the subconscious mind of the viewer as a sensation of conservation of the past in the present, while the duration of the experience with Borboletta's nuanced rhythmicity presents a way of being in time; a rhythm of duration that is distinguished from a discontinuous series of instants repeated identically—the following perceptual moment always contains over and above, the memory the latter has left it.

Borboletta is able to measure time as an emergent composite of two kinds of multiplicity. One is represented by space (or rather, if all the nuances are taken into account, by the impure combination of homogeneous time); it is a multiplicity of exteriority, of simultaneity, of juxtaposition, of order, of quantitative differentiation, of difference in degree; it is a numerical multiplicity, discontinuous and actual. The other type of multiplicity appears

FIGURE 2.6.4
Borboletta biodiversity activator.

in pure duration; it is an internal multiplicity of succession, of fusion, of organization, of heterogeneity, of qualitative discrimination, or of difference in kind; it is a virtual and continuous multiplicity that cannot be reduced to numbers.

PERCEPTION AND THE TRANSMISSION OF AGGREGATES

Borboletta's tectonic articulation is informed by architectural interpretations and extrapolations from Leibniz's *Monadology*; as defined by Leibniz, *monadology* may allow for the extrapolation of micro-behaviors of transmission between cells that telegraph effective alliances of perception.

Complexity of material systems, field conditions, and synchronicity of the collective articulate the combinatorial techniques used in Borboletta to activate the taxonomies of components and their environment in a holistic project.

Leibniz's thought is intricately constituted in a series of transfers and contaminations between physics, biology, mathematics, metaphysics, and theology. His concepts about monads manifest and actively deploy a conceptual materialism of high relevance to the field of contemporary design and computer-aided speculation; one could indeed offer the monad for architecture operations that engender material plurality. Monads are, on the surface, units—and unities—of thought, like concepts in the conventional sense.

Yet when considered microscopically, each monad is, arguably, infinitely subdivisible into further monads, smaller conceptual units, and is thus irreducibly non simple. Or to put it differently, the monad possesses a certain "architectural" unity but, on closer inspection, unfolds into numerous smaller, not necessarily synchronic, spaces, cavities, joints, seams, and components. These, by extension, define a contemporary expression for architecture, a rhythmic field of inherent ornament activated by digital design technologies.

This new expression introduces the idea of perception as a transitory state that contains and represents a multitude in the one, or in the simple substance, and in doing that it goes beyond the notion that represents the multiplicity in the monad as no more than a multiplicity of the various states.

According to Leibniz, whatever interchange of parts may take place between bodily aggregates in cases of veridical perception, the perceiving subject's experience in the total situation does not and cannot involve acquiring parts or properties from outside. Instead, it will be because its perceptual states occur as they do in harmony with the flow of other monads' perceptual states that one monad perceives bodies that are constituted by other monads.

TOWARDS A PULSATING PART-TO-WHOLE BIOLOGICAL SYNTHESIS

Given the capacity of digital design to generate a gradient-transmission between components, what is the status of the parts, the single pieces, the fragments in Borboletta?

Pulsation refers to the principles within living matter that pulsate, which the digital architecture approximates, attempts to reconfigure, or simulate, and that through the digital, the hope is that matter can be reborn in a new form but with the same pulse and pulsation that surrounds us and inspires architecture throughout history. Pulsation can also be thought of as the evidence of transformation, of metabolism, or the ability to chart time through some form of body, whether tectonic skin or digital mediation.

■ Eric Goldemberg

FIGURE 2.6.5
Borboletta details.

Pulsation in architecture can be assimilated to systems that reflect periodicity. Periodic systems show a continuously repeated change from one set of conditions to another, opposite set. The repetition of polar phases occurs alike in systematized and patterned elements, and in processes and series of events. This registers clearly in physiological examples:

- inspiration and expiration of the lungs;
- systole and diastole of the heart;
- in the nervous system the impulses occur serially and might, therefore, be described as frequencies;
- much the same applies to the active muscle system, which is actually in a state of constant vibration.

The more closely one examines the physiological rhythmic functions, the more evident these recurrent sequences become. Events, then, do not take place in a continuous sequence, in a straight line, but are in a continual state of constant vibration, oscillation, undulation, and pulsation.

This also holds true for the systematized structures present in Borboletta's morphogenesis. On the largest and smallest scale, we find serial elements, repetitive patterns, and the number of fiber stromata, space lattices, and reticulations is legion. Similarly, in the realm of pulsation and architectural effects, it can be shown that every part of the Borboletta installation is, in the true sense, implicated in the whole.

When looking at biological rhythms and histology—the science that deals with the structure of tissue—a good number of observations can be made that are relevant to the production of rhythmic effects in architecture; skin structure and tissue constitute the basic fabric of architectural envelopes, which reflect the deeper organization of systemic, sequential aggregation of units.

The very origin of the word *tissue* (Latin *texere* = to weave) is a significant comment on the prevailing conditions: cells are arrayed in rows, one pattern following another. The intercellular structures take the form of frameworks, networks, grids, families of elements continually repeated and following each other in regular sequence, forming a woof or weft whether looked at with the naked eye, through the microscope or through the electron microscope. The integument, the skin of animals, reveals that—apart from the cell tissue as such with its vast array of repeating elements—all the skin structures, scales, feathers, and hairs are arranged in serial patterns, in regular formations, in rows and tracts. Each structure is in turn a serial product. In the muscle tissues we do not find compact homogeneous masses but organized fasciculi of fibers with the elements arranged in rows, one bundle next to another. Series of fibers of this kind continue in sinews which irradiate into the ligaments and bones. Everywhere there are fibrillae, lamellae, and folia that develop into the spatial frameworks of sinew, ligament, and bone organizations.

The whole of periodicity is ubiquitous in nature's creation. In cell division in particular, in mitosis, the process of the regular repetition of polar well-characterized phases occurs as a function of space and time. The regular and consistent repetition of basic elements is not restricted to the major organ systems (integument and nervous, supporting, digestive, and procreative systems, etc.), we also find segments occurring serially, as it were, as elements of "style" in the general structure principles of organisms. But it is not only the structural elements that show a repetitive periodic character; functions also proceed rhythmically, in regular cycles and serial processes. This is exemplified by the pulsations of the heart's autonomic rhythmicity of the intestinal musculature and the serial action currents of the nervous pathways.

Similarly for the architecture of Borboletta, part-to-whole relationships are at stake, continuously being revised and resynthesized by explorations that range from thick modularity to surface fineness and the management of multiple elements with parametric relatedness, incorporating organizational strategies that distribute material effects at the level of ornament, a gradient of porosity and opulent form that disseminates tectonic fields with degrees of connectivity afforded by joinery understood as hyper-indexical spatial seams.

Such reformulated role of ornament in the morphogenesis of Borboletta and its potential to be proliferated as genetic pool has shifted and augmented our capacity to perceive and produce rhythmic form in space neighboring ecstatic states of distributed singularities capable of registering incremental difference.

WHAT IS RHYTHM?

Duration, Repetition, and Difference in Borboletta

Pulsation also applies to sound and rhythm, where a pulse provides a guideline for articulation, a thread to pull, which pushes back and pushes forward, a locus to navigate around and through.

Rhythm appears as regulated time, governed by rational laws, but in contact with what is least rational in human beings: the lived, the carnal, the body. Time and space, the cyclical and the linear, exert a reciprocal action; they measure themselves against one another; each one makes itself and is made a measuring-measure; everything is cyclical repetitions through linear repetitions.

Rhythm is born of moments of intensity, incommensurable accents that create unequal extensions of duration. Whereas meter presumes an even division of a uniform time, rhythm presupposes a time of flux, of multiple speeds and reversible relations.

■ Eric Goldemberg

FIGURE 2.6.6
Borboletta rhythm seems natural, spontaneous.

The paradox: rhythm seems natural, spontaneous, with no law other than its unfurling. Yet rhythm, always particular (music, poetry, dance, architecture, etc.), always implies a measure. Everywhere where there is rhythm, there is a measure, which is to say law, calculated and expected obligation, a project.

Periodic repetition encodes a milieu, but one must distinguish the measure (or meter) of such repetition from the rhythm that occurs between two milieus, or between a milieu and chaos (as the milieu of all milieus). Measure implies the repetition of the Same, a preexistent, self-identical pattern that is reproduced over and over again; whereas rhythm is the Unequal or Incommensurable, always in a process of transcoding, operating not in a homogeneous space-time but with heterogeneous blocks.

Rhythm is difference, or relation, the in-between whereby milieus communicate with one another, with themselves (as collections of sub-milieus), and with chaos. Rhythm is not a secondary by-product of a milieu's measure but a primary constituent of that milieu.

Consider the human body. Its internal milieu is made up of various elements—the heart, lungs, brain, and so on—each with its own rate of periodic repetition. The rhythms of the body, however, take place between various milieus and sub-milieus, the heart's regular measure, for instance, fluctuating in response to neural and hormonal stimuli, changes in breathing rate, alterations in the external environment, and so on. In a sense, the heart's periodic repetition produces rhythm, but not by reproducing an identical measure and not in isolation from other milieus. Its regular meter is a vital pulse, not a reproduction of the same, whose regularity and variability are inseparable from the inter-milieu rhythms of difference.

Hence, Deleuze and Guattari assert that

> a milieu does indeed exist by virtue of periodic repetition, but such repetition only has the effect of producing a difference through which the milieu passes into another milieu. It is difference that is rhythmic, and not repetition, which, however, produces it; but that productive repetition has nothing to do with a reproductive measure.

We know that a rhythm is slow or lively only in relation to other rhythms, but each rhythm in Borboletta's structure has its own and specific measure: speed, frequency, consistency.

Our sensations and perceptions, in full and continuous appearances, contain repetitive figures, concealing them. We contain ourselves by concealing the diversity of our rhythms: to ourselves, body and flesh, we are almost objects of periodicity.

According to Deleuze, a succession of instants does not constitute time any more than it causes it to disappear; it indicates only its constantly aborted moment of birth. Time is constituted only in the originary synthesis that operates on the repetition of instants and concerns a living present in which past and future do not designate separate instants but rather dimensions of a present that are involved in contraction.

Borboletta's architecture of pulsation celebrates duration, enhances our awareness in terms of time-passage indexed in the form; for Bergson, duration is the continuous progress of the past that gnaws into the future and swells as it advances. Duration involves a process of repetition and difference, it is irreversible since consciousness cannot go through the same state twice; we cannot live over and over a single moment. The notion of duration is embedded in rhythmic, throbbing, vibrating strategies for the articulation of membranes that extend the tectonic qualities to the spatial experience, a multitude of synchronized components that radiate micro-alliances between parts, distributing ornamental patterns that give character and atmosphere to the architecture.

Poetic Systems—the Art of Transformation

Stefan Mittlböck-Jungwirth-Fohringer

Based on the idea that we humans live in a world of systems, in which we humans already represent a system and live in symbiosis with many natural and artificial systems, poetic systems try to make systems visible that elude our human perception.

Systems in which we live. Systems that we are. Systems we have created for ourselves. The question arises what exactly systems are and what then, beyond that, poetic systems are. We assume here that everything can be a system, but always with a "human-centralistic" view—for the reason that it is about the human consideration, about the human perception. It is about the consideration, which we humans bring up towards a work of art or a certain circumstance and about the reflection process connected with it—intentionally or unintentionally. This "human-centralist" view does not mean that we humans cannot take the perspective of systems to be understood—on the contrary, poetic systems should help us to do exactly that.

Poetic systems do not distinguish between cognitive or technical, artificial systems—they try to act as a whole. Especially artificial and technical systems which are operated without human intervention, without being operated by humans, for example, a car or a house, may not be a system at first sight. However, assuming that a car or a house represents different values, which in turn have an influence on us humans—produces data, represents added value, is subject to the process of transience, can be observed and thus be recognized and is part of, let's say, a social value system, which remains below the human threshold of perception, in the context of poetic systems also those kinds of systems are included.

But what are poetic systems? Poetry in this case describes an artistic approach, the goal and the desire to visualize, to describe, and to make "something" experienceable. This means that poetic systems are systems that visualize "states" for us humans with the means of art, in order to make them perceptible for us. Art touches us humans in an emotional way and thus enables us to gain knowledge.

How can a communication, a sensual communication arise between us and the systems surrounding us? It seems desirable to create a system that communicates itself to us not only purely via the cognitive level, but also not only purely via the sensory level, but one that requires us humans to use both levels—sense and intellect. This striving results from the necessity to look at the world as a whole, at the systems surrounding us, in order to understand them with all senses. Niklas Luhmann writes in Art of Society, "We are still under the spell of a tradition that had arranged the construction of mental faculties hierarchically, assigning a lower position to 'sensuality,' which means perception, in comparison to the higher, reflective functions of understanding and reason."[1] This description illustrates a tradition we come from—it illustrates that we have neglected and disregarded parts of our mental faculties. But in order to understand our world and its increasingly complex systems, we need to rediscover all the capabilities at our disposal and especially perception.

Art can be helpful in this; it not only speaks to us visually or cognitively—it touches us on an emotional level. But what if we humans lack the necessary sensorium to perceive the systems we create and live with? Why do we need to perceive these systems? In consideration of the constantly growing artificial and technical systems of the technosphere surrounding us, it seems to be inevitable to deal with them in order to learn the ability, the necessity of collaboration with these systems in order not to fail. So it demands for systems—for poetic systems, which enable us to make these systems, which are inaccessible to us, exploratively accessible—they represent the recurring attempt to create again and again new ways of perception, in order to be able to gain knowledge.

Poetic systems transform processes and states with the instruments of art, in order to be able to be perceived by us humans. In this way, they open up new strategies and ways of thinking, which enable us to gain epistemic access. A transformation of the systems is inevitable for this process of perception. This transformation from one state to another requires a process of deconstruction. Deconstruction, in the searching, in the exploratory sense, means to disassemble in order to understand one's inner self. Transformation also implies the process of construction. Construction in the sense of creating, of the creative act. Creation in all its conceivable and feasible forms. Transformation is an essential component of poetic systems. These must therefore have the ability to grasp systems in a form that is not possible for us humans and at the other end of this transformation process find a form of representation that we humans can read again—are able to perceive. Perceiving also means recognizing—for Luhmann, recognizing means observing—that is, distinguishing and designating.[2] We thus create a poetic system that observes, distinguishes, and designates.

It transforms what we recognize into a form of expression that we choose.

The search for the poetic moment within the variety of systems that surround us humans holds the possibility of unique ways of looking at things, which have great creative potential, which allows artistic works to emerge in the context of art, technology, and society.

For the Ars Electronica Futurelab, establishing these poetic systems is a possibility for artistic expression that is reflected in the context of art and architecture, art in public space, and represents a design basis for artistic projects in this field.

The following three projects "Quell.Code," "ZeitRaum," and "insight | out" describe in practical application the approaches outlined previously.

SAP, as an enterprise that configures and provides an organizational setting for abstract business processes, is Source.Code's point of departure. Business processes that actually take place within the company's corporate structure are transformed into visualizations that populate the headquarters complex itself in the form of abstract creatures that react to visitors—for instance, timidly, politely encouraging, or even somewhat miffed. Thus, a visit to SAP Germany's new premises means an encounter with the actual residents of the business world: its processes.

It is an example of a poetic system that allows us to explore abstract digital processes within the system of a global company.

Watercourses form axes. They connect and mediate, they move and direct. And they do so in the new headquarters of SAP Germany too. Here, state-of-the-art technology and one of human culture's oldest navigational aids merge to form Source.Code (Quell.Code), a network of interactive signage pointing the way to the Visitors Center.

■ Stefan Mittlböck-Jungwirth-Fohringer

FIGURE 2.7.1
"Source.Code," Ars Electronica Futurelab, 2007.

From its spring near the parking lot, the water makes its way to a 27-meter-tall steel Stele that functions as both a landmark and an interactive architectural element. Physical contact makes its inner workings pulse with light to the rhythm of the respective visitor's heartbeat. From here, the watercourse flows toward the main entrance. Upon arrival, it morphs into a virtual current of data fed by the global processes of SAP software.

Every bit of system input and each line of recorded information is visualized as a "process-creature" swimming in a flow of data in which these virtual inhabitants interact with guests. The movement of the flow is taken up by the mechanically driven Data Wheel. The motive force for its rotation is provided by the "sum of all staff activities" in the SAP system.

The stream of data flows on, following the elevator car on its upward path with countless process-creatures along for the ride. Each of these swarms is formed on the basis of the attributes of the particular process that triggered it; the identity of the overall business process to which it belongs is revealed as a form of greeting in the headquarters' fourth upper level. This is the destination: the new Visitors Center.

The Aquarium provides access to the substantive contents that are assigned to each respective creature; those going over the Data Fall—depicted as symbolic torrent of 1s and 0s—pass through a display. Being "touched" by visitors bursts the links of these character chains, and they fall individually like raindrops back to the original source.

As a work of media art, this guidance system is meant as a statement that sets up a dialog between nature and culture—that is, human beings and architecture—and simultaneously opens up a lively, individualized way of looking at SAP's business and information processes.

ZeitRaum ("TimeSpace") is an interactive art installation the Ars Electronica Futurelab designed for the new terminal at Vienna International Airport. It creates real-time

Poetic Systems—the Art of Transformation

FIGURE 2.7.2
"ZeitRaum," Ars Electronica Futurelab, 2012.

interpretations of arriving and departing flights. ZeitRaum consists of a series of stations that accompany departing passengers on their way to their gates. The airport authority will also be using the installation for half of the available time as an ad medium.

At the core of this work is an imaginary space, one at the interface of all the world's airports. Passengers enter it when they pass through a security checkpoint prior to takeoff and leave it after touching down at their final destination. This space's boundaries are constantly shifting in accordance with current air traffic. Within its confines, cultures, languages, and nations segue into one another like adjacent time zones. This space hosts more than 5 billion people a year, men and women who are total strangers and yet feel that they're temporarily interconnected as fellow members of a transient community. This space has had no name until now. The Ars Electronica Futurelab calls it ZeitRaum.

insight | out, a work of media art by the Ars Electronica Futurelab, is a poetic system which portrays the Oberbank AG Linz rendered on a fragmented frieze made up of eight video screens. The medium itself thus evokes the multiplicity of influences that flow into this portrait—the values that this long-established financial institution represents, the names of the European regions in which Oberbank is present, customers and staff members going about their business in the facility, and finally, environmental phenomena such as the sun's position and the wind's strength.

Visually, the image is characterized by particles, the movements and flows of which engender a linear aesthetic akin to a pen-and-ink drawing or a brushstroke, with the lines' thickness varying over time. The particles have divergent mutual affinities—keeping their distance and seeking proximity. They obey the law of the swarm, attraction and repulsion, depending upon their distance from one another and the factors that influence them.

FIGURE 2.7.3 "insight | out," Ars Electronica Futurelab, 2017.

The red particles are attracted by visitors and/or by writing. Individuals interacting with each other are registered by a tracking system and "drawn" by the particles. The letters in the lines of writing that appear are "filled" by the red particles and thereby made visible. A few "lead particles" see to it that all of the particles are evenly distributed; the other particles follow them to their respectively assigned areas of the space to be drawn.

The particles have been conceived as an emergent element in the sense of "The whole is greater than the sum of its parts." They constitute a metaphor for the interplay of diverse factors and influences, such as the people (users), monetary flows and transactions that characterize a bank.

The magnitudes derived from the building's central control system, such as the position of the sun and brightness, minimally change the image's coloring over the course of the day—in the morning, bluish; in the evening, reddish. The wind strength measured imparts short-duration impulses that "blow" the particles in the corresponding direction. This is a metaphor for being situated in and acting in the midst of a local culture at a specific location.

People in the lobby are registered by the system and positioned in the space depicted in the installation, where customers and staff members can visually experience their influence on the particles and the system as a whole. The visualization swarms about the interacting individuals—a person appears to be both a driving force of and a source of resistance to the current in the ongoing flow of the "aesthetic of capital."[3]

NOTES

1 Luhmann, N. (1995). *Die Kunst der Gesellschaft*. Wiesbaden: Springer VS, p. S13.
2 Wikipedia. (2021). *Operativer Konstruktivismus*, aufgerufen November 28. https://de.wikipedia.org/wiki/Operativer Konstruktivismus
3 Kriesche, R. (2017). "die kunst, die freiheit und ihr wert," FIN/2 Liquid Music, Herausgeber Heimo Ranzenbacher.

Energy Flow Across Enclosures

Joseph Lstiburek

Buildings don't work the way they used to.[1] Folks are always saying stuff like this. But let me make the case regarding just one factor and you decide. There are other factors of course, but I want to focus on only one for the moment. This one overarching factor is the amount of energy exchange across the building enclosure.

I think that higher levels of thermal resistance and reduced heat gain across building enclosures has forever changed the performance of buildings—and not necessarily in a good way. And things are going to get worse before they get better. Sound familiar?

The lens I am going to use to look at this factor is moisture. Why? It is one of the principal damage functions acting on materials along with heat and ultraviolet radiation.[2] I think moisture is the key to understanding the performance of buildings in general—and in this particular case—in specific.

The consequence of this reduced energy exchange is beginning to be seen all over the place: mold, part load humidity problems, rot, and corrosion. Highly insulated building enclosures with reduced heat gain have low drying potentials and increased interior moisture loads. When they get wet, they don't dry. Stuff is beginning to stink, rot, break, and annoy.

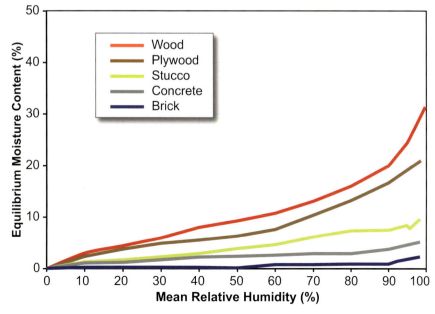

FIGURE 2.8.1 Sorption curve for common building materials. Note that moisture content goes up as relative humidity goes up. There is no temperature dependence or vapor pressure dependence except where temperature affects relative humidity or where vapor pressure affects relative humidity.

■ Joseph Lstiburek

There are two things to look at here. Levels of insulation and airtight assemblies and heat gain through glazing, roof assemblies and interior loads. Adding insulation and providing airtight assemblies reduces energy flow. That is a good thing, right? Well, no—not always. Less energy flows from the inside to the outside the colder things on the outside of the building get in the winter. The colder these things, the wetter these things get, and the wetter they stay. This is not good. Less energy flow from the outside to the inside in the summer and the less heat that is generated inside in the summer, the less the air-conditioning system runs. This is a good thing, right? Well, no—not always. We create something called "the part load humidity problem."

HIGHER LEVELS OF THERMAL RESISTANCE

How do we dry wet wood? We kiln dry it. We heat the wood so that the water in the wood is warmer than its surroundings. We add energy to the water, and it evaporates. There is a huge exchange of energy. When we put warm wet coffee beans in a room with very cold surfaces, we call it freeze-drying. The moisture leaves the coffee beans and accumulates on the cold surfaces. There is a huge exchange of energy. The greater the rate of energy exchange, the greater the rate of moisture movement. Drying cannot happen without an exchange of energy.

When my mom and dad bought their first house in Toronto, Canada, in 1957, there was no insulation in the walls, and the house was leaky to air—it had a high air change driven by a traditional chimney. We lived in a 1,200 square foot house, and in January, when the outside temperature dropped to 0 degrees F, Momma cranked up the 300,000 Btu oil furnace to maintain an interior temperature of 70 degrees F. The energy flow across the

FIGURE 2.8.2
The "Typical House": Built in 1965 in Cleveland, Ohio, with no cavity insulation in the exterior wood frame walls. No problems for 20 years. Insulation added to exterior walls in 1985, and within one year the paint begins to fail.

154

building enclosure was enormous, but oil was cheap, and we were comfortable and happy. The energy flow was so enormous the building enclosure was simultaneously kiln dried and freeze-dried. In fact, the drying potential was so high we were uncomfortably dry. As a result, Poppa insisted that the furnace have a newfangled gadget attached to it—called a humidifier. How things have changed.

Well, what changed? We've begun to insulate—and insulate exceptionally well—and we're getting the assemblies "tighter" to air change and convection. That results in two things—less energy exchange, therefore less drying potential—and things on the exterior side of the enclosure are colder in the winter. Things being colder on the outside lead to something most folks don't consider. Many building materials are hygroscopic (Figure 2.8.1). This means they absorb moisture based on relative humidity. Even more strangely, they don't care about vapor pressure except if it affects relative humidity. This is a big deal. In fact, it is a huge deal.

Quick, snap quiz, psychrometric chart stuff . . . as the temperature drops, and vapor pressure is kept constant, what happens to the relative humidity? Buzz/Clang/Bell. Yes, folks, you are correct, the relative humidity goes up. The implications are staggering. Just making things on the outside of your building cold, hygroscopic things, makes them wetter. Period, end of story. But, but, the moisture content of the outside air in the wintertime is low. Yes, grasshopper, it is, but its relative humidity is high. The amount of moisture in the absolute sense is low, but in the relative sense, it is high. And hygroscopic materials don't care about the absolute sense; they only care about the relative sense. Why? Second law stuff—isn't it always?

Check out Figure 2.8.2. Nice, normal, everyday type of house in Cleveland, Ohio. Twenty years old, no insulation in the wall cavities, built in 1965 (yes, the photograph was taken in 1985—we did have cameras back then). The house was perfectly happy at this point

FIGURE 2.8.3
Retrofit cellulose cavity insulation: Dry blown cellulose packed into exterior wood frame walls. Injected from the exterior at top of cavity. This author, very young at the time, amazed at how well the insulation worked. Cavities were dry when opened.

for 20 years. Then the homeowner decides to do something crazy. He decides to insulate the exterior walls to save energy and has the cavities blown with dry cellulose. What a dumb idea in 1985, eh? But nevertheless, it was a beautiful job, no voids. Yes, it can be done, and yes, it was done. No voids, no convection (Figure 2.8.3—notice how young this engineer once was). Next thing you know, the paint falls off, and the siding gets smelly, moldy, and begins to decay (Figure 2.8.4). Huh? The insulation did this? Yup. The drying potential is reduced due to the addition of the insulation so that the moisture entering the cladding assembly from the exterior due to rain and capillarity does not evaporate, and this is further exacerbated by the colder siding having a higher local relative humidity and thus a higher equilibrium moisture content due to the sorption properties of wood. Bummer. How to fix this? Easy, wedges were used to create a gap at the overlaps of the siding, reducing capillary uptake at the laps and increasing evaporation despite the cladding being colder (Figure 2.8.5). This early lesson in sorption and drying potentials taught this engineer to drain and back-ventilate claddings—especially those on highly insulated assemblies (Figure 2.8.6).

Let's extend this discussion to cavity insulation in general. The same thing happens to the cavity side of sheathing when we insulate cavities. It gets worse when the cavities also have no airflow or convection.[3] Sheathings get colder. If the sheathing is hygroscopic, its equilibrium moisture content also goes up. Why take the risk? Insulate on the exterior of the sheathing. This makes the problem go away. The risk is so high in cold climates that folks are no longer insulating the cavities in steel stud walls in places like Ottawa and Montreal—all of the insulation goes on the outside.

This is why insulating sheathing is pretty much the name of the game for highly insulated wall assemblies—or at a minimum, claddings should be back ventilated and back-drained—or better, do both. This is easy for new construction. The problem is what to do with the

FIGURE 2.8.4
Wet Cladding: Problems with mold and decay were worse on north and east elevations. Problems with peeling paint were worse on west and south elevations. Solar radiation cycled the cladding moisture content more on the west and south elevations stressing the paint. UV cross-linked the paint, making it less flexible. Less flexibility, more movement on the south, and the west led to the peeling paint. Less energy on the north and the east led to the mold and the decay.

Energy Flow Across Enclosures

FIGURE 2.8.5
Wedgie: So simple and so obvious. After the problem is understood. Wedges created gaps that reduced capillary uptake of surface water, promoted drainage and back ventilation.

existing building stock. What are we going to do if oil ever goes above $100/barrel? Dumb comment. Yes, but now we have a real problem. Folks cannot just go and blow/spray/fill cavities with a bunch of insulation without appreciating the consequences. This is not just a cold climate problem. It is a problem everywhere. In fact, it gets worse when we go far south. Read on, McDuff.

REDUCED HEAT GAIN

I am going to let you in on a little secret that us mechanical engineers don't often share with the rest of the world: air-conditioning systems only dehumidify when they run. Yup, when they don't run, they don't dehumidify. If there is no load, there is no dehumidification.[4]

Well, just make them run longer. How? They still make the air cold no matter how you run them. That is good if you need cold air. But what if you don't need cold air? What if you only need dry air? Well, you still have to make the air cold to get it to drop its water, and when you are done, you still have cold air. So now what? Well, you have to heat it back up if you want to use it. This is sometimes called cooling with reheat. There are other tricks we can do—read on—but at the end of the day, we have to add energy back to the air that we cooled. There is no other practical way to do it.

It gets worse when we over-ventilate with humid air—especially when it is cloudy and not so hot. Now all you are doing is bringing in moisture. But you are doing it when there is not much of a load—not much of a "sensible load" (heat gain across the enclosure and heat gain from lights and appliances and people—the load you can "sense") to run the

■ Joseph Lstiburek

air-conditioning system. This moisture that you are bringing in with the ventilation air is also a "load"—but it is a different kind of load that we have pretty much been ignoring up till now and getting away with it. The operative phrase to note is: "getting away with it." Mechanical engineers like me call this the "hidden load" or the "latent load" (as in "latent defect" or "hidden defect"), and our heads explode when we try to explain this problem to the indoor air crazies who think that only dilution is the solution to indoor pollution. I mean, how can too much outside air be bad?[5] Arrargah.

To take the water out of the air you need to use energy. To make the air comfortable/useful, the air can't be too cold after you have taken the water out of it. Typically heat (energy) has to be added back to the air. Traditionally this heat (energy) was available through lousy glazing systems, too much glass, black roofs with no insulation, poorly insulated walls, energy inefficient lights, and crappy appliances. Well, this traditional "re-heat" due to inefficiency and poor practice is disappearing. Now we are stuck. If we don't warm up the air after we dry it, we are going to get into trouble. We haven't been, and we are getting into trouble. The buildings are now getting too cold or too humid or worse, both.

Ah, this is easy, you say. Just make the air-conditioning systems smaller—"right size" them. Don't make me scream. I am getting tired of being told by energy weenies that my equipment is too big.[6] I still have to satisfy the "full load" requirement. If you make the equipment too small, it doesn't satisfy the cooling requirements under full load. Let the people be uncomfortable, you say. People should suffer, you say; we have had it too good,

FIGURE 2.8.6
Drainage and ventilation matt behind cladding. This is easy for new construction and recladding. Existing buildings are going to be a problem. Don't say you weren't warned.

you say. Yeah, sure, another greenie weenie value judgment that also makes me scream. I don't think we should suffer. I like it being good. I don't have a problem with using energy. I have a problem with wasting energy. Until now we have gotten pretty good at dealing with this part-load problem with face-bypass, run-around coils, hot gas bypass, and heat pipes, but we have reached our limits.

Building enclosures have gotten so good, glazing systems so good, interior load management so good, that we can't use the same equipment to handle the "sensible load" and the "latent load." Did I mention just how good the glazing systems have become? Did I mention the low SHGC thing? We used to just install air conditioners and only cared about making it cold inside. We used one piece of equipment to handle the sensible and latent load. The reason this worked is that the latent load was small compared to the sensible load. Not anymore. The sensible load has gotten smaller big time. And much to my chagrin, the latent load has gone up due to over-ventilation. The old systems can't handle the new sensible-to-latent ratios. We have to separate the two loads.

We need separate systems for the sensible load and the latent load. This is a big deal, and it results from the low heat gain in the modern enclosure. In other words, energy conservation and good construction practice is biting us on the butt. We sometimes refer to this second separate latent load control system as supplemental dehumidification—and we need it when we have a low heat gain enclosure and efficient lighting and appliances. Others call it "preconditioning" of outside air since the largest component of the latent load is the ventilation air or the outside air. Whatever you call it, we need this second system. We don't often get it, and it hurts us.

But, but these systems use energy. Yes, as the saying goes—there is no thermodynamic-free lunch. You need to use energy to make air cold, and you need to use energy to make air dry. We have been very good at making air cold. We now have to get good at making air dry. Think of it this way. For every 100 units of energy you save on the efficiency and on the cooling side, you are going to have to give back about 20 units of energy to be dry. You are still 80 units ahead. Problem is, if you are greedy and want the entire 100 units, your building fails, and your occupants get very uncomfortable and probably very annoyed.

It is pretty amazing to me, but the hotel industry figured this out first. They pretty much had the problem first, so it stands to reason that they would also figure it out first. Think about the typical hotel room. The drapes are pretty much closed all the time, the room is empty during the day, and you know the unit has been sized for the full load, with the drapes open, and the room full, and everything on, and you know that someone in some bureaucracy somewhere wants way too much outside air. Most of the time your latent load dwarfs your sensible load. So what do you do? You reduce the amount of outside air by installing timers on the exhaust fans, and you pretty much ignore the faceless bureaucrat. Then you only run the through-wall unit to control the temperature (i.e., make it the "sensible" system) and install a dehumidifier in each unit to control the humidity (the "latent" system) (Figure 2.8.6). A pretty primitive but effective "fix." In new design, we just "hide" the dehumidifier better—or better still, make it part of the ventilation system.

Guess where this technology is now making an impact—condos and apartments. Small houses are next. We are already separating the latent from the sensible on most commercial design—after all, it is the sensible thing to do.

■ Joseph Lstiburek

FIGURE 2.8.7
Hotel room fix: The through-wall unit controls the temperature (the "sensible" system). The dehumidifier controls the humidity (the "latent" system).

NORTH VERSUS SOUTH

So how come it is worse in the south than the north? In the north, it still gets cold, and the outside cold air is pretty dry—and walls tend to dry to the outside in the north—so the size of the moisture drying "sink," so to speak, has not changed. But in the south, walls also dry to the inside, and if the inside is humid because of the part load problem, the walls stay wetter because the moisture drying "sink" is smaller. Additionally, in the south the moisture drive from the exterior into the wall is greater, while at the same time the moisture drive from the wall into the interior is smaller as compared to the corresponding drives in opposite directions in the north. Let me translate. It is easier to get wet from the outside in the south than it is from the inside in the north. It is also easier to dry to the outside in the north than it is to dry to the inside in the south. With less energy available, it gets worse in the south faster than in the north.

Good air-conditioning design leads to dry interiors, and dry interiors allow walls to dry to the inside. Part load humidity problems lead to wetter walls. Higher levels of thermal insulation and lower heat gain lead to part load humidity problems. Not good.

160

NOW WHAT?

Okay, everybody relax. We want and we need much higher levels of thermal control (airtight, insulated assemblies) everywhere. We just have to be smart about it. We want and we need ultra-efficient glazing, lights, appliances, and reflective surfaces everywhere. We just have to be smart about it. And we want and we need the right amount of outside air whenever we need it. We just have to be smart about it. This is neither expensive nor difficult, just different. We have to modify our building enclosure and mechanical system paradigms. Get used to it or be steamrolled by the change.

Insulate on the outside. Back ventilate and drain your cladding. Separate your sensible load from you latent load. Don't over ventilate. Existing buildings are going to be a bear. And have a nice day.

NOTES

1 Yes, I know, pretty arrogant for a relative youngster to say. I am in my fifties, but when you get to this age, you spend as much time looking back as you do looking forward. My mentors tell me that it helps with perspective. It has been said that in order to understand the future, you have to understand the past. I am not so ambitious. I am only thinking of today. I think in order to understand the present, you have to understand the past.

2 Someone once said that 80 percent of all building-related durability problems are due to three principal damage functions (water, heat, and UV radiation) with 80 percent of the 80 percent being water. I don't know who said this. Can someone help me out? I might have just made it up, but I have been saying it so long I no longer remember if I did or not. Aren't footnotes great.

3 Air flow—air change and convection—increases energy exchange, therefore increases drying potential. My Canadian friends' heads are now going to explode because they have been taught that air leakage leads to "wetting" from interior sources. Yes, in extreme climates with high interior moisture loads. Think humidified buildings in Canada. Not everywhere else. Come visit the United States, the dollar exchange now works for you, and air leakage improves drying potentials.

4 Sensible load. I know you knew that I knew this, but some of the emails I have been getting from you folks have been quite picky, which is good, but I want to head off the obvious emails, so continue to be picky, but not on this.

5 Some folks don't seem to care about the energy thing either. I mean health is paramount, and we should always err on the side of caution. How can we argue against health? Easy, when the "healthy" measures are "unhealthy." Over-ventilation can be unhealthy—and energy wasteful. Read on. This is leading to interesting discussions in the Standard 62 committees. Apparently, the Standard 62 committees are not about energy. Apparently, energy security is not a 62 problem, nor is climate change, nor are operating costs. Apparently, it is some other committee's problem. How about the energy committee (Standard 90.1)? Except that the energy committee does not want to touch ventilation. Cowards. My insider's perspective (on 62.2 at least) is that there is a lot of mileage to be made by scaring people about under-ventilation, and folks are rising to the occasion. Unfortunately, over-ventilation in hot, humid climates and in mixed humid climates has led to more indoor air problems due to mold resulting from part load issues than under-ventilation anywhere else—in my not-so-humble opinion. And speaking of health and under-ventilation, where are all the dead bodies? Where is the causal link between health and specific levels of specific indoor contaminants? In my not-so-humble opinion, all of the rates have been just wild assed guesses without a sound epidemiological basis. But the resulting mold from over-ventilation is real and demonstrable. Just to make it clear, I have been guessing

at "rates" as well, but I have not been afraid to call them "guesses" or tried to hide the guesses behind a lot of bad science. And one more thing, this LEED stuff is making me crazy, the part where you get extra points when you ventilate at an even higher rate than what Standard 62 calls for. What a bunch of green sustainability hypocrisy. Doesn't anyone at the US Green Building Council know anything about energy and part load humidity?

6 Don't go there. Just don't go there.

3
CONCLUSION

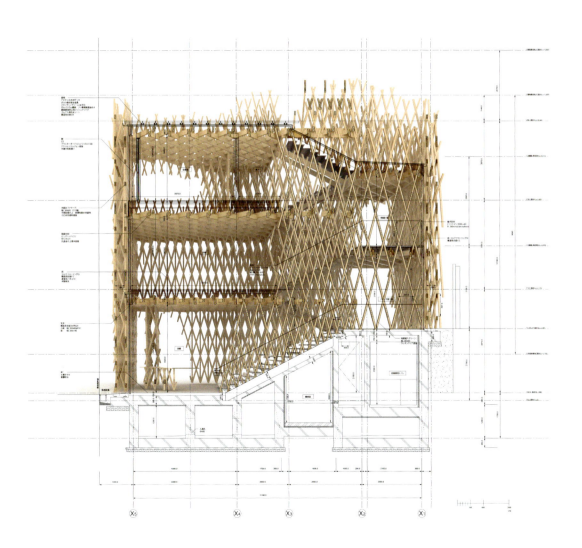

Digital Fabrication by Kengo Kuma

Professor Kengo Kuma

My search for a method that would replace concrete as a building material resulted in my finding digital fabrication. The fact that concrete is such a huge competitor made it possible for me to realize the potential of digital fabrication.

The twentieth century can be summarized as being the "Age of Concrete." The material known as concrete dominated the twentieth century because it can be easily obtained anywhere in the world, an adequate level of strength can be easily secured, and it easily enables interior and exterior spaces to be separated. The twentieth century is called the century of concrete and steel, but while steel is suited to the construction of high-rise buildings in large cities, it is not a material that has a low level of fabrication difficulty that can be easily used anywhere in the world, which is the reason it has not attained a high level of universality.

In addition, steel does not have the same level of performance as concrete in separating interior and exterior spaces. A system which completely isolates interior space from the outside and manages the environment in the interior space with air-conditioning is a basic OS of the twentieth century during an age of cheap oil. When constructing a building with steel, an additional year is required to isolate the inside from the outside. When concrete is used, that additional year is not needed, with the inside and the outside being isolated by simply pouring the concrete.

Clearly separating interior and exterior spaces and selling the spaces that are created was another basic OS that was very compatible with the twentieth century. The economy of the twentieth century was supported by this construction isolation system. Ambiguous space such as eaves, which is neither interior space nor exterior space, is not very compatible with this isolation system. Thick concrete walls have the power to create an illusion of secure ownership of space, and concrete was very compatible with the twentieth century from this perspective.

Thus, concrete was a basic OS to facilitate smooth operation in the twentieth century. It was not really a basic material, but it became the basic OS for operation of the economy during that age.

I began my search to find a new OS to replace the OS that has been used up until now. The first thing that I focused on was traditional wooden architecture in Japan. Before concrete came to Japan in the twentieth century, architecture and cities in Japan were operated with an OS that consisted of frame structures made using wood. This system resembles the steel frame structure, which was the basic OS for high-rise buildings in the twentieth century, but it is much more open than steel and is a system with a high level of universality. First, wood is much lighter than steel, allowing materials to be carried around by people without using heavy machinery. That is to say, there were carpenters who built houses everywhere, no matter how small the city or town. Compared to steel, which can only be handled by

■ Professor Kengo Kuma

FIGURE 3.1.1
Milano Salone 2007 Cidori-Castelo Sforzesco.

Digital Fabrication by Kengo Kuma

FIGURE 3.1.2
Milano Salone 2007 Cidori-Castelo Sforzesco illuminated at night.

specialized steel companies and construction companies, wooden structures in Japan consist of a much more democratic OS.

Furthermore, the interesting thing about wooden structures in Japan is the fact that they were included in the forests, which produce the trees. Wood represents a portion of a link in a local circulatory system. While iron ore is contained in mines that produce it, wood is the most familiar material and is available anywhere in Japan. The proportion of land in Japan which is forested is 70 percent, which is an exceptionally high percentage as a developed country. Carpenters in villages all over Japan were able to use lumber produced by thinning forests to easily build wooden structures.

In addition to being easily available, wood is the lightest material compared to other construction materials such as brick or stone, and the energy required to transport wood and CO_2 emissions are the smallest. Wooden structures in Japan were the most democratic in the world, as well as the most sustainable building system.

Furthermore, a modular system has been popularized for wooden structures in Japan that consists of units measuring approximately 900mm, and in addition to the wooden frames being modular, exhaustive efforts were also devoted to making the modularization of the secondary materials that are used to fill the space between the frame members (e.g., tatami mats placed on the floor), and there was a custom of people bringing the tatami mats with them when they moved. This represented a more advanced modular system than the modular system proposed by Le Corbusier. It was already the de facto system in Japanese society.

This wooden structure system in Japan provided me with a big hint while I was looking for a new building OS to replace concrete. However, I felt that the 100mm square sectional size of traditional Japanese wooden structures based on fixed 900mm modules was too cramped to accommodate the very quick paced and complicated conditions in modern cities.

FIGURE 3.1.3
Milano Salone 2007 Cidori-Castelo Sforzesco up close at night.

Digital Fabrication by Kengo Kuma

FIGURE 3.1.4
Milano Salone 2007
Cidori-Castelo Sforzesco
details.

A pavilion called Chidori (2007, Milan) that was built based on a hint from the joints used in wooden structures in Japan called Chidori represented the first catalyst to overcoming the cramped quality of wooden structures. Over the years, carpenters in Japan have honed their skill at joining wood members to each other without using nails, screws, or adhesive by innovating the shapes of joints. There is a high possibility that joints that are made with metal will deteriorate due to rust with time, but the creation of joints that do not use metal enabled the building of sustainable wooden structures. The biggest difference between traditional Chidori and the Chidori that I designed consists of the dimension of the pieces of wood that are the unit.

Normally, Chidori joints often consist of a system in which wooden members measuring about 600mm square are assembled. On the other hand, my Chidori system uses an extremely small unit of 30mm square section pieces. The use of this small unit enables the same 30mm square section unit members to be used to build the furniture and other items that fill the space, in addition to the structure itself. Furthermore, since no nails or screws are used, the structure and other items can be easily disassembled and reused. Thus, only these small units can be used to configure space in a world which is very complicated and fluid.

I realized while I was designing this system that it was not possible to study the potential of this system without the help of computers. First, there are infinite options for the sectional size, and there are also infinite possibilities for the span between different joints. Therefore, examination and analysis by computer were indispensable in order to determine the optimum solution for the structure, design, and economy out of the infinite number of

■ Professor Kengo Kuma

FIGURE 3.1.5
Sunnyhills sketches.[1]

FIGURE 3.1.6
Sunnyhills elevation.

sectional size options and span options. Professor Jun Sato, who is a structural engineer, will be performing on time analysis of the options that we have proposed.

Computers were also utilized with this system when doing the wood working to make the joints that have complicated shapes.

In recent years in Japan, computer-controlled machines are generally used to cut wood for traditional wooden houses, which is called precut wood. Many houses in Japan continue to be built with traditional wooden house technology, and computational precut technology has progressed due to the chronic shortage of craftsmen. It can be said that I was able to create my Chidori system because of this technological background.

FIGURE 3.1.7
Sunnyhills entrance.

■ Professor Kengo Kuma

I started to take on the challenge of creating space, which has a higher level of freedom and fluidity using the same small units as the next step after my Chidori system. The use of computers has opened up a way to transcend traditional wooden construction, which is dominated by right angles and modularized dimensions. The flow that consisted of the CG Prostho Museum (2010), Dazaifu Starbucks (2012), and Sunny Hills Japan (2013) was a flow in a process to achieve freedom, but it also was a flow in order to integrate architecture, furniture, and various small articles during my challenge to expand the scale of the "totality," which is comprised of these units. This also consisted of a challenge of breaking down the twentieth-century norm that large and strong architecture can only be built with concrete.

FIGURE 3.1.8
Sunnyhills side.

Digital Fabrication by Kengo Kuma

This challenge transcended the limitations of wood before long. The Water Branch House at the Home Delivery Exhibition which was held at MOMA in New York had the most provocative character. I selected polyethylene containers used to hold water as the unit for the Water Branch House.

Polyethylene containers are lighter than lumber and are more democratic than lumber from that perspective. The weight of polyethylene containers can be adjusted by changing the amount of water they are filled with. This overturns the major premise in architecture that one material has only one physical property. Structural stability can be achieved by making the lower units heavier and the upper units lighter. Computers need to be relied upon for the weight distribution. Water can be channeled between the polyethylene containers by joining them together.

Architecture that is built with polyethylene containers and the overall environment can be controlled by controlling the temperature of the water that flows through them. Highly efficient environmental control of a higher level than floor heating can be achieved since the polyethylene containers are used for the floors, walls, and ceiling. Furthermore, these polyethylene containers can be combined to make beds, chairs, bathtubs and kitchens. The polyethylene containers are like stem cells in an organism, and the stem cells can create all types of organs by means of reproduction and differentiation. According to classic biology, an

FIGURE 3.1.9
Sunnyhills at night.

■ Professor Kengo Kuma

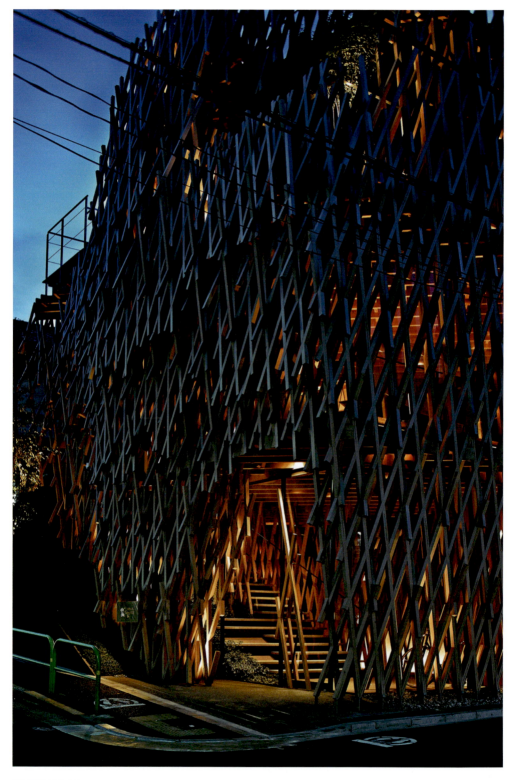

FIGURE 3.1.10
Sunnyhills entrance at night.

Digital Fabrication by Kengo Kuma

organism was an aggregation of organs, but in modern biology, life is defined as an aggregation of cells. In the same manner, the Water Branch House is an aggregation of cells, and fluid continually flows inside the cells and in the gaps between them.

A computer must be relied upon to control this overall flow. Concrete architecture was divided vertically. That is to say, the structure, facilities, and interior were all separated, and they were designed and managed by different people. Therefore, concrete architecture

FIGURE 3.1.11
Sunnyhills interior stair.

FIGURE 3.1.12
Sunnyhills interior space.

175

■ Professor Kengo Kuma

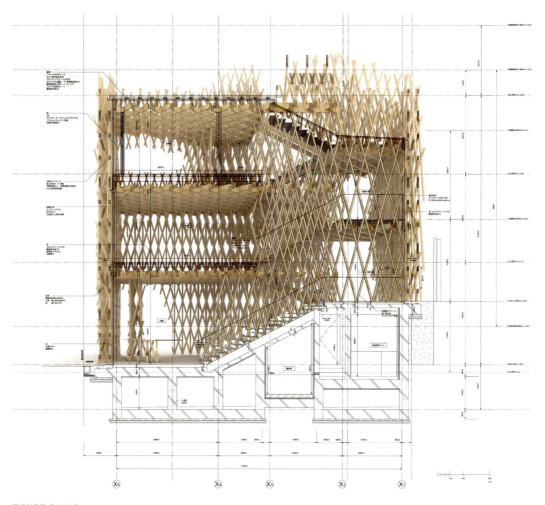

FIGURE 3.1.13
Kengo Kuma Sunnyhills section drawing.

was dead architecture. Since nothing can be done with concrete once it has hardened, it is extremely difficult to update a concrete building after it has been completed. However, there is no vertical divide in architecture that is configured as an aggregation of small cells, so there is no death. Division of the structure, facilities, exterior, and interior is eliminated, and architecture continues to be updated and change. One might say that this gives life to architecture. Consequently, digital fabrication consists of a transformation from architecture being something that is dead into a living organism, rather than a revolution in fabrication.

NOTE

1 This shop, specialized in selling pineapple cake (popular sweet in Taiwan), is in the shape of a bamboo basket. It is built on a joint system called "Jiigoku-Gumi," traditional method used in Japanese wooden architecture (often observed in *Shoji*: vertical and cross pieces in the same width are entwined in each other to form a muntin grid). Normally the two

pieces intersect in two dimensions, but here they are combined in 30 degrees in 3 dimensions (or in cubic), which came into a structure like a cloud. With this idea, the section size of each wood piece was reduced to as thin as 60mm × 60mm.

As the building is located in the middle of the residential area in Aoyama, we wanted to give some soft and subtle atmosphere to it, which is completely different from a concrete box. We expect that the street and the architecture could be in good chemistry.

Conclusions

The Significance of Design Build Studios

William Carpenter

INTRODUCTION

The conclusion of this study identifies a possible growing trend in North American architectural schools. This trend is creating productive results and fervor among architectural students and faculty. Each program appears to adapt the ideas of construction in the design studio in idiosyncratic ways. Some of the program studies foster an altruistic social agenda where societal needs are primary and synthetic. These programs layer this sociopolitical obligation onto the basic intent of the design and construction based studios. This is most evident in the work at Auburn University, where community needs have been identified with stunning abstractions of the Alabama vernacular. The work of the Southern Polytechnic State University students in Atlanta focuses on a more urban condition. Students begin with urban planning projects and move to site-specific installations, which begin to solve larger city-based issues, such as community identification and the definition of park and public urban space. The community has responded to these students in an unparalleled manner and expanded and reified the need for experimental and high-quality design.

Some of the programs studied are more insular in intent. At Cranbrook Academy, for example, the students work on campus. They have built lighting, bridges, entry pavilions, gatehouses, mail centers, and gallery installations. The students' craft-based work continues the Saarinen-based traditions in that they cast bricks in special shapes and colors, cast metals for fittings to a jeweler's level of perfection, and use the projects as full-sized study models. Because they do not need to go through the rigors of city-run permit processes, they have more freedom in the construction process.

As the trend grows in North America, it is important to recognize the often profound effects this type of learning has on architectural students during schooling and after graduation. Employers state that these students are much more helpful in the office setting and more comfortable with site-based work. One student explained that he has now become a general contractor, electrician, master plumber, and architect. By integrating other aspects of the construction, he believed that the design could be more rounded (Kreiling, 2002). The Prince of Wales in 1989 stated the necessity for the profession of architecture to incorporate aspirations, needs, and feedback from clients and the community into the design process. Along this line, in 1960, Sweeny and Sert have already argued that architecture could benefit from relating back to the community and the environment. They warned against the tendencies toward pure aesthetic approach or preoccupations with technology-driven design.

THE POSSIBLE SIGNIFICANCE OF DESIGN BUILD STUDIOS

As shown in this study, the recent advent of DBS programs indicates that the recent design and construction integration taking place in the construction industry has made its way into the architectural curriculum. The case studies in this study suggest that this type of learning may be an improvement over traditional educational pedagogies. The most immediate benefit for architectural students is the direct connection they have to architectural practice. In the Yale program, for example, students prepare a complete set of construction documents, present them to the city commission, and work closely with their clients to control the budget schedule and scope. This experience as part of architectural school appears to have an almost direct transference to architectural practice.

The DBS appears to have a strong effect on the architecture culture. In North America, these projects are popular amongst architectural periodicals as a way to showcase student work. The ownership and pride, which develops in the students, has a strong collaborative air to it. Students seem to learn how group interaction can improve the design process. Most recently, the Whitney Museum in New York City—which has identified artists Mark Rothko, Jackson Pollack, Richard Serra, and Willem DeKooning through the Biennial, the most prestigious revealing of new talent in the United States—chose to present the work of architects. Its curatorial staff chose to showcase the work of the Auburn Rural Studio, giving them an entire room in the spaces exhibition. The show offered evidence that this respected art museum has identified the connection between art, architecture, and culture. The show displayed several well-crafted models on sculptural bases rendered in basswood and found objects. In a respite area, it screened a commissioned film titled *Proceed and Be Bold*, which showed students in action and interviewed luminaries in the architecture culture who spoke of the importance of the DBS movement and the Rural Studio.

PRACTICAL SKILLS AND FIELD WORK IN ACADEMIA

The essence of intelligence is skill in extracting meaning from everyday experience (Miller, 1988). Laboratory and field work are integral elements of the architectural programs at Yale and Auburn Universities. This approximation of practice, while diverse and conceptual, allows for learning objectives to be met. In these courses, it is essential that student performance be assessed and given adequate weight in the final grading. Further, Miller made an analogy to the fundamental role of laboratory work in the pedagogy of science.

Architectural education cannot be based just on theoretical principles. Any study of science that is based entirely on lectures and reading lacks an essential ingredient—that of knowledge from direct observations of natural phenomena and changes that occurred there (Miller, 1988). There are indications that architectural professionals expect students to be able to enter the workforce more prepared than they are. Studies indicate that this approach to architectural education could lead to graduates who could address design problems faster (Carpenter, 1997).

Students of languages, including their own language, are often encouraged to participate in drama or write poetry or prose. Students who have learned a new language, such as French or Italian, are sometimes immersed in a culture in order to accelerate their command and to discover nuances in the language that a professor in a classroom would have a difficult time teaching. Education in other fields, for example in social and cultural sciences, has long established direct engagements and experiences as a means to learn the discipline (Miller, 1988). Along this line, the Rural Studio exemplifies the transfer of this model into architectural education. It offers a complex process of immersion: students learn teamwork, design, racial integration, social work issues, and construction skills simultaneously.

ASSESSMENT AND THE DBS

Determining an appropriate system for grading in the DBS is a complex undertaking and deserves some rigorous focus in this conclusion. This is one of the inherent weaknesses to date in the DBS, and some uniformity amongst assessment criteria might improve the process. The creation of clear and cogent learning objectives and outcomes is the most important educational paradigm. Practical experience courses often use a pass/fail or satisfactory/unsatisfactory grading system, which has serious reliability issues. The often incomplete or inaccurate system can leave both the student and the authoring professor wondering if a fair assessment of the course work was granted. The setup could start from identifying the strengths and weaknesses of each student. It is not enough to simply rely on satisfactory grades (Miller, 1988). Considering the flaws in the two-point system of grading, it is important to look at other alternatives.

A number of new systems exist to grade studio, collaborative, and practical experience. One particular system that could prove more accurate was used by the faculty at the University of Hong Kong in their diploma in social work. This system appears to align with the intent and learning objectives of the DBS (Danelo, 2017).

Proposed Assessment System for Fieldwork

Knowledge (25 percent)
Skills (40 percent)
Values, attitudes, and professional development (35 percent)

These categories are then subdivided into criteria, or "expected behavior/attitude" (Miller, 1988).

This approximates the typical grading system used in North American education. This six-point scheme could help DBS professors quantify student work:

A = excellent
B = good
C = fair
D = pass
F = fail
G = badly fail

This grading system is not without weaknesses. For example, a B achieved on a project is somewhat ambiguous because the variation in quality between a B+ and a B– grade is astounding. The Fieldwork Handbook also reveals a set of criteria that can be used by teachers and supervisors in the DBS and that is similar to the criteria currently used in North American architectural schools. For each of the letter grades, it is proposed that the following items be used to assess fieldwork:

Competence
Initiative
Task completion
Understanding

It is also important to question the validity of the learning objectives set forth by the professors who design the DBS courses. Miller asks, "How close to real-life experience is the field experience program? Do students (interns) have the same responsibilities as qualified practitioners?" (1988).

It is unclear whether or not this grading system provides indicators of the student's success in real practice. Although students do not have the same skill sets as actual practitioners, they will likely assimilate into industry more successfully.

We can infer that a student diary, a video production of the team actions, or even personal interviews cannot accurately portray the student's work. The faculty and course designers should not expect to be present for every action either; in fact, this could actually weaken team performance. Having the teacher present at all times can provide a cushion not always found in the industry. Many of the decisions involved must be solved on site with the team interacting and formulating their own solutions.

"Problem-based learning" is an important element of the DBS. Boud (1988) offers us a problem-based learning system in which "the prime focus is on a problem or problems rather than a discipline or body of knowledge." He goes on to describe the three elements of assessment he suggests for problem-based learning:

The importance of careful specification of learning objectives and criteria for assessment
Assessment as a process rather than as a measurement activity
Assessment for the benefit of student learning

So the learning objectives emerge again as the primary sextant to guide DBS course designers. Each course designer will have nuances or curriculum-driven assessment criteria, such as the NAAB requirements in North America.

The following questions adapted from Miller (1988) may be useful:

What tasks were students able to perform at the end of the DBS that they did not know how to do at the beginning?
To what standard or level of craft were they required to perform the task (entry level, high standard, etc.)?

Miller also offers us a set of skills that are directly transferable to the DBS. They can be used by course designers in the conception of new DBS courses and are illustrated in the following diagram:

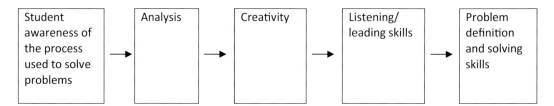

FIGURE 3.2.1
Miller's transferable skills.

From the nursing field, Faletti et al. (1993) offers us a usable system of problem-based learning and what he calls "inquiry-based learning." His description is included at length for help in summarizing the DBS assessment model. This model relies on analyzing a case study in a small group of students. The group would analyze a set of limited data on a real or simulated study case, often with the aids of guiding questions. It aims to cultivate their analytical skills to diagnose a clinical situation. Essential in this model is in preparing a well-defined study case that relate to multiple learning objectives. The analysis intends not only to diagnose the condition but also to identify further topics of study and organize learning tasks. This setup leads to an independent study for each student. The closing of each session includes a review of each personal contribution to the learning process. The learning that occurs is open and flexible and draws on the diverse skills of faculty and students alike. Faculty become co-learners in the DBS who can guide, with their own expertise, the students to achieve goals and solve problems. Students then assume some of the responsibility for their own learning.

INTERACTION WITH CLIENTS

Interaction with clients provides one of the most tangible benefits of the DBS. In most architectural education programs, the professor asks the students to "pretend" they are the architect and "pretend" the project is real. The benefit is that it allows students to imagine clients and lets them design projects with no constraints. The drawback is that when they actually work with a client postgraduation and realize the difficulties involved, they are often surprised and disillusioned. The practice of giving students "real-life" experience is common in other fields, as Miller points out. It would prepare students to real-life scenarios that requires interactions with various entities related to a practice, including clients, other professionals, and staffs (1988).

The DBS exposure is helpful in that it provides diverse exposure to the students so that their strengths can be identified. One person may emerge as a good leader, while another a good craftsperson. It would benefit in identifying talents, strengths, and weaknesses in each student relative to the field of study. This educational approach could help to build up these student's potentials (Gerndt, 2003).

CONCLUSIONS

Many architects have stated that architectural schools are out of touch with practice. The DBS may be one way to reconnect academia with practice. Some of the relevant conclusions reached are as follows:

- As demonstrated in Section 4.5, within the DBS exists a psychological interaction between the emergent design concept and the project team. As we have seen with learning by doing studios at the Bauhaus and at Yale and Auburn Universities, the project is integral to the DBS.
- As described in Sections 2.2, 2.3, and 4.5, the DBS is vibrant and changes with the existent dynamic forces, which are exerted, unlike the Ecole des Beaux Arts model, which was insular. While it emulates the flux and problems of real-life experiences, it simultaneously presents a compelling array of concurrent scales and enhanced decision-based thinking. The DBS brings practice-based methods into an academic realm, giving students direct experience.
- As described in Chapter 3, within the DBS, students learn to cope with crisis nonsequentially and are better prepared for practice.
- As discussed in Chapter 5, the construction process adds a level of reality to the design process, which can sometimes be positive and sometimes negative but always affects the design process and thus the learning in a cognitive way.
- Chapter 5 also demonstrated that architectural education is behind in terms of technology and building methods when compared to practice.
- As demonstrated by the Yale model in 4.2, the DBS is more effective as an integral part of the curriculum rather than a stand-alone course. It appears to allow skills from other courses to be tested.
- As demonstrated by the Auburn model in 4.3, the interaction between design concept and the project team in the DBS enhances the student's education.

RECOMMENDATIONS

The following are recommendations based on the findings of this study:

INCORPORATE CUTTING-EDGE TECHNOLOGY

In future DBS projects, professors should use more cutting-edge technologies in the studios to explore future uses and methods of assembly. Several that would be most appropriate for the DBS are CATIA-based design processes, full-scale prototyping and experimental materials, such as carbon fibers, succulent plant roofs, gel-foams and hybrid plastics. Linking these studies to industry would create a direct link between the teachers and students and the material production methods, and would potentially provide research grant income for schools.

ALIGN WITH INDUSTRY

DBS projects should work with existing DB firms and contractors. This would link the school to practice, providing valuable access to materials suppliers and subcontractors. Manufacturers often offer research grants to programs such as the DBS. An example of this is if Gehry Technologies sponsored a DBS to build full-scale prototypes of new projects and offered a research grant to the host school.

DEDICATE TIME TO PROGRAM EVALUATION

The DBS should incorporate more research and increase the degree of critical thinking and evaluation. For example, the Auburn case study reveals a connection with the Deep South, the politically charged Civil Rights Movement, and the optimism of early American culture. The Yale model reveals a successful management simulation model, but design exploration and development is in question due to the strict guidelines imposed by the chosen client, Habitat for Humanity.

INTEGRATE THE NOTION OF THE UNIT OF PRODUCTION

Integrating the notion of the unit of production would allow the DBS to concentrate on a replicable element of construction. This is demonstrated in the following two images: Frank Lloyd Wright's textile block construction, which weaves concrete masonry units with steel threading, and Jean Nouvel's woven wall of operable windows, which calibrates to sun levels like a camera lens. Like Kahn's or Piano's light diffusers (discussed earlier), both of these practice-based models could inspire exciting and transferable potential DBS projects.

SLOW THE PROCESS DOWN, MOVE IT FORWARD

Through the process of slowing down the DBS, new technologies and the concept of research can be integrated. The pressure of completing an entire building can be overwhelming for a one-semester project. Selected DBS projects could concentrate on research-based projects, which deal with concepts such as sustainability, lighting design, cutting-edge materials research, and prefabrication techniques.

SEEK INTERDISCIPLINARY COLLABORATION

Within the context of the DBS as a transferable model, the notion of interdisciplinary collaboration becomes paramount. If students and professors from other disciplines were involved within the context of the DBS, the projects could have valuable learning objectives and outcomes and could make the student experiences more diverse. One example of this is the recent addition of law and social work students working with the Rural Studio. Another is the computer science and industrial design students working along with architectural students at Southern Polytechnic State University in Marietta, Georgia.

CREATE AN URBAN DBS

Schools of architecture that are located in urban areas or have satellite studios within city contexts could incorporate an urban DBS. Alliances with nonprofit and city agencies could be formed, such as the alliances by the Yale and Auburn DBS with public officials. Issues such as urban planning, homelessness, and adaptive reuse of existing structures could be considered, and this would enhance the learning outcomes of the DBS.

ENCOURAGE COLLABORATION ON THE EMERGENT DESIGN CONCEPT

Through learning objectives and syllabus design, DBS professors should encourage students to allow the emergent design concept to be a team creation. This could be done through several introductory exercises, which would help prepare students for the larger DBS project.

PLACE THE DBS THROUGHOUT THE CURRICULUM

The DBS should be an integral part of the curriculum rather than a stand-alone course.

CONTRIBUTION

The contribution this study makes to architectural education is that it is the first to recognize the connection between the DBS paradigm and the enriched emergent design concept within the collaborative project team. Specifically it recognizes how real-life forces can affect an academic experience and allow the students to experience real-life situations in practice. This study not only clearly catalogues the current movement of design build studios in the United States, but it reaches beyond with suggestions for their improvement and development, incorporating newly emerging technologies of materials and process. It is the first to encourage DBS professors to look to cutting-edge ideas in architectural practice in order to progress. This study contributes to future students who endeavor to enter these studios, faculty who plan them, and in the end, to the practice itself, for a better-equipped graduate will help contribute to the profession of architecture.

REFERENCES

Boud, D. (Ed.) (1988). *Developing Student Autonomy in Learning*, 2nd edn. London: Kogan Page.
Carpenter, W. (1997). *Learning by Building*, New York: Van Nostrand Reinhold.
Danelo, D. (2017). *The Field Researcher's Handbook: A Guide to the Art and Science of Professional Fieldwork*, Washington, D.C.: Georgetown University Press.
Faletti, J., Patterson, H., Thornton, R., Lipson, J., & Spring, C. (Eds.). (1993). Computer-Based Concept Mapping. *Journal of College Science Teaching, Generations*, 8, 35–38.
Gerndt, A. (Architect). (2003, January 1). Discussion with the author.
Kreiling, M. (2001, January 15). Student in discussion with the author.
Miller, A. H. (1988). *Student Assessment in Higher Education*, B. W. Imirie and K. Cox (Contributors). London: Kogan Page.

Index

abstraction 28, 31, 47
academic approach to design education 4
academic model of design pedagogy 28–29
activism 5
air-conditioning systems 157, 158, 159, 160
Albers, J. xii, xiii, xiv, xviii, 44, 46, 79; *Homage to the Square* 40; material and matter studies xix; preliminary course xx, 40; "Werklicher Formunterricht" xviii–xix
Alias software xxxvii
American Collegiate Schools of Architecture (ACSA) 54
American Institute of Architecture Students (AIAS) xxii
American University of Sharjah 52, 53; Display Wall 57; *see also* Design Build Initiative (DBI)
Amisano, J. 7
analogical model 29
Angerer, F. 43
animal laborans 26–27, 28
anthropomorphism 27
apprenticeship 5, 125, 126
aptitude 29, 30; *see also* skill/s
Architectural Division of the American Composites Manufacturers Association (ACMA) 50
architecture xxi–xxii, xxxv, 16; education xxxiii, 121, 126, 179–180; French schools 114; pulsation 144; skin-in approach xxxvi; *see also* design
Architecture Europe Study Abroad Program 83
Arendt, H. 26–27
Aristotle 38
Ars Electronica Futurelab 149; insight | out 151, 152; Source.Code 149, 150; ZeitRaum 150, 151
artifacts 29, 35
artistic education xl
art/s xix, 148, 149
assembly/ies xl, 27, 154; versus making 15, 16
assessment: design build studio (DBS) 180; fieldwork 180–181
Atlanta xxiv–xxv, xxxii, 7; Mad Housers xxv; Miss Matties Garden xxvi, xxvii; Reynoldstown Gateway Park xxviii
Auburn University 79, 83, 178; Rural Studio 5

Audi-Fab design build project 58
automation 59, 67
AVM Pavilion project 59, 60
axiomatic thinking 30, 31

back ventilation 156, 161
Baker, E. 58
Barcelona Fish xxxvi–xxxvii
Barnsdall House xiv
Bauhatte xiii
Bauhaus xii, xiv, xl; glass workshop xviii; influence on Virginia Tech's pedagogy 83; learning by doing xiii; Manifesto xv, xix; mentors xv; pedagogy 4, 5; school-based commission xiv–xv; science course xviii; talent xvii; vocational training 4; *see also* Itten, J.; learning by doing workshops
Becker, E. 103
Beckmann, H. xix–xx
beginning design 5, 31
Behrens, P. xvi, xvii
Bell Aircraft 3
Benjamin, W. 7
Bergson, H. 142
Biaxial CMU modules 84
Bill, M. 83
Black Mountain College 5, 46, 79, 105
Blankenship, K. 84
Bloomer, K. 5
Blue Book 79
Borboletta 139; in Buenos Aires 140, 141; in Miami/Venice 141–142, 143; periodicity 145; in Pisa 141; pulsation 143, 144; rhythm 145, 146–147; support structure 142
Breuer, M. xiv, xx; Wassily chair xl
bricoleur 27–28
Buchanan, P. 66
Buenos Aires, Borboletta in 140, 141
building/s xv, xxi, 27; air-conditioning systems 157, 158, 159; design and lii–liii; enclosure 36, 37; energy exchange 153, 155; insulation 154, 155, 156; insurance 117, 119, 120; licensure 117, 118; moisture

186

Index

153, 154, 157, 158, 160; over-ventilation 161; pedagogy 120, 121; permit 117, 131; zoning 117
Burchard, C. 79, 83, 105
Burton, J. lvii
Burton Architecture PLC lv, lvii
business process 149

Cage, J. 79, 83
Cal Poly Pomona 47, 48
Canizaro, V. 61
Carpenter, W. J. 7; *Learning by Building: Design and Construction in Architectural Education* xxii
carving 7
Cary, J. xxii
cavity insulation 156
cement, ferro- xxxiv
Cereghetti, J. 139
changes of form 27
Chavez, D. 57
Chidori 169, 172
Clemson University 50
climate sensitive design 140, 141
CNC 59, 76, 108
collaboration xliv, lii; Carter + Burton lvii; Elk Run Ridge lv, lvii; interdisciplinary 184
Collins, P. 29
color 40, 44
column 46
community 48, 178
computer modelling xxxiv
computer-aided manufacturing (CAM) xxxix
computer-aided three-dimensional interactive application (CATIA) xxxvi–xxxviii, xxxix
concept/s xxi, lix, 26, 28
Concept-test model 29
concrete 165, 175, 176
Cone Studio 84
conoid studio liii
constraints 32, 40, 47, 49
construction xv; computer-aided three-dimensional interactive application (CATIA) xxxvi–xxxviii, xxxix; de 149; drawings xlvi, li; fiber-reinforced polymer (FRP) 49, 50; Nubian Vaulting xlvi, li; technology transfer xxxiii–xxxiv; textile-block 184; *see also* building/s; fabrication
constructional thinking xix–xx
constructivist elementarism xiii
contrast xvii
control offices 119, 120
cooling with reheat 157
Corbusier, xvii
corrugated cardboard 48
countertops, digital fabrication 67, 76, 78
Covid-19 xxiv

craft model of design pedagogy 28–29
Crafts Movement xiv
craftsmanship xiii, xvii, 7; techniques of experience 27
Cranbrook Academy 178
crease pattern 46
creativity xvii, xviii
culture xliv, lix; language 179–180
curriculum: Design Build Initiative (DBI) 56; Interior Design 57; Southern Tech School of Architecture 4
curve-crease folding 40

Davis, L. xlvi, li, lii
De Carlo, G. xxi
deconstruction 149
Deleuze, G, 146–147
design xv, xix, xxi; beginning 5, 31; and building lii–liii; carving and joining 7; climate sensitive 140, 141; Fibonacci Nook 22; integrated xxxiv; knowledge 29–30; multilayered 32, 35; problems 26, 37; problem-solving 28, 29–30; rule-based 26, 30; standardization 26; thinking 6, 29
Design Build Initiative (DBI) 52, 53; Audi-Fab design build project 58; AVM Pavilion project 59, 60; curriculum 56; faculty 54, 61, 62; furniture making 56, 57; grants 55; implementation 57, 58, 59, 60, 61; infrastructure 55; *Neonomads* 60; prototyping studio 58, 59; *Tarkeeb Gatehouse and Garden* 60, 61
design build/design build studio (DBS) xv, xxii, xxiii, xxxiii, xxxix, xl, 5, 179; assessment 180–182; faculty 52, 53; first-year 30, 31, 32, 35; French model 123, 124, 125, 126; Gjerton on 52; interaction with clients 182; internships 124; issues and challenges 61, 62; leading 52, 53; modules 6–7; problem-based learning 181–182; reality xxxv–xxxvi; recommendations 183–185; regulatory framework 118; service-learning model 122; Small Center 135–136; technology and xxxix; third-year 35, 36, 37; Tulane 128; urban 184; Virginia Tech 83–84; *see also Practicing for Practice*
design education: academic approach 4; engineer-technological approach 4–5; vocational training 4
Design for Humanity studio xxvi
design/built program: First-Year Building Project 5; Rural Studio 5
Dessault Systems xxxvi, xxxvii
Deutsche Werkbund movement xiii
Dewey, J. xiii, xviii, 4, 5, 28
diagramming 31, 35
dianthus blooming facade 36
diffused light xxxv
digital fabrication 54, 59, 66, 176; screens and countertops 67, 76, 78
discovery xviii
Disney Concert Hall xxxvi
DIY tactics 23

187

Index

doing 26–27, 37
domain shift 27
drawing/s xxxvi, xliii, xliv, 31; construction li; fabrication xlvi, li; observational 31, 32
Dunay, R. 84
Durand, C. N. xii–xiii
duration 147

École Nationale Supérieure des Beaux-Arts 47
Ecole Polytechnique xii–xiii; pedagogy 4
Ecole-des-Beaux Art 28–29
economy of materials xx
Edge, K. 103
education xix; *see also* pedagogy
Eisengarn xl
Eisenman, P., *Visions Unfolding: Architecture in the Age of Electronic Media* xxxv
electronic media xxxv–xxxvi
elements 35, 145
Elk Run Ridge lv, lvii
energy exchange 153, 154, 155
Engel, H., *Tragsysteme/Structure Systems* 45, 46
engineer 27–28; model 28–29
episteme 38
equilibrium studies xix
evolution 27
exercises, material xix–xx
Experience Music Project (EMP) xxxvii
experience/experiential 40; learning 28, 65, 66–67; techniques of 27, 28
experimentation xviii, xix, xl, xliv, 17, 28, 29, 40; Fuller on 105; materials xxxiv

fabrication xxxiv; computer-aided three-dimensional interactive application (CATIA) xxxvi–xxxviii, xxxix; digital 54, 59, 66, 176; drawings xlvi, li; foldable composites 49, 50; hybrid approach 61; La Riviera Bistro (*see* La Riviera Bistro); project management 20; rapid prototyping xxxiv; shops 5, 6
facade 36, 37
faculty: Design Build Initiative (DBI) 54, 61, 62; design build studio (DBS) 52, 53
fax xxxv
Ferrari, O. 79, 83
ferro-cement xxxiv–xxxv
fiber-reinforced polymer (FRP) 49, 50
Fibonacci Nook 22
fieldwork, assessment 180–181
filmmaking xliii
first-year studio 30, 31, 32, 35
flexible teaching xix
flow 172, 175
foldable: composites 49; structures 40, 43, 47, 48, 50
folded-plate structures 45

folding 40, 47, 49; crease pattern 46; curve-crease 40; paper 49, 50
fold-inspired structures 44, 45
Forbat, F. xiv
form 43
framing xxiii
France: architecture and building, regulatory framework 114, 117; building permit 118, 119; collaborative teaching 122; control offices 119, 120; design/buildLAB 123, 124, 125, 126; residential projects, regulation 120
Freedom By Design 15
Freyssinet, E. 44, 45
Froebel, F. xiii
Fuller, B. 79, 83, 86, 105
full-scale modelling xxxiv–xxxv
funding, Small Center 136
furniture making 56, 57
FutureHAUS 86, 87, 90, 92, 98

garden structure xxvi, xxvii
Gehry, F. xxxvi, xxxvii; *see also* computer-aided three-dimensional interactive application (CATIA)
generative rules 30, 31
Géométrie Constructive 47
Georgia: industrialization 3; *see also* Atlanta; Marietta; Southern Tech
Gesamtkunstwerk xiii
Giesen, M. 54
Gjerton, G. 52, 53
glass workshop xviii
Glymph, J. xxxvi, xxxvii
Glyph, J. xxxix
Gokchepinar, J. 139
Golconde li, lii
Goldemberg, E. 139, 140
grading *see* assessment
graffiti 13
Graham, B. xxxvii
grant/s: "Skillset Development" 55; "Special Initiative Funding" 55
Great Society 5
Gropius, W. xii, xiii, xiv, xvi, xviii, 79; Bauhaus Manifesto xv
Guattari, F. 146
Guggenheim Museum xxxvii

Hanover Bus Stop xxxviii, xxxix
haptic xvii, xxxv–xxxvi; cognition xl
Hayes, R. 5
Heatherwick Studio, *Paternoster Vents* 45
"Heimatsil" xiii
Helvetica Design lvii
heuristic thinking 28, 29
Hilker, K. 103

Index

histology 144
Hochschule für Gestaltung 46, 47, 83
Hodge Prototype Day Care Center 84
Holt, J. 87
homeless residents/homelessness xxvi
homo faber 26–27, 28
Hu, J., "The Problem with Blaming Robots for Taking Our Jobs" 67
Hurricane Katrina 129–130
Hurst, H. 83–84
hygroscopic 155

imagination 6, 27
implementation, Design Build Initiative (DBI) 56, 57, 58, 59, 60, 61
industrialization xiv, xv; Georgia 3
informality xxii, xxiv–xxv, xxviii, xxxi
innovation xxiii
inquiry-based learning 182
insight | out 151, 152
instrumentalism xviii
insulation 154, 155, 161; sheathing 156, 157
insurance 117, 119, 120
integrated design xxxiv
integrated thinking 66
Interior Design 57
internships 124
interstitial urban space xxiv
Italy xxiii
Itten, J. xii, xiii, xiv, xvii, xix, xx; glass workshop xviii

Jackson, P., *Folding Techniques for Designers: From Sheet to Form* 46
Japan lii, 165, 168; Chidori 169, 170
Jara, C. 29
Johnson, L. B. 5
joinery 7, 31, 32, 170; Chidori 169; orthogonal 27; *see also* wood/woodworking
Jones, D. 84
Judd, D. xxi

Kahn, L. I. xxxv
Kalo, A. 57, 59
Karimi, Z. 18
Kennesaw State University 3, 26; Fibonacci Nook 22; Tactile Urbanism course 23; Tactile Urbanism (TU) 18, 20, 22; *see also* Urban Design Build Studio, projects
kinetics 36, 37
kiosk, Welty Design Build Studio 16, 17, 18
Klee, P. xiv; glass workshop xviii
knowledge 26–27; design 29–30; episteme 38; praxis 38; techne 38
Koolhaas, R. xxiv–xxv

La Riviera Bistro 108; ceiling skeleton 110; countertop, fabrication 106, 108; fabrication 106; flowers (ornament), fabrication 113; foam ornament (bar), fabrication 108, 110; foam ornament (wall), fabrication 110; front panels, fabrication 108
Laboratory of Excellence for Architecture, Environment, and Constructive Cultures 114
Labrouste, H. xiii
labs 179; Design Build Initiative (DBI) 55
Lahti, A. 47, 48
Lamina 110
language 179–180
latent load 159
layout 65
Le Corbusier, xvi, xxxvi
lead glazing xvii
leading a design build studio 53
learning 29; experiential 28, 65, 66–67; inquiry-based 182; by making 29–30; problem-based 181–182
learning by doing xii, xiii, xviii, xx, 4, 16, 29; design problems 26; shops 5, 6; woodshop 31, 32
Leibniz, G. W. 143
Lew, R. lvii
light/ing 57; *Boy Lights Fire* xliii; diffused xxxv; *Table Top Lamp* xliii, xliv
lightness xx
Limaçon Design xlvi
Lipari, F. 139
Live Project xiv–xv
LOOP Pavilion 137
Luhmann, N. 148
LumenHAUS 86, 87
Lynch, D.: *Boy Lights Fire* xliii; *Table Top Lamp* xliii, xliv
Lyons, B. M. 126

machines xvi
Mad Housers xxv, xxvi, 7, 9
making xl, lix; versus assembling 15, 16; components 26; film xliii; furniture 56, 57; learning by 29–30; procedure 27; space- 31; thinking-through- 6
manufacturing, computer-aided xxxix
Marietta, Bell Aircraft 3
Martin, S. 84
Masonic Amphitheatre 98, 99, 103
masonry liii
mass production xiii, xiv; computer-aided manufacturing (CAM) xxxix
mastery xv
material/s xvii, xviii, xix, xxxiii, xl, 31; concrete 165, 175, 176; corrugated cardboard 48; economy of xx; exercises xix–xx; experimentation xxxiv; ferro-cement xxxiv–xxxv; folding 40; hygroscopic 155; metal 27; newspaper xx; paper xviii–xix; plywood liii–liv; polyethylene 173, 175; spray foam xliv;

189

Index

steel 165; studies xix; wood 165, 168; *see also* wood/woodworking
Matta Clark, G. xxviii
matter studies xix
media, electronic xxxv–xxxvi
medium-density fiberboard (MDF) 108
memorial garden, Reynoldstown 12, 13
Menil Gallery xxxiv
mentorship 120; Bauhaus xv
metal 27
metamorphosis 27
methodical thinking 30, 31
Meyer, A. xiii, xiv
Miami, Borboletta in 141–142, 143
Miller, A. H. 179, 181, 182
Miss Matties Garden xxvi, xxvii
Mitchell, K. 29
Mitchell, W. xxxvii, 29
mitosis 145
Mockbee, S. xxi, xxii, xxv, 5, 7
model/s 30, 31, 38; academic 28–29; analogical 29; computer xxxiv; Concept-test 29; craft 28–29; digital xxxix; engineer 28–29; full-scale xxxiv–xxxv; heuristic 29–30; paper 40, 46, 47; social science 28–29
modernism 43, 44
modules 6–7, 22; beginning design 31; Biaxial CMU 84; prefabricated 90, 92
Moholy-Nagy, L. xvii, xix
moisture 153, 154; air-conditioning systems 157, 158; north versus south 160
mold 161–162
monadology 143
montage xvii
Montessori, M. xiii
Moore, C. 5
morphology 31, 47; Borboletta 142, 144
Morris, W. xiv; "The Seven Lamps of Architecture" xvi
multi-person space 32, 35
multiplicity 142, 143
Munari, B., *Good Design* 43, 44
Museum of Modern Art (MOMA), Home Delivery Exhibition 173

Nagy, M. xiii
Nakashima, G. li, lii, liv
Nakashima, M. lii–liii, lv, lvii
Nakashima, T. xliii
nature-facts 140
Neighborhood Housing Services of New Orleans (NHS) 131
Neonomads 60
Nervi, P. L. xxxiv
New Orleans 129–130; LOOP Pavilion 137; *see also* URBANbuild

New River Train Observatory 103, 105
New York City xxviii
Newman, H. 5
North America: architecture and building regulation 117, 118, 122; design build studio (DBS) 179; service-learning model 122
Nouvel, J. 184
Nubian Vaulting xlvi, li

objectivity xvii
observation/al 27, 31; drawings 31, 32
operative rules 30, 31
origami 40, 43
orthogonal joining 27
Ove Arup and Partners xxxiv
over-ventilation 161
ownership xxxi

Pallasmaa, J. 66, 121
Pallathucheril, V. 62
paper xviii–xix, xx; curve-crease folding 40; folding 40, 46, 49, 50; models 40, 46, 47
particles 151, 152
passive systems 35
Paternoster Vents 45
Paxton, J. xvi
Peccioli Charter xxiii–xxiv, xxxii; *see also* prototypes
pedagogy xv, xviii, xxv, xxxiv–xxxv, 17, 20, 179; academic model 28–29; analogical model 29; Bauhaus 4–5; Blue Book 79; building 120, 121; Concept-test model 29; craft model 28–29; design problems 26; Ecole Polytechnique 4; engineer model 28–29; heuristic model 29–30; learning by doing xviii, 16; material studies xix; pragmatism 28; social science model 28–29; Southern Tech 3–4; Tuskegee Normal and Industrial Institute 5; Virginia Tech 79, 83; *see also* learning; learning by doing
perception 143, 148, 149
perforated doors 67
performing 26–27
personal space 35
photography xxxv, 36, 40
Piaget, J. 29
Piano, R. xxxiv, xxxv
Piedmont-Palladino, S. 87, 105
Pisa, Borboletta in 141
place xliv
plastic-injection molding 113
plywood liii–liv
poetic systems 148; insight | out 151, 152; Source.Code 149, 150; transformation 149; ZeitRaum 150, 151
pole structures 83–84
polyethylene containers 173, 175
practice 27, 179

Practicing for Practice 114
pragmatism 28
praxis 38
preconceptions xxi
preliminary course xvii; Albers' xx, 40
problem-solving 28, 29–30, 37
procedure/process 27; business 149, 150
programmatic forces xxi
project management 20, 22
prototypes/prototyping 13, 24–25, 36, 50, 58; heuristic 60; Mad Housers xxv, xxvi; Miss Matties Garden xxvi, xxvii; precedents 35; Reynoldstown Gateway Park xxviii; URBANbuild 132, 133; *see also* rapid prototyping
Prouve, J. 27–28
pulsation 143, 144
Puryear, M. xliv, xlvi, l–li

rapid prototyping xxxiv
reality xxxv
reflection 6, 27, 28, 32
regulation: French architecture and building 114, 117, 122; North American architecture and building 117, 118; residential projects 118
relative humidity 155
repetition 27, 31, 146
representation xl
request for proposals (RFP) 136
research: agenda, Small Center 138; through teaching 50
residential projects, regulation 118
resiliency xxiv
Resilient Communities xxiii–xxiv
Reynoldstown Gateway Park xxviii, 13
Rhodes, P. 60
rhythm 145, 146–147
Rice, P. xxxiv–xxxv
Riggs, R. 103
Risher, C. 84
robots 67
roundhouse 13
routine 27
Rowe, P. 29
rule/s 31, 35; -based design 26; generative 30, 31; operative 30, 31
Rural Studio 5, 179, 180
Ruth, D. K. xxii, 5

Salama, A. 4; survey of design pedagogy 28–29
SAP 149, 150
Sarnecky, B. xii, 56, 60
Schillig, B. 84
Schlemmer, O. xiii
school-based commission xiv–xv
Schwarz, R. 43

screens, digital fabrication 67, 76, 78
sculpture xl
self-discovery 37
Semper, G. xiii
Sennett, R. 6, 26, 27
sensible load 159, 161
Sevebeckee, B. 84
Shahn, B. liv
sheathing, insulating 156, 157
shops 5, 6
Simmons, G. 29
simulation 40, 49
simultaneity xxiii
site forces xxi
skeletal system 43; La Riviera Bistro ceiling 110
sketching 87
Skidmore Owings and Merrill (SOM) xxxvii
skill/s 27, 30, 179, 182; craft xviii
Skillset Development Grants 55
skin-in approach xxxvi
Sky Scraper system 84
Small, G. 47, 48
Small Center for Collaborative Design, The 128; curricular calendar/schedule 135–136; funding and project intake 136; LOOP Pavilion project 137; mission 134–135; research agenda 138
Smith, R. xxxvii, xxxix, 29
Smythe, E. xxxvii
social science model of design pedagogy 28–29
software: Alias xxxvii; Lamina 110
Sommerfeld House xiii; glass mural xiv; glass windows xvii
sorption 156
Source.Code 149, 150
Southern Tech 3, 178; interdisciplinary mindset 4; pedagogy 3–4; School of Architecture 4
space 142, 172; -making 31; multi-person 32, 35; personal 32, 35
Spaw, G. 60
"Special Initiative Funding" grant program 55
specialization xv
spray foam xliv
standardization 26
steel 165
Stern, G. 83–84
Stoekel, J. 84
Storm King li
storytelling 7
structures: foldable 43, 47, 48, 50; folded-plate 45; fold-inspired 44, 45; pole 83–84; solid 43; surface 43
Studio 804 65; digital fabrication of four screens and two countertops 67, 76, 78
supplemental dehumidification 159
surface structures 43

191

Index

sustainability 35
systems: poetic 148, 149; SAP 149, 150

Tabbarah, F. 61
Tactile Urbanism (TU) 18, 20, 22, 23
talent xvii, 27; *see also* skill/s
Taliesin 5
Tarkeeb Gatehouse and Garden 60, 61
Taut, B. xiii, xiv
teaching: flexible xix; through research 50; *see also* pedagogy
techne 38
techniques of experience 27, 28
technology xxxiii, 90, 183; and the DBS xxxix; transfer xxxiii–xxxiv
temporary appropriation xxii, xxiv; Mad Housers xxv, xxvi; Miss Matties Garden xxvi, xxvii; odd lots xxviii, xxxi; Reynoldstown Gateway Park xxviii
tensegrity lab 83
tents 43, 50
Texas A&M University 105; *see also* La Riviera Bistro
textile-block construction 184
thermal resistance 154
thinking 26–27; axiomatic 30, 31; design 6, 29; heuristic 28, 29; integrated 66; methodical 30, 31; -through-making 6, 38
third-year studio 35, 36, 37
three-dimensional printer xxxix
Timberlake, K. xxxiii
time: duration 147; pulsation 143, 144; rhythm 145, 146–147
tissue 144–145
tools 6–7
traces 27
Tracy, K. 59, 60
training: artistic xl; technician 4; vocational 4
transformation 27, 32, 35, 149
Trask, E. xliv
Tulane School of Architecture 128; design build history 129–130; *see also* Small Center for Collaborative Design, The; URBANbuild
Tuskegee Normal and Industrial Institute 5

under-ventilation 161
United Arab Emirates (UAE) 54
University of Cincinnati 29
University of Kansas 65
Urban Design Build Studio, projects 7; Mad Housers homeless shelter 9; Reynoldstown Gateway Park 13; Reynoldstown memorial garden 12, 13; Welty Design Build Studio 15, 16, 17, 18, 20, 22, 23; Wheelbarrow Summer Theatre 7, 9
urban space, interstitial xxiv

URBANbuild 128; methods and iterative process 131–132; mission 130; project sites and proximities 130–131; prototypes 132, 133

van der Rohe, M. xvi, xvii, xliii
Venice, Borboletta in 141–142, 143
ventilation: under- 161; back 156, 161; over- 161
Veruchshaus xiii; foyer table xiv
Virginia Tech: Bauhaus influence on pedagogy 83; design and construction of the Masonic Amphitheatre 98, 99, 103; design build 83–84; digital fabrication labs 86; Environmental System Laboratory 86; experimental structures 86; FutureHAUS 87, 90, 92, 98; international experience 87; LumenHAUS 87; NRTT design build project 103, 105; pedagogy 79; *Practicing for Practice* 114; prototyping 86; Studio Residency program 87; Washington-Alexandria Architecture Center (WAAC) 87
vision xxxv–xxxvi
Vkhutemas 28–29
Vlock Building Project 5
vocational training 4
volunteerism 5

War on Poverty 5
Waseda University lii
Washington, B. T. 5
Wassily chair xl
Water Branch House 173, 175
weaving 27
Welty Design Build Studio 15, 16, 17, 18, 20, 22, 23
Wheelbarrow Summer Theatre 7, 9
Whitney Museum 179
Wilkinson, N. 4
wisdom 7
wood/woodworking xix, li, lii, lii–liii, 6–7, 31, 165, 168; carving 7; joining 7, 27, 31, 32; thermal resistance 154
workmanship xii
workshops xv; glass xviii; Les Grands Ateliers 124
World Economic Forum 66–67
Wright, F. L. xiv, li, 5, 184

Yale School of Architecture, First-Year Building Project 5, 179

Zalcberg, V. 139
Zawistowski, K. 84, 98
Zawistowski, M. 84, 98
ZeitRaum 150, 151
zoning 117
Zumthor, P. 29
Zyberk, E. P. xxii